SURF FISHING
WITH THE EXPERTS

SURF FISHING
WITH THE EXPERTS
Richard Reina • William A. Muller

L.I.F. Publishing Corp.
Sag Harbor, New York

Copyright © by Richard Reina and William A. Muller

All rights reserved. No part of this book may be reproduced or utilized in any form or by any means, electronic or mechanical, including photocopying, recording, or by any information storage and retrieval system, without permission in writing from the Publisher.

L.I.F. Publishing Corporation
Post Office Box 1994, Bridge Street,
Sag Harbor, New York 11963.

Manufactured in the United States of America
Designed by Richard S. Reina

Table of Contents

Acknowledgments vii
Preface ix
PART ONE—General Information 1
CHAPTER 1—What is Surf Fishing 2
  by William A. Muller
CHAPTER 2—Perspectives on Yesterday 8
  by Fred Schwab
CHAPTER 3—Gear to Get Started 16
  by Tom Fitzsimmons
CHAPTER 4—The Very Basic Basics 27
  by William A. Muller
CHAPTER 5—Casting 42
  by William A. Muller
CHAPTER 6—Effects of Winds, Tides, and Moon 49
  by Fred Schwab
CHAPTER 7—Women in the Surf 58
  by Joyce Daignault
CHAPTER 8—Starting or Joining a Surf Fishing Club ... 64
  by Tom Fitzsimmons

PART TWO—Game Fish Approaches and Techniques .. 71
CHAPTER 9—The Big Three: Bass, Blues, and Weaks .. 72
  by William A. Muller
CHAPTER 10—Artificials 88
  by John Fritz
CHAPTER 11—Baitfishing 104
  by John Fritz

CHAPTER 12—Releasing Fish 120
  by Fred Schwab

CHAPTER 13—How to Catch Flounder and Fluke 130
  by Gerald Hahn

CHAPTER 14—How to Catch Porgies and Blackfish . . . 146
  by Gerald Hahn

CHAPTER 15—How to Catch Mackerel, Whiting,
  Kingfish, etc. 160
  by Gerald Hahn

PART THREE—Regional Game Fish 173

CHAPTER 16—Montauk 174
  by Fred Schwab

CHAPTER 17—South Shore Ocean 190
  by John Fritz

CHAPTER 18—Inlets and Jetties 201
  by Fred Golofaro

CHAPTER 19—Long Island Sound West 207
  by Andy Regina

CHAPTER 20—Long Island Sound East 220
  by William A. Muller

CHAPTER 21—Cape Cod 229
  by Frank Daignault

Acknowledgments

I wish to express my thanks to many people who helped to make this idea a reality. To my mother, who gave me abundant love and understanding throughout my life and then insisted that a young and unenthusiastic student write and rewrite compositions and reports until they were "right." To my late father who instilled in me a sense of determination, hard work, and pride as well as a thirst to strive for excellence. To my wife Susan who provides help, support, understanding, and patience even though she suspects I fish too hard and knows definitely that I assume far too many responsibilities than I can reasonably handle at one time. That she loves me so thoroughly is one of the great joys of my life.

To L.I.F. publisher Rich Reina who was willing to join me in this project and who supplied encouragement and support throughout the period of its preparation and then mobilized the facilities of the publishing corporation to bring it to the public in a timely fashion. He is friend as well as colleague and his friendship has meant a great deal to me for many years.

To all the writers and artists who took time out from fighting for conservation and resource management, surf fishing, family obligations, and community activities to write their chapters. To a person, they gave more to the effort than was reasonably expected. It is evident from reading their contributions that many researched less familiar aspects of their assignments thoroughly and each freely shared private information and opinions about surf fishing. Some of these people are among the best surf fishermen in the world and we are privileged to be able to benefit from a collective surf experience that spans more than 200 years. Each has his or her share of trophies, prizes, awards, and recognitions.

To the staff of The Fisherman who willingly accepted another publishing task although the pressures of publishing three weekly magazines already pushes their time and energy to the limit. To the printing arm of L.I.F. who similarly took to the task with a smile.

Thanks, and deepest appreciation to all.

Preface

In recent years, surveys have shown that there is a growing interest in surf fishing in the greater New York Metropolitan Area, as well as nationwide.

For the most part, marine anglers are being lured to the surf by its beauty and serenity. It's hard to beat a quiet night in the surf with stars lighting up the heavens and fish breaking close by. Catching fish under such circumstances is a bonus. The scene described above is not atypical of the spring and summer surf scene. Although not as serene, the crashing surf and fast-paced fishing during the fall migration also has its romantic and satisfying appeal. In many ways then, surf fishing offers a variety of pleasures to the shore-bound angler. In addition to placid summer surf and thunderous fall surf, the stars and full moon magic, there are the animals one encounters on the land in the wee hours—nocturnal animals that shy from exposure during the day.

In addition, for many people with high-powered jobs and long hours, there is the convenience of surf fishing. Most fishermen can find good action close to home in their own backyards if they take a little time to explore beaches only fifteen minutes to half an hour from their homes. A surf fisherman can have dinner with the family and still make a tide nearby for several hours of peaceful relaxation and exercise.

This book has been put together with these people primarily in mind. That is, it is a book of basics designed to get the novice started and help the recent newcomer improve his or her catch. That is not to say that the book will not be of interest to more experienced surf fishermen. Indeed, we have planned for that and we hope they, too, will find value in many chapters. We believe the chapters on history and species will prove interesting reading for all, and we suspect that even the seasoned pro will pick up many helpful hints from the how-to and where-to chapters.

The philosophy of this fishing book is much different than most. It was our aim to get together New York's finest surf fishermen and ask them to write chapters that they were most knowledgeable about and comfortable with. That is precisely what we have done. Each tells of his or her own experiences and expertise in his or her own way. Then we added the perspective of two of Massachusetts' best and most famous surf fishermen, Joyce and Frank Daignault, in order to provide information for one of the East Coast's most glamorous surf fishing locations: Cape Cod.

We intend for this book to entertain as well as inform. There is a lot of "nitty-gritty" stuff in this book. Each of these accomplished and well-known surf fishermen has shared many of their secrets with us. Surely, this is a golden and unique opportunity to pick the brains of the world's best surf fishermen.

PART ONE
General Information

CHAPTER 1

What is Surf Fishing?
by William A. Muller

Whenever anyone asks me this question, I'm immediately both enthusiastically anxious to share my love for the sport and fearfully anxious about where to start. I wonder if my words alone can convey what I really feel. Some years ago I found at least a way to begin when I came across a quote that's been attributed to Frank Woolner, senior editor of *The Salt Water Sportsman*.

The quote is: "Surf fishing is a war, and the battle is renewed every night." Perhaps that doesn't sound very appetizing, but a closer look reveals much about the sport and the men and women who participate in it. Hopefully, the discussion in this chapter will help clarify that quote.

Perhaps today's world was never really meant for people. Psychologists tell us that stress, pressure, anxiety, and future shock often make it difficult for people to cope. Thus, psychologists and psychiatrists urge us to find healthy and socially acceptable outlets for these emotions as a way to cope with our lives and remain reasonably adjusted. I translate this to mean that we need passions in our lives. I do not mean our loved ones or our jobs, since love of family is too intimately associated with our normal daily routines and love of job can be consuming of our health and sound mental outlook. In addition, we are urged to find physical outlets in sports. Apparently physical activity calms the spirit and funnels anxiety and stress through our bodies and out. Perhaps spouses, children, and bosses won't be offended when I repeat that many of us benefit from having a passion in life.

For me that passion is surf fishing. Actually, I love to fish whether it's in a boat, from the beach, from a dock, or at the side of a lake. All fishing is relaxing to me, but surf fishing offers something special and I'd like to tell you why it's special for me and what I think it is all about.

Let's start with what may be obvious to some. Surf fishing is done from the shore. It doesn't have to be the churning south shore ocean to be considered the surf. The back bays, the inlets, and Long Island Sound also represent surf fishing locations. In that sense, then, the term "surf fishing" is a misnomer to a degree. Perhaps "shore fishing" would be better. Nonetheless, through conventional usage we say surf fishing. In surf fishing the angler has his or her feet on the ground or on some structure that, in turn, is attached to the ground, such as a jetty or pier or dock. In other words, if you aren't in a boat, then you are surf fishing. A person might wish to split hairs over one aspect of this fishing. There are some people who insist that fishing from a bridge doesn't qualify as surf fishing, while others insist that it is a form of surf angling. I have my own prejudices, and I feel that bridge fishing isn't really surf fishing because many of the unique characteristics of surf fishing that I'm about to describe don't apply to this unique form of angling. Bridge fishing is an approach unto itself and in its own way has as many challenges and skills as other types of fishing. I only contend here that it isn't surf fishing.

What do I like so much about surf fishing? First, there is the frequent solitude. Most of the time the best fishing for the biggest specimens is done at night. There are few fishermen prowling and even fewer everyday citizens. There are few cars, often the wind is still, and the world seems to calm.

Second, I like the challenge. Surf fishing is the hardest form of fishing there is, especially in New York waters where there are just enough fish in the surf to tantalize, but not enough to guarantee frequent blitzes. In order to catch game fish consistently, in order to consistently catch large game fish, in order to be respected as an accomplished surf fisherman, one must sharpen skills to the cutting edge of excellence, one must practice in the surf long hours, and one must learn to respect the fish and begin to think like the hunted, not the hunter. That's a challenge. One must never stop learning, listening, or thinking. One must constantly search for better techniques and better odds. For many, the challenge is a great stress and they cannot adjust. They fall out of surf fishing almost as fast as they fell into it. For me, this challenge offers little stress. Quite the contrary, because the challenge is so different from the stresses of my career. Thus, the challenge becomes an outlet rather than a stress and all the hustle and bustle, the long hours, and the hard work is a way to drain the tensions from me. After all, I do not have to fish if I do not want to, but I do have to go to work. I do not have to work so hard at fishing if I do not want to, but I must work hard at the job. When I'm in the surf I think of nothing else; I am a thousand miles from nowhere and I haven't a care in the world.

Third, there is the companionship of good people who share your passion and your dreams. We all learn much from these people, and eventually the day comes when others will learn much from us. Such is the cycle of it. The people we encounter in the depth of night tides are not alien to us even if we do not know their names. They are comrades, they are part of the family. If they, too, are so dedicated as to be prowling in search of fish at 2AM, then they surely must be colleagues in the battle.

Fourth, there is the fun. Feeling the strike of a good fish and its powerful runs straight out from the beach allows a fish to display its God-given abilities in the purest light possible. There is no boat for the fish to drag around and there exists no security to swim deep. The fish is in very shallow water, it is not comfortable there, and when hooked has only one way to go—OUT! The angle of the line is not up and down, but out. It is harder to use the flex of the rod to tame a fish at this angle and ultimately the fish must be dragged through the surf zone where it will panic, and where every fish poses the real threat of breaking off.

Fifth, there is the satisfaction of doing something well that is very hard. Each large fish is its own triumph and a memory to be savored for a long time.

Sixth, there is the unknown that adds mystery and suspense. In the surf at night the next fish could be fifty pounds or it could be a pound. The size of the fish you last caught often tells you nothing about the size of the next one.

Seventh, there is the convenience. If I compare surf fishing to flounder fishing, a sport I dearly love, in terms of preparation time, I find that flounder fishing takes the most time. In fact, in spite of the fact that many beginners perceive that surf fishing requires a great deal of preparation before each trip, the exact opposite is true. Yes, there is considerable winter preparation, but during the season it is possible to structure things so that preparation time is about five minutes and most of the five minutes is consumed getting dressed. I've got a large box in my trunk where I keep the tackle bag, web belt, gaff, sweatshirt, hat, etc. The rod is on a rack on the wall of the garage, and rod racks are on the car all season. Sure, every so often I'll have to change line, clean the reel, change plugs and sharpen hooks, but I can do these any time and need not be pressured right before leaving for the beach. Here's what I do:

1. Put the waders and top in the trunk
2. Tie a new knot on the leader or snap
3. Put the rod on the car
4. Get in the car
5. Take out the correct pass
6. Go fishing

Some people believe that all good fishing spots are far away. Not so! All spots are potentially good. You must study an area, learn it, fish it often and try new ideas until you get it to work.

The convenience of fishing nearby, with little preparation, makes surf fishing a desirable after-work nighttime activity.

To further illustrate how and why these things are important to me, let's reconstruct a day during a typical run of quality fish. Either you find the fish or someone calls and puts you into them. It doesn't matter; the point is, you're in. The first night you don't have the right plugs or you aren't sure what to bring. You take a variety and you take too many. The plug bag bulges. You know you'll fumble with plugs later and regret taking so many. There are big bass in one of the south shore inlets. The tide moves at about 11PM. By sunset, you are ready to go and you're anxious, but you know the time isn't right.

You finally leave home with enough time to arrive as the tide gets going. You're itchy during the drive, your heart pounds when you think of those fish. You hope you don't blow the chance. You arrive at the spot and see signs of feeding fish. You throw out your plug, but after twenty casts you have no hits. You switch plugs, the plugs tangle, and you curse yourself as you knew you would. You try artificial after artificial but the bass ignore your offering. You know you can't fish bait here because of rocks and a swift current, so you've got to find an artificial that works. You're daydreaming, thinking of something new to try when you get a hit. Later, you beach a 25 pound bass. Why this fish? You remember now. Just before the fish struck you swatted a mosquito that caused the rod to twitch. You throw the plug out and twitch the rod as you retrieve. You get another hit, but miss the fish. Then the fish move off—gone until tomorrow night.

All the way home you think about what happened and you decide on several different plugs and make a commitment to use the twitch. You get a couple hours of sleep and go to work. The usual problems inundate you at work and you handle them well in spite of the fact that you're tired and you can't wait until tonight. You are efficient because the pressure can't get to you. You are insulated from it by the prospects of surf fishing. You hope there's not a weather change.

Later, you eat dinner and take a nap. Your wife isn't delighted about an absentee husband taking a nap any more than she is pleased with your long hours on the beach, but she loves you and knows she wouldn't have the man she fell in love with if you didn't fish so hard. She resigns herself to this and watches TV either alone or with the older kids. Maybe she goes bowling, plays cards, but whatever she does, she knows she'll be doing it without you, at least until this run of fish is over. She also knows that she'll be hearing blow by blow accounts of each night's experience too—for awhile yet.

The alarm gets you up around eleven. You dress, put the rod on the car and off you go. There is the same anticipation as last night and the same anxiety, too. You arrive, you fish with new enthusiasm and new approaches, and you take four nice fish. You get increasingly less sleep every night that the run continues because the tide gets later every night and the bass require hooks be sharpened and adjustments made in tackle. Blues wreak more havoc, but big bass do their share, too. So it goes, night after night, until the fish leave. After a few nights you do well with only two to three hours of sleep. You won't let your work suffer because of your fishing; you have too much pride for that. So, you go to work everyday and you fish every night. While the run of fish lasts, you have no headaches, no job fatigue, and the passion of the hunt fills your life. Your bones hurt, but it's a good hurt. Your fingers have cuts all over from hooks and gill plates and spines, but you don't complain: they are battle scars to be accepted. The waders give off a stink that a skunk would run from, but you accept that, too. You battle the weather and other natural elements, too, but you love each and every second of it because you're a surf fisherman. Indeed, "Surf fishing is a war, and the battle is renewed every night." So may it be for a thousand, thousand years. Come join us. Be one of the few and the proud.

CHAPTER 2
Perspectives on Yesterday
by Fred Schwab

The first men to toss baited hooks from a beach probably did so several thousand years ago, and it's reasonable to conclude that their only motivation was to obtain food. Their hooks were probably made of bone, shell, or perhaps stone. And the line—well, that's anyone's guess. The first fishing reel was in the far distant future; in fact, the first book written in English on fishing, "A Treatise of Fishing with an Angle" (1496), makes no mention of a reel, and "The Art of Angling" (1651), describes a very primitive one.

Despite their primitive gear one can assume that eventually they were rewarded for their effort, and in time, men began to associate success and failure with varying conditions. Gradually, perhaps at first by chance, they improved their gear and technique. Man had already evolved into a competitive, egotistical creature, thus one can assume that the excitement and envying glances generated by his dragging a large catch into his settlement, and being regarded as a good provider, swelled his pride. It follows that he would begin to consciously experience both the pleasures and frustrations inherent in locating, outsmarting, and landing the fish and that his competitive nature would prompt him to strive to outfish those around him. While obtaining food remained the primary objective for generations to come, the seed of recreational surf fishing had been sown, and its fertilization and maturity awaited only the passage of time.

Just when and where a gathering of anglers led to the

formation of the first surf fishing club, is unknown. But on May 31, 1865, the "Cuttyhunk Fishing Association" was established and some early members of this Massachusetts group were also members of Rhode Island's West Island Club which antedated the Cuttyhunk Association.

Being men of great wealth, the members of the Cuttyhunk Club, which flourished until 1907, built a large and apparently very comfortable clubhouse on the Massachusetts island of the same name. But despite the resultant comforts and their great wealth, they reportedly were hard fishermen with a love for angling in the surf for striped bass. Their method of surf fishing was largely, but not entirely, dependent upon chumming and casting from stands or piers extending 30 to 50 feet from shore. Their competitive spirit, ceremonious weigh-ins, devotion and innovations to surf fishing, and extensive record keeping attest to the legitimacy of the claim that this group was among the pioneers of modern day surf angling.

Whether they were the first to employ fishing stands in the surf, and just how widespread that method became, is unknown. But it is of interest to note that photographs taken in 1927 and 1930 show such structures beneath the Montauk Lighthouse, and at least one was still in use during the very early 40s. Rickety, and jutting over, and sometimes under the breakers, those determined men who used these platforms often tempted fate.

During the years that the Cuttyhunk Club flourished and until after World War II, the surf anglers' equipment improved at a slow and rarely dramatic pace. By the 1930s, the reels, with now-forgotten names such as Cozone, Perez, and Vom Hoff, were reportedly quite good, but linen line, Calcutta cane and split-bamboo rods were mainstays requiring constant care and frequent replacement. While rubber boots were becoming popular, high leather boots were still the dominant footwear and waders, quite dissimilar from those in use today, were a rarity in the early 30s.

With the advent of World War II, science and industry turned to the task of developing equipment, materials and manufacturing techniques applicable to the war effort. Accelerated research led to undreamed of applications for materials already in use, the discovery of a broad range of synthetics, and more efficient, less costly production methods.

Following the war man began adapting his new finds to peacetime uses. The application of durable, lightweight synthetics and rust resistant metals vastly improved the fisherman's tools. Nylon, followed by monofilament, replaced linen line, while glass replaced split-bamboo and cane rods. Waders were no longer a rarity and increasingly affordable four-wheel drive vehicles arrived on the scene. By the early 60s a few imaginative New Yorkers had broadened their range by adapting the wet suit to angling. In fact, if the wet suit's use in the surf did not originate on Long Island, it certainly was there that its use was finely honed and most broadly applied.

But of all the changes occurring after WW II, none had the impact on angling that the introduction of spinning gear had. While a few were already in use, it was not until about 1952 that such gear was no longer viewed as an oddity on the beach. In just a few years it replaced conventional equipment as the dominant gear and by the early 60s, on "most" East Coast beaches, just a scattering of fishermen had not made the change. Curiously, fixed spool or spinning reels were apparently in use outside the United States in the early 1900s, but if any of these early designs reached our shores, they were not widely accepted.

Spinning emerged at a time when a burgeoning population was experiencing increased wages and leisure time. Many people turned to fishing as a leisure time activity, and because casting with spinning gear was easily learned, and such equipment relatively maintenance and trouble-free, the surf anglers ranks swelled at an unprecedented rate. Spinning revolutionized the art and efficiency of surf angling. Gone were the days of thumb burns, maddening backlashes, snarls of nightmarish proportions, and month, even years of practice before one mastered the art of handling the surf fisherman's gear. No longer was there a built-in weeding out process—that prolonged learning period when repeated frustration discouraged a high percentage of beginners from staying with the sport. That period during which only the most determined and dedicated reaped enough rewards to justify the hard work that surf fishing is.

During the conventional era, principally because of the gear, even moderate success demanded an accumulation of a sizeable store of knowledge, and only the most knowledgeable and skillful caught fish with consistency. With spinning gear, lighter, more realistic lures with built-in action, could be handled effectively with little know-how, and in a relatively short period of time the beginner learned to make long casts, thus the first few fish from the surf came comparatively quickly.

But spinning also brought crowded conditions, added pressure upon fish stocks, and for those already on the scene, rather fast changes and a lessening of certain accustomed benefits derived from surf fishing—the most notable of these being diminished opportunities to fish in solitude, and increased numbers of anglers at traditionally productive locations. Those and other changes are mourned by survivors from the conventional era, and some silently curse the day spinning came along.

Most of today's surf anglers did not experience the pre-spinning era, and comparing the two types of gear invariably leads them to conclude that spinning was clearly a positive addition. That, in the final analysis, is a correct assumption for the positive aspects of spinning far outweigh the negatives. This is especially true nowadays, for without this more effective gear the angler's catch would likely be far less than it is, due to more people competing for less abundant resources.

A discourse on the development of any mode of fishing usually leads to comparisons of past and present levels of fishing productivity and fish stocks. Historical catch statistics compiled by the Federal Government go back to about 1880, but are very fragmentary. In fact, most official reports list data for New York on just 12 of the 49 years through 1928. But most significantly this data relates only to the recorded commercial catch.

Such data is used to indicate fishery trends, but the further back one goes the trickier the analysis becomes. In addition to fragmentary statistics there are changes in gear and technique, and events and circumstances which immeasurably alter the data but have nothing at all to do with the overall population of a species. For example, climatic changes which alter migratory patterns, and social or economic factors which affect fishing effort and/or cause shifts in marketing outlets.

It is senseless to take on the impossible task of analyzing such statistics, none of which relates to surf angling, and since records of any sort prior to the late 1800s are scanty, comment prior to that time is limited to one observation. In describing the striped bass in New England waters in 1614, Captain John Smith has been quoted as follows: "There are such multitudes that I have seen stopped in the river close adjoining my house with a sands out tyde so many as will loade a ship of 100 tons. I myself at the turning of the tyde have seen such multitudes that it seemed to me that one might go out their backs drishod."

One has to be impressed with the magnitude of the abundance in Smith's day. Of course, that was before the industrial revolution, the damming of many spawning rivers, contamination of our waters with lethal chemicals and all those unwanted goodies that man fouls his nest with, and long before unregulated, indiscriminant, and intensive netting with sophisticated gear led to overharvesting.

Of course it's not possible to make comparisons over a 100-year period and draw absolutely certain conclusions, but reasonably accurate assumptions are possible. In making comparisons one must bear in mind that today's anglers have superior tackle, lines, lures, accessory items, the means to cover more ground, the benefit of media reports and, in part thanks to their predecessors, more knowledge of the sport. Recognition of the comparative restraints placed on anglers of the past adds substantially to the significance of the following bits of information.

From published accounts, the Cuttyhunk Association's records indicate that the quantity and quality of bass that they caught from 1865 to 1878 was quite high and that throughout this group's 42 years large fish were caught. During the club's closing years the quantity dropped, but reportedly so did fishing effort.

Charles Church is a name which evokes images of big striped bass, for he caught many large fish and his 73 pounder taken on August 13, 1913 held the all tackle record for over 60 years. Apparently, Church fished mostly from rowboats, but given the primitive gear and the fact that he left behind records of his catches, the entries in his fishing log hint at the potential during that era. From July 27 through September 4, 1915, Church's log lists one bass of 50 pounds, four in the 40s, three in the 30s and five in the 20s. Presumably, he did not list lesser fish during the period.

From fishing articles written during the 70s, one old-timer reported that in the late 30s, weakfish were more plentiful in the surf than bass and bluefish. But two others with memories of that era agreed that fishing was better then, and that a lot more big bass were caught from the beach in those days.

Lou Cihlar was an outstanding fisherman and one of a handful who pioneered in surf angling at Montauk. Cihlar's career in the surf spanned some four decades beginning shortly before 1920, and apparently he kept good records, at least from 1920 to 1947. Reportedly, he averaged about 300 striped bass a year, and a sample of his log entries indicates a 48 pounder in 1936 and one of 51 pounds in 1937.

Most long-time surf anglers have a few old fishing magazines gathering dust somewhere around their house. My collection includes several 1951 issues of the defunct publication entitled *Fishing Long Island Waters*. In one, a lad is pictured with his conventional gear and 11 surf-caught bass ranging from 18 to 45 pounds. Another shows four lads with 27 "visible" surf-caught bass, with the smallest appearing to be about 12 to 14 pounds. Nowadays, how often do you hear of quality and quantity catches in that magnitude?

One Long Island surf regular who keeps accurate and detailed records, averaged 132 game fish (bass, bluefish, weakfish and pollock) per year from 1962 through 1971, but despite increased effort his average dropped to 105 for the following 10 years. His combined bass and bluefish average for the same time periods fell from 129 to 74. Since there was no change in the angler's gear and his fishing effort actually increased, it's logical to conclude that the drop in his catch, during this 20-year period, was due to a reduction in resource abundance.

Prior to the middle 70s many Long Island regulars maintained a yearly average well in excess of 100 game fish from the high surf, and while bluefish were not as large then, those who applied themselves to the task took them with regularity throughout the fishing season. Bluefish and bass blitzes in broad daylight still happen but, especially with respect to bass, they are a rarity these days. Gone are the days when undulating clouds of gulls were seen with regularity during the fall, working over vast schools of feeding game fish along the entire south shore of Long Island.

Gone, too, since the early 60s, are the spring and late fall pollock runs in the Montauk surf. This action lengthened the season, with the fall run filling the void left by departing bass and bluefish, and prompting the hardier souls to ply the Montauk surf for big pollock well into December. Kingfish, once fairly abundant in the surf, have become a comparative rarity during the past decade. Until the middle 60s several surf locations at Montauk often produced sizeable catches of platter-sized porgies. Even the pesky and once abundant blowfish, prized by some, scorned by others, is scarce. Weakfish, all but non-existent in northern waters for years, made a strong and welcomed comeback in the early 70s, but their numbers are again on the decline. One could fill a book with bits of information on the fisheries and the productivity of surf fishing, past and present, but the message is a repetitious one. In general, most species are less abundant today, and largely due to excessive fishing pressure, periods of non-productive fishing are more frequent and longer lasting.

But there are still fish to be caught. The chance for a prized 50 pound bass, an alligator bluefish, a tiderunner weak, a stubborn rock-hugging blackfish, or an impressive catch of flatfish still remains. Surfcasting is still a constant source of anticipation and unexpected happenings, and it remains the most challenging mode of angling if one is determined to be successful at it.

But catching fish is just a part of the pleasure to be gained from this activity, for other benefits of immeasurable value abound. There are still magnificent sunrises and sunsets to be seen and the awe-inspiring sight and sound of an angry surf to be witnessed. As always, a bright moon still projects a dancing jewel-like path on the water's surface, and one can still find an isolated stretch of beach where moments in peaceful thought can whisk an individual away from the artificial and regimented world of man. Or, one can share precious moments with others having kindred interests.

For those who are most observant, and fortunate enough to be in the right place at the right time, there are moments when one is privileged to see a rare species of wildlife or observe some unusual form of wildlife behavior. For the fisherman's children, the seashore environment is a source of never-ending wonder. A vast outdoor place of learning. A classroom where a child can grow to understand and respect the works of nature and its various life forms. A place from which memories of carefree childhood days are carried into adulthood years.

While certain qualities of surf angling may have diminished, our changing times have heightened the value of others...the magic is still there. But it can all be lost if anglers do not remain alert, fighting to retain their right of access and demanding effective resource management programs.

CHAPTER 3
Gear to Get Started
by Tom Fitzsimmons

Before you can undertake any new hobby or sport, you should be prepared with the proper equipment for the job. Surf fishing is no different, and perhaps, in some ways, this preparation is more important than in some other activities.

The conditions encountered in fishing the surf are rigorous and demanding on both the fisherman and his equipment. It must withstand the pounding surf, corrosion due to contact with saltwater, abrasion from the sand, and the lack of attention that it sometimes receives after a long night of fishing. For these reasons the equipment you purchase, or make yourself, should be of the highest quality your budget will allow.

In this chapter I will provide you with a guideline for equipment that will help you get started in an exciting, challenging and very demanding sport.

RODS

The type of rod you use can vary depending upon the type of fishing you do and the species of fish being sought. For light tackle, a seven or eight foot rod with light or medium action should work quite nicely for small lures and line to 12 pound test. When you start to use those larger, heavier plugs, trying to gain better distance, or presenting larger baits for bigger fish, rods from nine to twelve feet with medium to heavy action, for line weights from 15 to 30 pounds are called for.

There are many excellent rods available manufactured by Fenwick, Lamiglass, Shakespeare (Ugly Stik), and Daiwa, plus many others. These rods come equipped with guides made from various materials. Try to select one with stainless steel or aluminum oxide guides. The blanks themselves also vary in construction from fiberglass, S-glass or Fenglass (my choice because of their lighter weight and greater strength than fiberglass), graphite, boron (both excellent but expensive) and the Ugly Stik (a quality material made from a combination of graphite and fiberglass). Look for rods that have reel seats constructed of chrome-plated brass or the new Fuji graphite style. For the bigger rods you may not want any reel seat at all so that you can tape the reel directly to the rod with friction tape. Custom-made rods are also available at many tackle stores. They can build a rod to your specifications or specific fishing style.

When selecting a rod, as with the reel, your local tackle dealer can be of assistance in putting together a good combination of reel, rod and line that will best suit the type or style of fishing you are interested in.

Light tackle rods can run between $30 and $60 for ready-made, and up to $150-plus for a custom-made rod. Heavier rods from nine to twelve feet cost from $50 to $90 for production line rods, and climb to about $200, or even more, for custom rods, depending upon the materials used.

REELS

The main consideration you should keep in mind in the selection of a reel, is to make certain that you purchase one that can withstand the damaging effects of saltwater and sand. Avoid buying a cheap reel that is not constructed for saltwater fishing or strong enough to stand up to the heavier type of fishing encountered in the surf.

Look for reels that are constructed as simply as possible. The less mechanical parts you have, the smaller the chance of breakdowns. Also, try to buy a reel that uses quality engineered parts, such as gears and bearings made from stainless steel and bronze. Look for drags of Teflon alternating with metal washers, which will give you very smooth action when fighting a fish, with less chance of the drag stuttering and breaking the line.

For spinning reels, the Penn 710Z, 712Z Spinfisher or 550SS; Shakespeare Sigma 050/060; Daiwa BG 13 or 15; or the Quick 2001, 3001, are all fine reels for light tackle fishing with line capacity up to about 12 pound test. These range in price from $25 to $70.

Top row: Penn Squidder, Ambassadeur 7000, Newell 229. Bottom row; Ambassadeur 5500, Shimano Mag 50. Equipment courtesy of Merrick Tackle.

Top row: Daiwa BG15, Shakespeare Sigma 060, Quick 2001, Penn 712Z. Bottom Row: Shakespeare Sigma 070, Quick 5001, Penn 706Z. Equipment courtesy of Beckmann's and Merrick Tackle.

Spin reels for heavier tackle, with line capacity from 20 to 30 pound test, include the Penn 704Z, 706Z Spinfisher or 750SS; Garcia Cardinal 59; Shakespeare Sigma 070/080; Daiwa BG 60 or 90; and the Quick 4001, 5001—all good quality reels averaging around $40 to $90.

In this heavier class range, usually available through private sales, you may wish to purchase what is considered by many to be the ultimate surf reel, the Crack 300, for about $130.

For light tackle fishing with conventional reels, the Garcia Ambassadeur 5500 or 6500 series; Shimano Bantam 300 or 400; Daiwa PS7 or PS10 are all excellent reels for line capacities to about 12 pound test. These reels will range in price from $40 to $90.

For heavier tackle with line capacity to 30 pound test, the Penn Squidder 140; Garcia Ambassadeur 7000; Shimano MAG50 or Triton; and the Newell 229M or 235M will all give you the quality and dependability needed to fish the heavy surf. The price for these reels can run from about $40 to over $100.

When purchasing a reel, your local tackle dealer can again be of aid in helping you put together a well-balanced combination of rod and reel, depending upon what type of fishing you intend to do.

LINE

One of the greatest problems you will encounter with your line is abrasion. This is caused by contact with the fish you're fighting, plus sand, rocks, mussel beds, and other subsurface structures that you pull your line through or across while retrieving a lure or bait rig. There is no way to overcome this problem other than to purchase a quality line that has good resistance to this abrasion.

When fishing, you should remember to check your line periodically for nicks that can weaken the line and cause it to break when you hit a fish. A good practice to follow is to cut back on your line, by stripping a few yards off the spool when these nicks are discovered, or after you catch a few fish. You should also strip some line off each time you begin a new fishing trip; this will help eliminate the line from breaking due to line fatigue from constant casting the night before. Changing the first 100 yards or so of line several times during the season (more often depending upon the number of times you fish), will also eliminate problems in connection with damage by ultra violet rays, salt, nicks in the line you don't readily notice, and general deterioration from usage.

Stretch in your line is another consideration to look for. When that hook has to be set, you need to strike hard, and if the line stretches too much, it will only make it more difficult, if not impossible, to drive the hook home. That frustration of not being able to hook up time and time again is a feeling we all want to avoid.

Good quality monofiliment lines include Ande, Stren, Berkley "Trilene", and Maxima. For bait fishing, Cortland/Micron is favored by many anglers because of its low stretch and small diameter (per pound test).

You can have line put on your reel by most tackle dealers, or you could purchase bulk spools and do it yourself. If you buy spools, try to get the larger ones (if your budget allows). This can help eliminate problems of line set caused by tightly wound smaller spools, which can give you casting problems.

For light tackle, lines from 8 to 12 pound test will work well when using lures up to one ounce. As the season progresses and larger fish are being sought, or when bait fishing with chunks of mackerel or bunker, lines of 15 to 30 pound test should be used.

BASIC LURES AND BAIT RIGS

Specific types of lures, bait rigs and their uses will be discussed in greater detail in other chapters, so let me just state that a good selection of lures is essential when you are out on the beach. In most cases it is a long walk back to your car if you do not have the lure that the fish are responding to. Standing and watching other people catch fish, knowing the lure you need could have been in your surf bag, can make for a very disappointing evening.

For light tackle fishing, carry a good basic selection of plugs between 3/8 and 3/4 ounces by Rebel, RedFin and Rapala, in a combination of floaters, sinkers and jointed plugs, plus a selection of colors of each type. Try to include a few bucktails, Alou Eels or Tri-Fin Eelworms. Some poppers, and tins, are also necessary for fishing at sunset and sunrise. Tins by Kastmaster and Hopkins, poppers by Atom and Creek Chub should fill your needs.

Heavier tackle calls for plugs from one ounce and up in weight. Again, they should be carried in a variety of styles from surface swimmers, sinkers, deep divers, darters, plus a selection of tins, poppers and bucktails, again with an assortment of colors. Good quality plugs in this range are available from Atom, Stan Gibbs, Rebel, RedFin, Rapala and Super-Strike.

When baitfishing, you will need a good supply of sinkers, terminal tackle and floats. These should be carried in a separate bag to avoid the hassle involved with switching your bag from plugs to bait rigs.

SURF BAGS

Although it is impossible to carry all the lures you would like to when you go fishing, the use of a surf bag will help you to carry a large enough assortment. A good surf bag should be constructed with fasteners, clips, buckles, etc., that are not affected by saltwater and provide you with at least ten or more inserts large enough to allow you to carry as many large plugs as you have divisions, with enough room to double up on small plugs or provide you with an assortment of both.

To my knowledge, there are only a few surf bags on the market. One, manufactured by Shoreline, that sells for about $32 at local tackle stores, comes in two sizes with five or ten inserts made of aluminum. The bag itself is made of canvas, with six pockets sewn in front to carry tins and an adjustable shoulder strap. It provides you with enough room behind the aluminum inserts to carry droppers and leaders, and there are also "D" rings on the shoulder strap that you can fasten miscellaneous equipment to.

The Shoreline and Bronco surf bags. Equipment courtesy of Merrick and Beckmann's Tackle.

A new bag that is on the market is called the Bronco and is available in a deluxe model. They sell at your local tackle store for about $30 for the Bronco and $40 for the deluxe bag. The Bronco comes with ten plastic inserts and has six pockets on the front for tins, plus an adjustable shoulder strap. The Bronco is best suited for smaller plugs (up to 5½ inches), and has storage space for leaders, etc., behind the inserts. The deluxe bag has the same features, but is about an inch and a half taller and comes with larger inserts, not only in diameter, but also in height, which are necessary to carry large plugs like Atom 40s and three ounce Gibbs swimmers. Extra inserts are available for both bags for approximately $14 apiece. The deluxe bag also provides you with a pocket, on the end, to carry extra spools, a knife, hook sharpener and other miscellaneous equipment. This deluxe bag should prove to be a very versatile and useful piece of equipment.

Although all three bags are made of canvas (which becomes heavier when it absorbs water), they are the only reasonably priced, quality bags that I am aware of.

The Surfcaster, a mail order firm in Darien, Connecticut, does handle a very high quality bag made of Dacron (which sheds water), has polystyrene inserts, compartments for an extra spool, pliers, etc., and an extra wide shoulder strap that is more comfortable than bags with narrow straps. This bag costs about $130, with extra inserts available for about $23 each.

WADERS

Depending upon your degree of commitment, waders can be an optional item. The two styles available are the chest high and hip waders. The latter type is best suited for calmer waters, back bay fishing, and when deep water is within easy casting distance from the beach. However, hip waders in my opinion, are better left to freshwater fishing. For surf fishing, hip and chest waders with boots attached, are more practical than the freshwater stocking foot type. Some of the more popular, quality brands of hip waders include Red-Ball, Ranger, Converse and Marathon, ranging in price from $45 to $80. Other inexpensive brands are available but they will not stand up as well.

Chest waders are a much wiser choice for surf fishing. Not only can they be used in calm water situations, but will provide you with better protection in heavy surf. They enable you to wade out deeper to reach fish breaking further off the beach. And in rough weather or fast currents, they protect you from getting wet and catching a chill, which can put a quick end to your evening of fishing. Red-Ball, Ranger, Marathon, Uni-Royal, Converse and Gray-Lites are good brands to look for when purchasing chest waders. These can range in cost from $60 to $150 (for Gray-Lites), the cost also depending upon whether you purchase insulated or non-insulated styles with special soles. If you intend to fish heavily, the insulated style will help ward off the effects that standing in cold water for long periods of time can have on your stamina.

If you intend to fish the jetties, cleated sandals may be purchased to help insure more secure footing. In fishing areas with moss-covered rocks, felt-soled sandals will better assist you against slipping. If subsurface rocky conditions prevail in the area you fish, felt soles may be glued directly to your waders. But constant walking on sand beaches will soon destroy the felt; therefore, for varied fishing conditions, separate sandals are a better long-term investment.

Some die-hard surf fishermen will even go to the extreme of wearing wet suits. This enables them to wade out neck deep, or swim to sand bars or rocks located far off the beach, which is why these are very popular at Montauk. A quality wet suit consisting of a top, bottom ("farmer John" style with shoulder straps), soft style booties and a hood can cost anywhere from $150 to $250.

If your approach to surf fishing is very casual, limited to maybe one trip a week for a short period of time, waders, as I stated earlier, can be optional. But once the water turns cold, this can be very limiting. So, even for casual fishing, it would be better to purchase an inexpensive pair of waders for about $25 to $30.

MISCELLANEOUS EQUIPMENT

A necessary accessory to have when you wear chest waders is a web-type belt (corrosion resistant), secured at the waist. It could aid in saving your life by preventing water from filling up your waders if you should lose your footing and fall. The belt is also a good place to hang a gaff, stringer and knife. An Army issue pistol belt is ideal because of construction, ease of removal, and the number of holes available to aid in attaching various equipment.

Carrying a hand gaff with a handle about 15 to 18 inches long, equipped with a stainless steel hook, in a sheath attached to the belt with a telephone extension cord, will be an aid in landing that big fish. A good quality gaff and sheath should run about $20 to $30, or you could make your own using a one inch diameter birch dowel, and purchasing a stainless steel gaff hook.

A good knife, compound cutting pliers, or needle-nose pliers, plus a hook sharpening stone carried on the belt or in your surf bag, are also valuable aids. Cutting pliers, such as those made by Manely or Sargent, help when cutting line, removing the hook from a fish's mouth and, if need be, cutting the barb off a hook that found its way into your hand rather than the fish. Pliers can run anywhere from $10 to $20.

Carrying a stringer for those fish you catch can also be secured to the belt (with a quick release snap). Look for one made from chain, or make one yourself from brass sash or jack chain. They hold up better than nylon cord. The longer the stringer (about 12 feet), the better; this length enables you to pull the fish back down the beach easily while you walk in the water, thereby eliminating the strain of hand-carrying the fish back. Perhaps more important, this length will allow you to let the fish drift behind you while you are still in the water. This can eliminate an unpleasant close encounter with a shark should they be cruising the area. Long stringer or not, remember it is far wiser to leave your fish up on the beach than to take a chance meeting a shark in his home turf.

As with any style of fishing, there are numerous amounts of terminal tackle that you will need with you: snaps, swivels, leaders, sinkers, etc. These items will be discussed in greater detail with information as to their specific use, in

U.S. Army pistol belt with chain stringer attached to quick release clip. Gaff and sheath with telephone extension coil and clip (carried on surf belt). Justin neck lamp and battery pack, Flex-light, needle nose pliers (stainless steel), Manley cutting pliers and sheath.

other chapters. The best snap I have found is the Duo-Lock brand, which comes in various sizes and is available with a black finish to reduce reflections, thereby possibly eliminating a fish from striking the snap and breaking the line. Black swivels are also available in various sizes, made by Sampo or Crane. These can be carried on the outside of your bag, for easy access, by hanging them from a large split ring or sinker release snap. Plastic coated leader wire is available (also in black) in a variety of pound tests, depending upon your needs. Buying bulk coils will allow you to make leaders, combined with a snap and swivel of various lengths depending upon your requirements.

Two more items that are helpful are a hat and rain top. A hat helps during cold weather by limiting heat loss from your body. A wool knit Navy watch cap is a good type. The rain top should be a pullover style that is lightweight, with elastic cuffs, drawstring waist, zipper neck and a hood. A top helps protect you not only in rainstorms, but keeps you dry when you get hit by a wave. The pullover style will keep out water much better than the snap-front type. A very good quality top is available by mail order from L.L. Bean for about $50.

One final accessory that is helpful for tying knots or changing rigs when night fishing is a neck lamp. The old standby light manufactured by Justin is very good, but is heavy because of the four "D" cell battery pack that hangs on your hip. It sells for about $14. The much smaller and lighter "Flex-Light" is also very good. It takes two "AA" batteries and provides a much tighter beam of light. The Flex-Light sells for around $9.

This basic outline is simply a guide to help you get started as a surf fisherman. As you continue to fish and talk with others on the beach, you will pick up on many new ideas and methods of making yourself more efficient concerning the equipment you need and its usage. As you gain experience, you will also develop your own likes and dislikes for certain rods, reels, etc., that for one reason or another do not live up to your standards or conform to your style of fishing.

CHAPTER 4

The Very Basic Basics
by William A. Muller

I have been a member of the High Hill Striper Club for about ten years now and as a member, I have enjoyed meeting many new recruits to surf fishing, as well as veterans who know the sport inside and out. Throughout this decade of close contact with surf fishermen of varying experience I have been repeatedly impressed by the need to be well versed in the basics.

Other authors appearing in this book have discussed a vast array of basics related to diverse categories from lures, to bait rigs, to equipment. Each one in their own way has provided the interested reader with a wealth of advice on basics. It is not unusual for experienced surf fishermen to stress basic skills and basic knowledge. Many of these veterans have learned the hard way how many fish can be lost and how many golden fishing opportunities can be squandered when a surf fisherman is lacking in the basics.

It is also not unusual for the beginner to surf fishing to believe that success lies in knowledge of secret spots and secret weapons. They sometimes are convinced that success in surf fishing can be instantaneous. Well, I'm here to tell you that in more than 25 years fishing the surf I've never met a surf fisherman who was an instant success. Sure, once in awhile a newcomer enjoys a short-lived modest success. However, similar to the sophomore jinx in sports, the second fishing season becomes a lot more frustrating than the first.

I've also not come across too many secret spots and secret weapons in all the years I've prowled the surf. My advice is not to hold out hope for secret weapons because if you truly

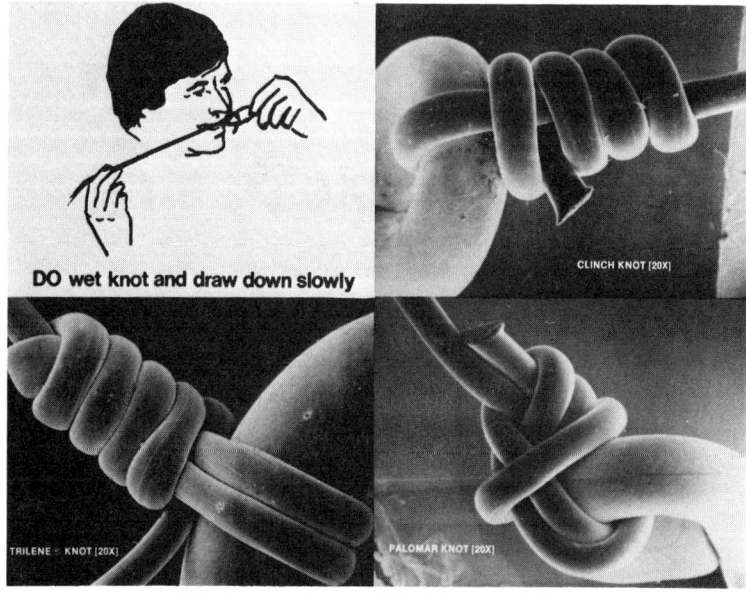

Photo courtesy of Berkley and Co.

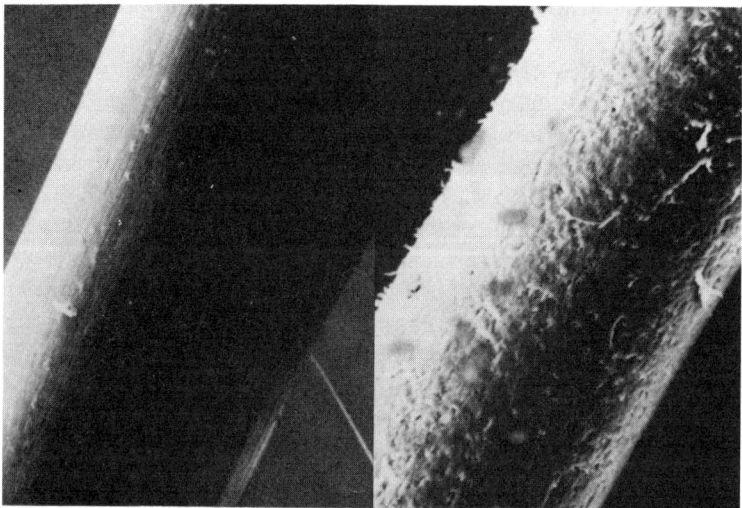

New, ten pound test nylon mono (left) and used, heavily fished ten pound mono (right) enlarged 200 times on an electron microscope. Photo courtesy of Berkley and Co.

believe in the search for secret weapons instead of "putting your time in," as the regulars say, you may be disappointed and turned off.

Although spending a lot of time on the beach is an excellent way to learn and improve your success, paying attention to details and learning the basics will also be a big asset. Since other authors have discussed specific basics in other chapters, I thought it might be apropos to review some of the general basics in a separate chapter.

Let's start with the fishing line. Change the line often. Do not use it when it loses its color, is frayed, or no longer possesses resiliency. Worn-out lines will exhibit poor knot strength and will have lost their stretch. Worn-out line will contribute to more lost fish, lures, and bait rigs. If you fish five or more nights a week in season, change the line every few weeks. Keep monofilament line out of the direct sun as much as possible and keep it dry between trips. Both water and sunlight weaken monofilament line. Strip ten feet of line off the spool after each trip, and tie a new terminal knot immediately before leaving for the beach. The last ten feet of line tends to take the most abuse while fishing, and removing it will mean you eliminate a small length of worn-out line. Do not use a reel that is not properly filled with line. Over-fills cause wind loops and birds-nests and under-filled reduces casting distance and increases the drag strain on line towards the center of the spool that has been previously compressed by line when the spool was originally properly filled.

Another often overlooked aspect of line is knots, since, after all, knots are tied with line. To begin with, never use a knot twice. That is, a knot that has held through one outing will probably not hold during the next. In fact, if you are enjoying a profitable night of fishing—making numerous casts and catching many fish—it is wise to retie every hour or two. Knots take tremendous abuse from the power of the cast and even more when a good fish is fighting hard to escape. The coils of a knot get tighter and tighter with each pull and whatever resilience was in the monofilament when the knot was tied is lost in a short time. The line in the knot and directly behind the knot becomes fatigued. The fatigue leads to fractures and breaks—at just the wrong moment. Tie your knots very carefully. Sometimes we get careless about the quality of our knots. We're in a hurry, our fingers are cold, the fish are swirling in front of us, others are landing fish around us. There are a thousand reasons for being careless with knots, but none of them are good reasons. Remember, quality fish are hard to come by and many plugs today cost five dollars or more. There are many good knots to choose from: the improved clinch knot, the Palomar, and the Uni-knot, are a few examples of knots that retain close to 100 percent of the line strength and are very reliable. Whichever knot you prefer, tie it carefully according to the directions. Tie it slowly and wet the knot and surrounding line with saliva before pulling it tight. The saliva will lubricate the line and prevent excessive and unequal stretching. Pull the knot tight with a uniform motion. This will improve the quality of the knot by causing the line coils to assume proper and non-overlapping positions. It will also prevent unequal stretching of the line. Make sure, when the knot is complete, that its characteristics conform to diagrams or pictures of the knot. Do not accept a knot that is irregular in any respect.

I cannot emphasize the preceding statement strongly enough. DO NOT ACCEPT ANY KNOT THAT IS IRREGULAR IN ANY RESPECT. If it is irregular, cut it, and make a new knot. For example, my favorite knot is the improved clinch knot. When the tie is complete, the coils of the knot should stack up one behind the other and the end of the line should exit smartly between the first and second, or the second and third coil. If any of the coils overlap others, cut the line, and make a new knot.

Some fishermen would disagree with me on the next basic, but I've found it valuable over the years. That is, I prefer to use a leader about 18 inches long instead of tying directly to an artificial. The leader allows the surf fisherman to use a line of slightly greater strength than the test of the spool line. This provides minimum diameter on the spool line for casting ease and distance, and at the same time, provides a margin of safety near the plug to ward off gill covers, spines, teeth, rocks, and shells. In addition, a large black barrel swivel can be used at the spool line end of the leader. In this remote position the large swivel should not spook the fish and yet its free swiveling should help prevent

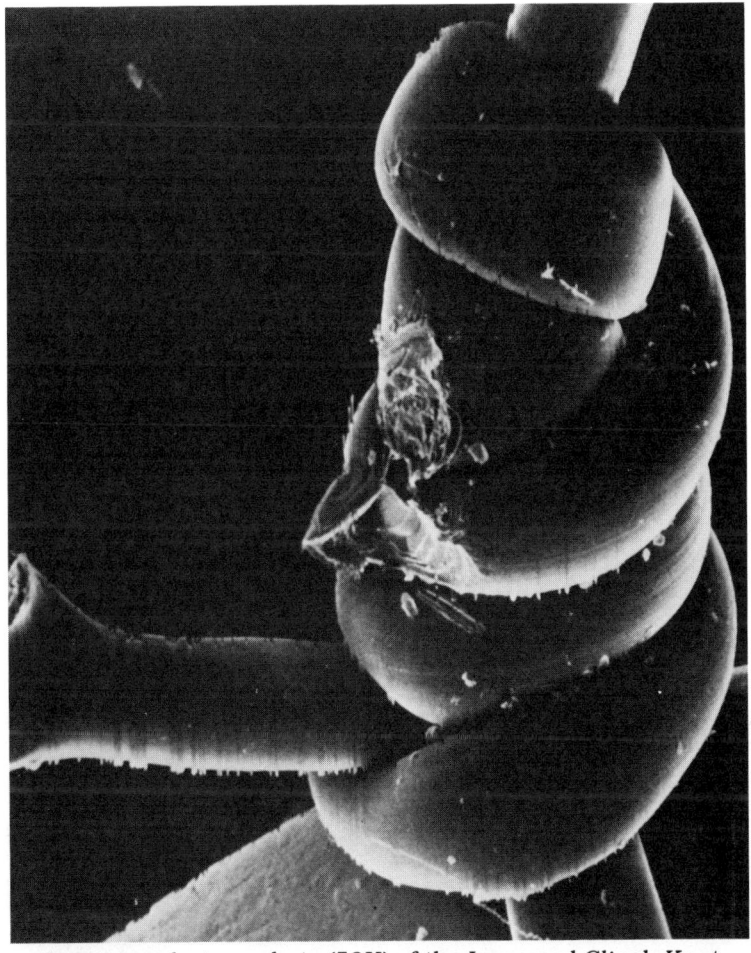

Scanning electron photo (50X) of the Improved Clinch Knot in ten pound test Trilene XL monofilament with the knot accidentally damaged by clipper when mono tail was trimmed off. Photo courtesy of Berkley and Co.

line twist. At the other end of the leader use a reliable snap such as the Duo-Lock snap.

Many fishermen may agree with the concept described above, but elect to use a "shocker leader" instead. A shock leader is a length of line of greater strength than the spool line and is long enough to extend from the artificial, through the guides, and make several turns around the spool. The shocker is tied to the spool or main line with a blood knot. Blood knots must be tied carefully, as any knot must be.

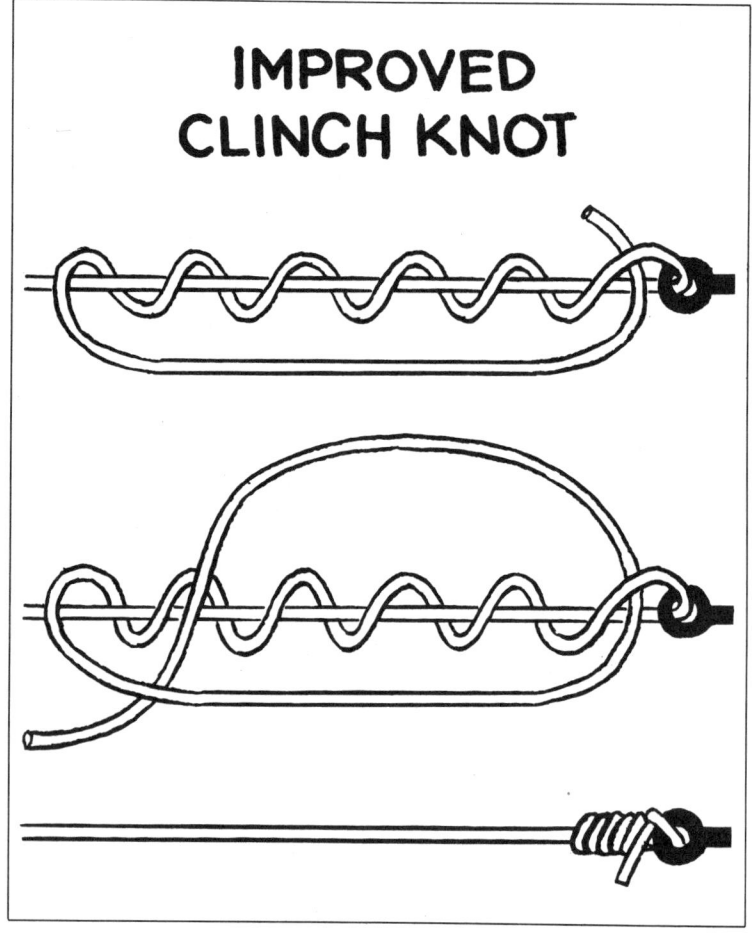

When completed, the ends of the two lines should extend out of the coils of the knot in opposite directions: 180 degrees. The coils should be non-overlapping. Blood knots can become unreliable and difficult to tie when the difference in pound test between the two lines becomes too great. Here are a few examples to provide you with guidelines on the strengths of the two lines. If you're using 10 pound test on the spool, 15 pound test on the shocker might be best, although some would use 20 pound test. Ten

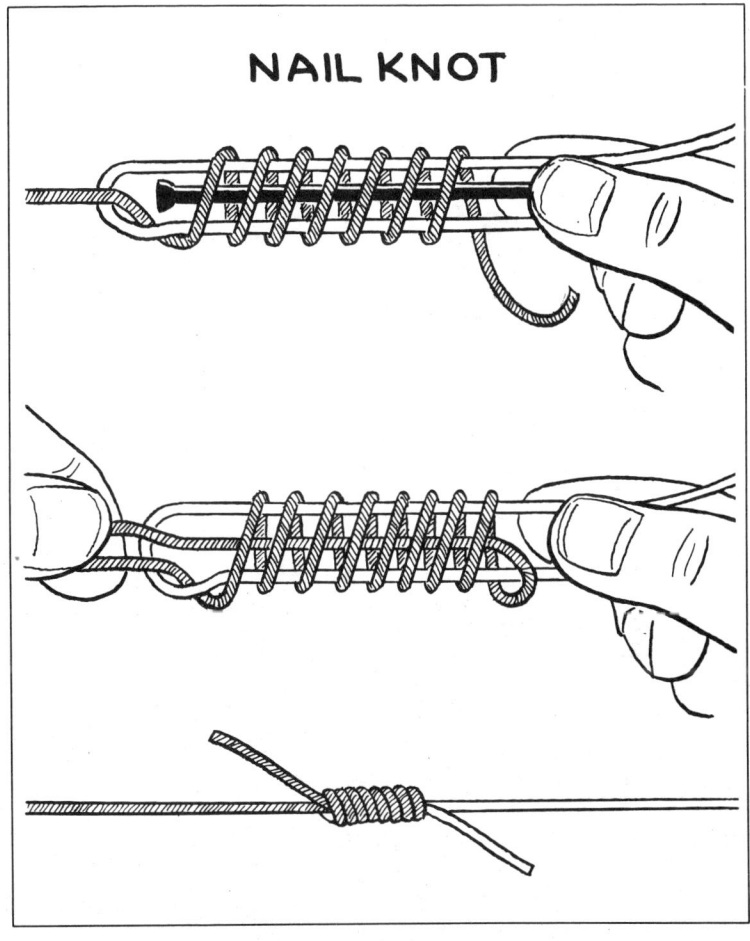

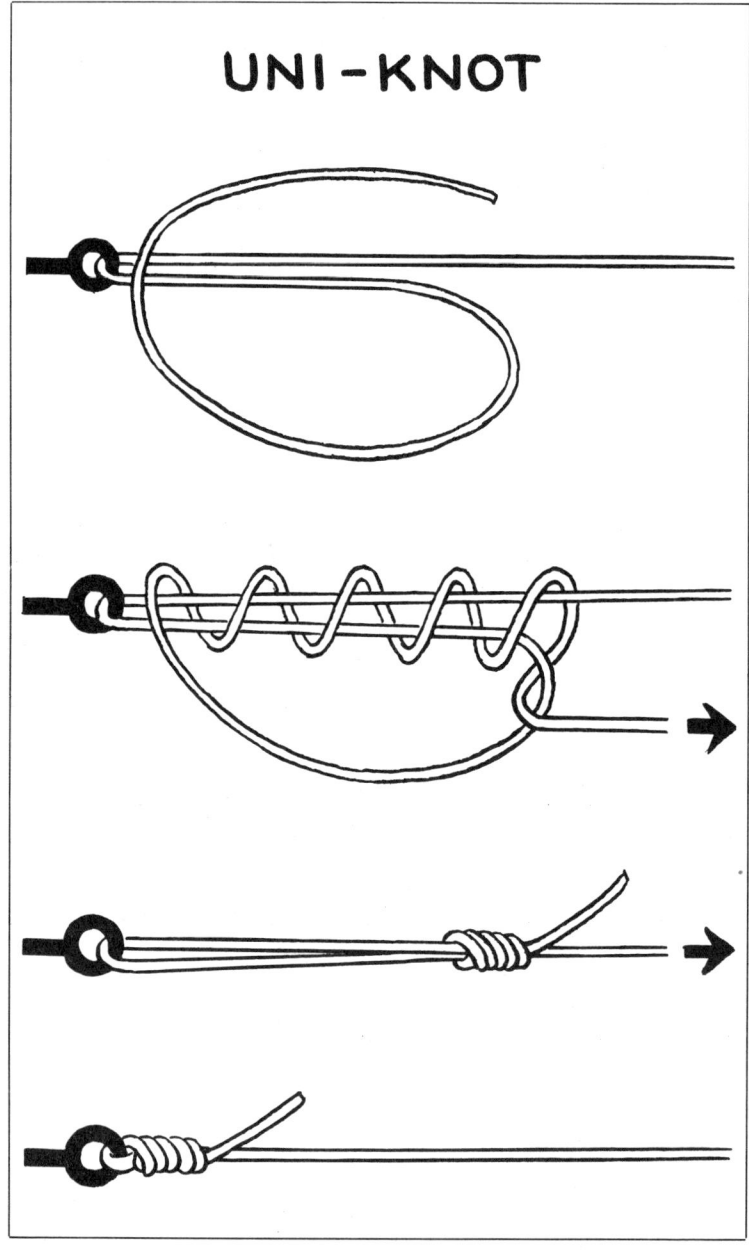

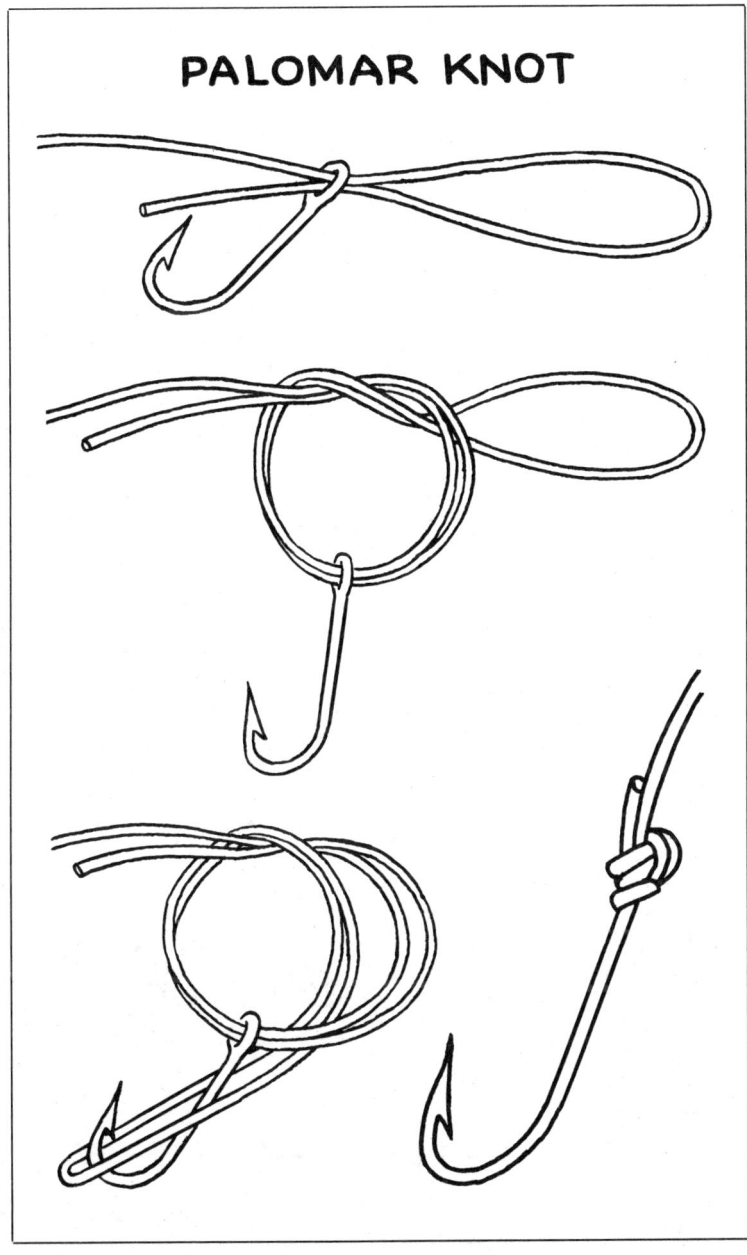

pound line blood-knotted to 30 pound test would be extremely difficult to tie and if you made a knot, that knot would be unreliable. With 20 pound test line, however, a 30 pound shocker might work out okay—if you took pains in making the knot.

The advantages of the shock leader include the added strength near the artificial, also indicated as an advantage for a plain leader. Also, the shocker provides extra strength

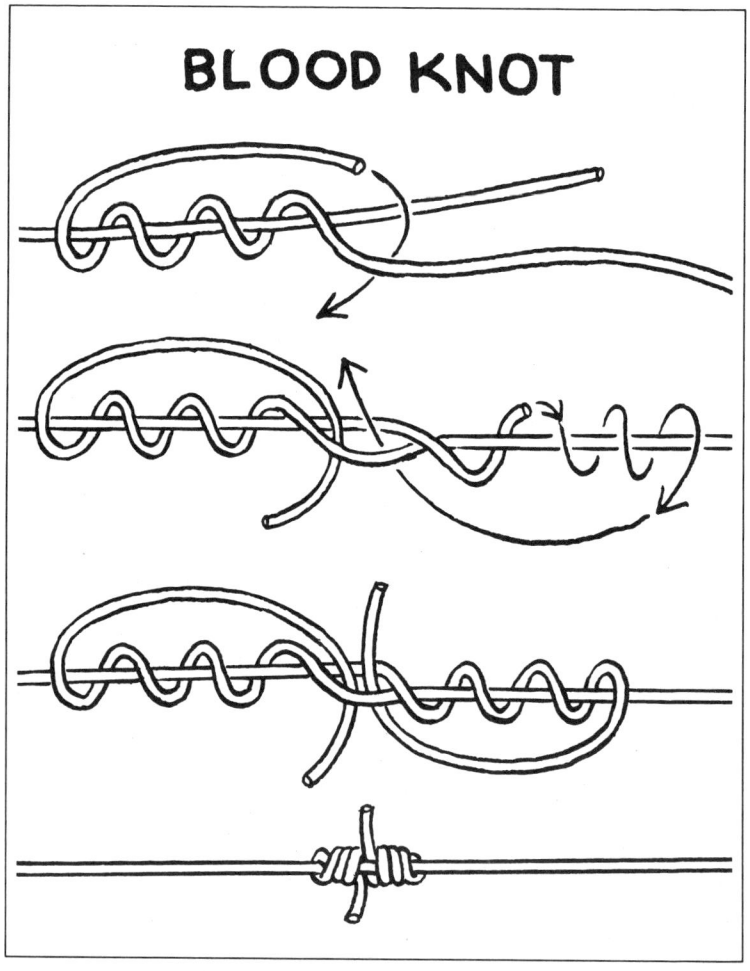

on the cast because the leader will absorb the force of the cast or the shock of the cast; hence, the origin of the leader's name. For many, the shock leader is the ideal solution to combining strength on the cast while being able to use thinner spool line for longer casts. However, I feel compelled to explain why I avoid the use of a shock leader. Over the years I have used shockers on and off because others indicated their success with this leader. My experience was always the same. I found that the blood knot would hit the guides during the cast, reducing the length of the cast and weakening the knot. Eventually the knot would fail, usually at precisely the wrong time. I have found, therefore, that the terminal leader is a better alternative. The reader may wish to experiment with both approaches and reach his or her own conclusions.

As long as we're discussing the terminal end of our tackle, let's pause a moment to consider bait fishing rigs. Many of the same principles apply. Bait fishing rigs used for species other than blues and tied with monofilament should be retied before each trip. Line should be checked for nicks often. When using wire leaders, test the crimps before using. I generally do this by sinking a strong nail into a beam of the basement ceiling. I secure the snap over the nail and pull the barrel swivel with a pliers. If the crimps are strong, there will be no slippage. Wire leaders can be used again. But if the wire under the nylon coating begins to corrode or rust, or in the case of non-coated single strand wire, the wire kinks, discard the leader. Also, if bluefish eat away at the leader do not use it. Finally, the life of wire leaders and rigs is not infinite. Therefore, after a few uses make a new one. The snaps and swivels can be used again and again, however.

Another very important basic basic is hooks. It must be impressed that hooks should be sharp and kept that way. Hooks out of a box, whether they are on a plug or loose, are not sharp. Buy a jeweler's file at a hardware store and sharpen all hooks carefully. The file can be a small one and inexpensive. Stroke the point of the hook towards the very tip only and work around the tip until all sides have been

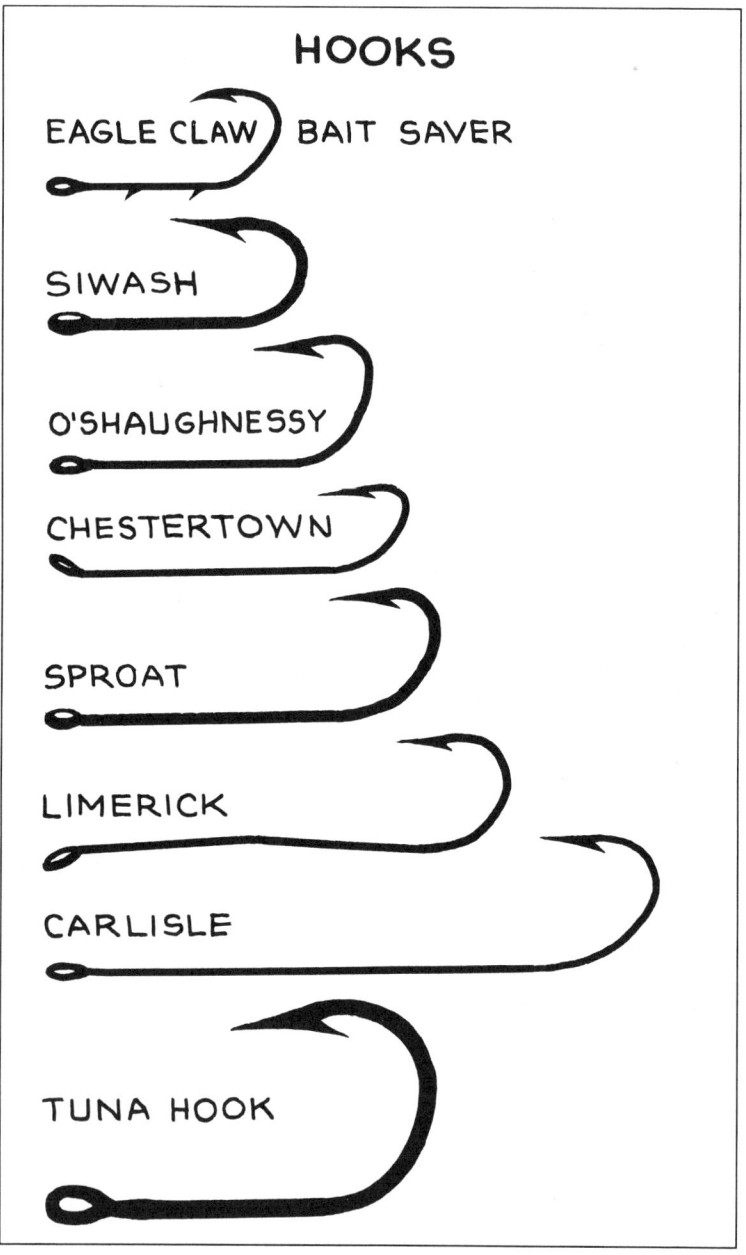

touched. Test for sharpness by gently placing the hook in contact with the nail on your thumb. If the point of the hook grabs the nail without pressure, the hook is sharp. If it does not, continue to sharpen. You may struggle with this technique in the beginning until you find the proper angle of the file and the precise stroking motion. However, after a few attempts you will become proficient.

When hooks begin to rust they should be taken off the plug and replaced. Do not scrimp on the cost of replacement hooks. Get the best and strongest you can buy. Remember that the hook is what holds you to the fish—even a trophy fish. Do not open and close the eye of a hook repeatedly. Even the best of today's hooks cannot be opened and reclosed after the first use. If you have to remove a perfectly good hook for some reason, such as repainting a plug, discard the hook(s) and replace with a new, sharpened one. Incidentally, hooks become dull through oxidation even when not used. Therefore, check for sharpness before each trip and sharpen those hooks that need sharpening. Hooks used for baitfishing will dull quickly because they are being dragged through sand and/or against rocks. When baitfishing, bring the file with you and check for sharpness after every cast. It takes a very sharp hook to penetrate the hard bone and tough cartilage of large game fish.

Many of us overlook our reels. We take their smooth performance for granted. However, reels are subjected to sand and salt constantly and we should take pains to keep them in tip-top working order. Here are some of the problems we can run into if reels are not stripped and cleaned regularly. Saltwater intrudes into crevices in the reel. When you hang up the reel the water dries, leaving salt crystals behind to mix with grease and dirt. In severe cases, the result can be a cement-like substance that can stop a reel from turning. Sand can easily work into a reel. Once inside it can damage the sides of spools, drag mechanisms, bearings, and shafts. Grease and oil do not have infinite life spans. Saltwater, heat, cold, sun, and dirt rapidly reduce the efficiency of lubricants. Dried and caking lubricants can do more damage than no lubricants at all. If you fish often and

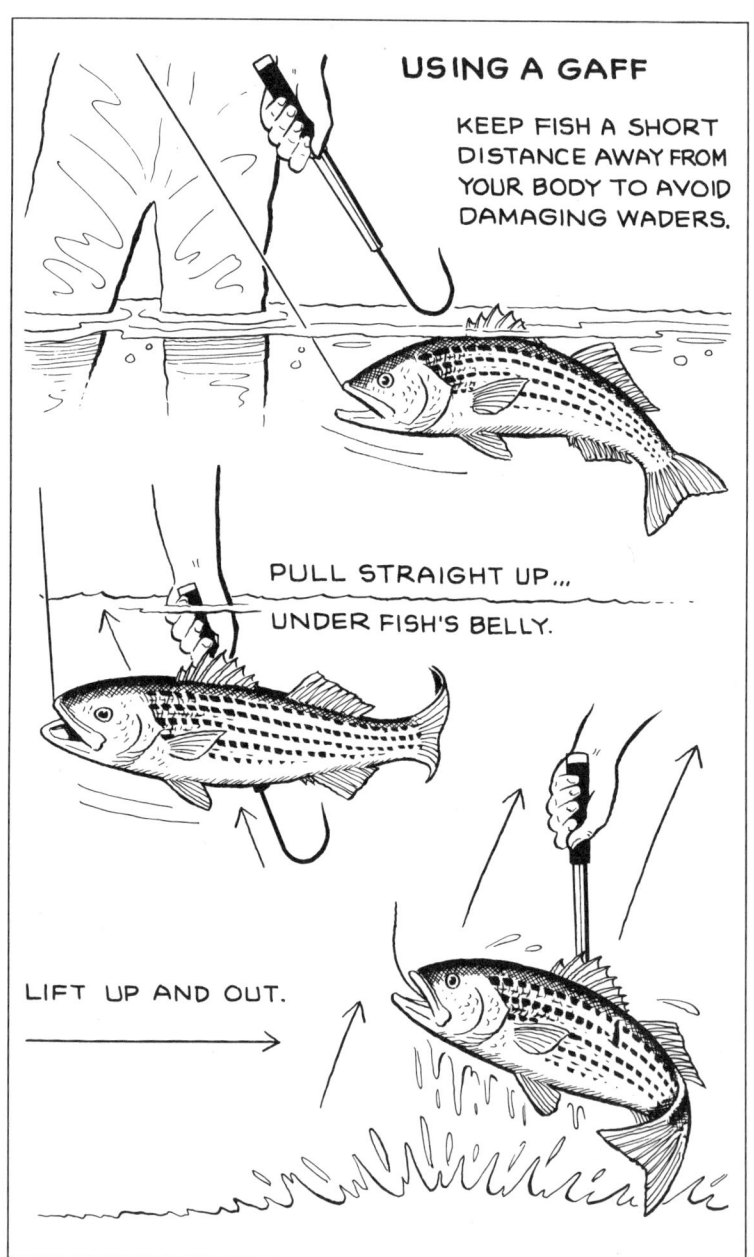

hard, strip the reel down at least once a week. Remove dirt, salt build-up, and any sand. Replace the lubricant.

Many fishermen have a habit of washing their reels in fresh water when they return from a fishing trip. Fresh water will wash away surface salt and dirt, but is not likely to penetrate deeply into crevices. Even if it does and dissolves the salt, it will remain there and when this water dries, the salt will again be left behind. Instead, it is recommended that fishermen spray their reels thoroughly with WD-40 or similar silicon spray. These lubricant sprays penetrate deeply and replace water. Therefore, you can lift away the water and salt and leave behind a film of silicon.

Rods need attention, too, and I'm not referring to winter refinishing. Instead, check the guides for cracks and corrosion that can cut through line. Check reel seats and/or tape for corrosion and deterioration.

Last, but not least, keep a log. A log does not have to be a fancy record of everything you do, although some surf fishermen are fastidious in keeping long-standing records of their fishing successes, experiments, and failures. There is no set format for record keeping. You can keep track of dozens of facts and figures, or you can choose to keep the record to a minimum. At the very least, we suggest the following:

Date
Tide stage
Hours fished
Artificials or bait used
Location(s)
Number and species of fish caught
Sizes of fish
Wind, moon, sky

You might be surprised at how easily memory fails and confuses. The log will allow you to look back and spot fishing patterns that repeat year after year and simplify your decisions about where, when, and how to fish. One of the keys to consistent success is improving the odds of catching fish. A log goes a long way to make that possible and thus makes a log a very basic basic.

CHAPTER 5
Casting
by William A. Muller

The purpose of this chapter is not to make expert casters out of those who read this. Such a goal would be very ambitious and would require not only many more pages than are available to us in this book, but also personal lessons from an expert caster. I am not an expert caster, and over the years that I have been surf casting, I have met very few expert casters. Most of us do a good enough job; we get the lure out where it might catch a fish and with decent accuracy.

Many of you know how to cast and probably, if we're honest enough to admit it, with a few bad habits. This chapter becomes superfluous for the experienced. However, for those of you who are new to surf fishing or who have watched others on the beach and noted certain distinct differences between your casting method and theirs, this chapter may be of some help in orienting you towards more controlled, comfortable, longer, and more accurate casts. Thus, what we offer is a chapter of some basics. Each of you should feel comfortable adapting these basics to your own style of fishing. After all, the key is to get the job done.

In some parts of the world precise casting is very important. That is, imperfections in style cut down on the distance of the cast and the accuracy, and because the fish may be much further off the beach in those places than they are in Long Island waters, reduced distance equates to empty stringers. In some parts of Europe and in Australia, the development of surf casting skills has become both a science and an art. We'll give you a little flavor of that when we discuss "power casting."

SPINNING—SMALL STICKS:

During some parts of the season, particularly in spring when seeking weakfish and school bass, quiet waters and close-feeding fish means a surf fisherman can use one-handed sticks effectively. Few people have trouble with these outfits because they are light and can be handled by people of almost any age and size. The only suggestions I would make for the recent convert to surf fishing is to keep the spinning reel under the rod and to keep the casts overhand for more accuracy and to avoid catching the

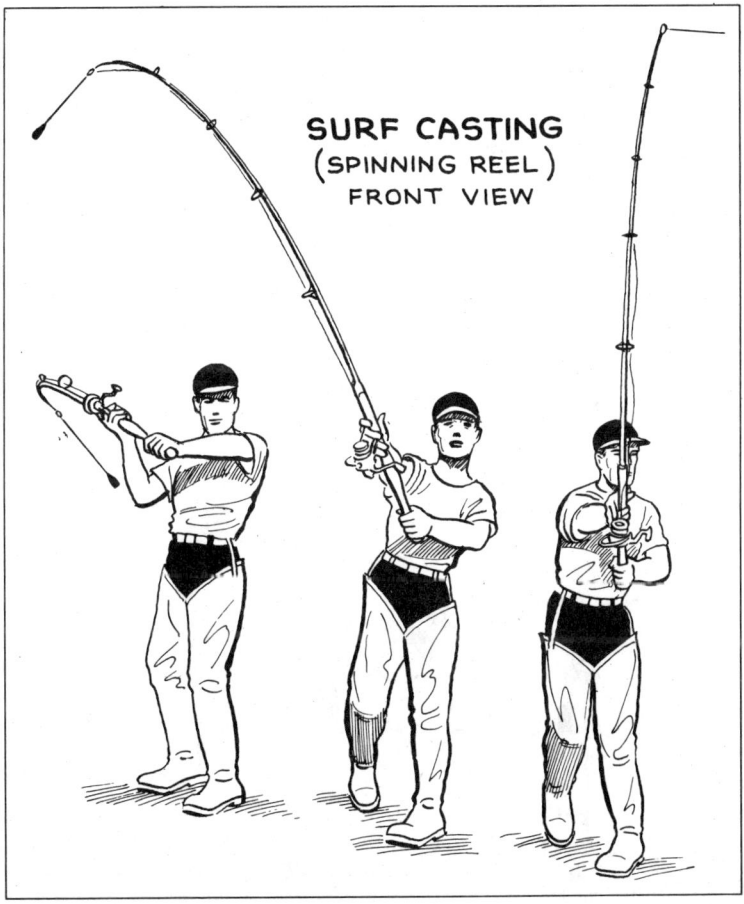

person fishing next to you. If the spinning reel seems awkward under the rod, you might want to consider exchanging that reel for one of opposite handedness. That is, a right-handed reel for a left-handed model, etc.

SPINNING—LARGER TACKLE:

For the most part, we'll let Fred Guardineer's drawings explain casting with bigger spinning tackle in the surf. Let me point out several keys to making a good cast. First, lift the line with your index finger to make sure it isn't wrapped around the tip. Then, swing the rod to a position perpendicular to your body and behind you. The rod should be parallel to the water or beach and your upper torso should pivot towards the rod. Keep your elbows in. If your elbows flare out towards your shoulders, you will be casting with only the strength of your forearms, torso, and legs. If the elbows are closer to the body you will propel the lure with both forearms and upper arms adding more force and a

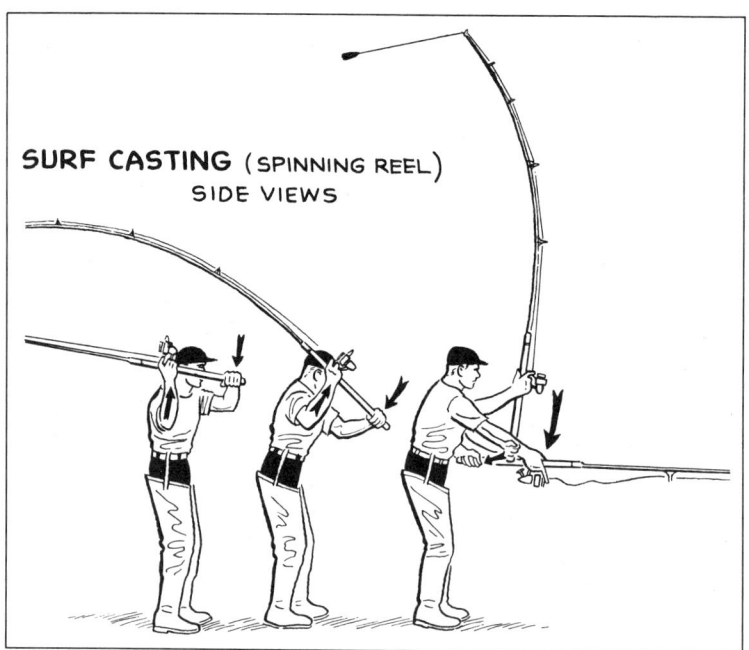

SURF CASTING (SPINNING REEL) SIDE VIEWS

better follow-through for distance and accuracy. As you begin the forward motion, step forward slightly with the foot opposite to the side you have pivoted. Sweep the rod over your head, keep the spinning reel forward as the rod swings, and keep your head straight. As the rod swings to a forward postion of about 60 degrees relative to the beach, or eleven o'clock if you use the imaginary clock approach, release the index finger press on the line. Let the rod continue to swing forward and down as a follow-through and extend the arms fully. Bring the other foot slightly forward to a position next to the first foot. Take a small step backwards to regain the original position.

The surf fisherman who has never used a big stick before might profit from a short practice session on a field. Use a one ounce sinker without hooks. Select a large field with no one around (we wouldn't want to hit a child with that sinker). A football field can be the best place for this practice because distances can be approximated easily. Accuracy can also be assessed better on some kind of a marked field.

CONVENTIONAL TACKLE:

More and more surf fishermen are returning to conventional tackle. There are several very good reasons for this. First, modern conventional reels have anti-backlash features and are much easier to use. Second, conventional tackle is thought by some fishermen to provide a better "feel" and sensitivity when baitfishing.

Make no mistake. Even with anti-backlash features conventional reels are still more difficult to cast with. An educated thumb is still a caster's best friend, and a backlash, although they occur infrequently, is still a horror to work out in the dark. Don't let me turn you off to using conventional gear. Far from it. I love conventional tackle. However, don't take up this tackle with rose-colored glasses on, either. Most quality conventional reels of recent vintage have a pressure control nut. By turning the nut you can either increase or decrease the effect of the anti-backlash mechanism. High pressure will virtually eliminate any chance of a backlash, but will reduce casting distance. A nut

Steve Petri demonstrates proper form using a conventional outfit to cast bait rig into the south shore surf. Photo by William A. Muller.

that is thoroughly loosened will increase the casting distance, but increase backlashes. Thus, each angler has to find a suitable combination of anti-backlash activation, casting distance, and subtle thumb pressure on the spool. The casting process is virtually the same as for larger spinning tackle, except that the reel will be under the rod and face away from the angler's back when the rod is brought back prior to the forward motion. Imagine a clock that goes around the angler from front to back so that the rod tip points to three o'clock with the rod in the back position prior to the cast, and so that the thumb pressure is released when the rod is swung forward and the tip is in the eleven o'clock position. Again, extend the arms forward on the cast and barely touch the revolving spool to prevent the line from overrunning the motion of the spool and thus prevent a backlash. When retrieving the line on a reel without a level-wind device, wrap your thumb (of the hand not used to turn the reel handle) around the line in front of the reel and work the line slowly back and forth across the spool so that the line is distributed evenly on the spool. Unevenly spooled line will produce backlashes.

POWER CASTING:

Power casting is a technique developed abroad where very long casts (300 to 500 feet) are needed to traverse broad beach shelves and place the bait in deeper water where the fish feed. There are significant differences between standard casting techniques and power casting. The most obvious difference is that a pendulum motion is established on the back cast so that greater momentum is added to the lure or sinker and bait. This technique places more strain on tackle, knots, and rigs than standard casting. The beginner in this technique may break off rigs easily at first until the exact combination of motions is coordinated properly. Thus, successful power casting requires the angler build up confidence both in his or her technique and tackle.

The accompanying diagrams show clearly how the rig is swung backward so that the bait or sinker arcs back and upward. The torso rotation is more exaggerated in order to achieve a proper pendulum that can generate considerable power.

With practice the technique can be mastered. Not every caster gets the same distance out of a power cast. In the

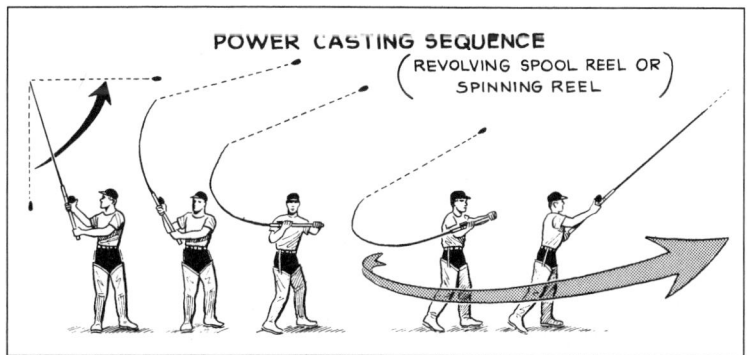

U.S., power casting is most commonly seen at casting tournaments. One must remember there is a big difference between casting conditions at a tournament and on the beach; so don't expect a 500 foot cast with a slab of bunker, a pyramid sinker, and a fish finder rig.

The application of power casting in the U.S. is limited. I have tried it on a few occasions while fishing with big plugs into a stiff wind in an attempt to gain extra distance. I got that lure out a bit further, but I doubt it was worth the effort. Certainly I didn't catch any fish because of the extra distance. I've been reluctant to try it with bait rigs because I already generate enough force with a standard cast to break off 20 pound test line from time to time.

Remember that casting propels a lure or rig. In standard casting, the rod develops a bend as the tackle is swung forward. As the bend recovers it catapults the lure or rig out over the water. A significant portion of the success of a decently long cast also has to do with the aerodynamics of the plug, the weather conditions, and the momentum of the lure or rig; and that is related in part to its weight. In power casting, the idea is to add distance by increasing the momentum of the lure or rig and increase the bend in the rod, thus increasing the catapult effect.

Power casting was originally developed for use with conventional gear, but in the last couple of years, the technique has been adapted to spinning as well, and in some quarters is being highly touted. I believe there is good reason why the technique has not caught on in America. That's because usually our fish are close. There are a few spots where a lot more distance might help. However, one is usually up to one's armpits at such places and that makes power casting much more difficult, if not impossible.

CHAPTER 6
Effects of Winds, Tides, and Moon
by Fred Schwab

A serious surf angler always strives to improve his chance of a successful fishing effort by basing the selection of where and when to fish on a combination of existing, and/or anticipated circumstances. Of course, there's never any certainty that fish will be caught at a particular location, but experienced anglers know that for every spot fished there are conditions which increase the likelihood of fish being present.

Among the factors to be considered, the subjects of this chapter are high in the order of priority, and none place higher than tides. All fishing locations yield fish most frequently during a particular tidal period, and in many cases, it's a wasted effort to fish at other times. Anglers who do not learn which tides are best, or who fail to apply such knowledge can never expect to achieve an even moderate rate of success.

It would simplify matters if it could be stated that a particular tide is best at all places; however, that's hardly the case. Not only do the most favorable tides differ between locations, but there are other variables to be considered as well. For the beginner there are shortcuts to learning which are the best tides for the more popular locations. He can ask or observe others, join a surf fishing club, or glean the information from media reports. These are ways in which the beginner can get started in the right direction, but simply knowing what the best tides are for a few locations is not enough. The road to success is much more complicated than that!

A basic understanding of what causes tides, what they have to do with fishing success, and what can alter their effectiveness, is information which broadens the angler's range. It is knowledge which allows the angler to adapt to varying conditions, and to effectively fish in areas new to him.

While the sun's gravitational pull is a factor, tides are primarily caused by the moon's gravity. In fact, tides follow the moon's position as it relates to the earth, with high tide (high water) occurring directly below it and on the opposite side of the earth simultaneously. Low tide (low water) occurs in areas situated at right angles to the moon's position. Incidentally, the earth's rotation on its axis creates the illusion that the moon revolves around the earth roughly once a day. In actuality, it takes over 29 days for the moon to complete one revolution around the earth.

The two differing water levels, high and low tide, each occur twice during a period of about 25 hours. This variance, in terms of the 24-hour day, explains why the tides occur some 30 to 60 minutes later each day. High and low tides are the maximum and minimum ranges of the tide, and in actuality, under normal conditions, each lasts less than a half hour. The period from high to low water is described as the falling, dropping or outgoing tide; while low to high is usually referred to as the rising or incoming tide. Normally, the duration of these periods of change are about six hours. Because it takes time for water to move from one place to another, the occurrence of a particular stage in a tide varies from one location to the next. The greatest variations occur where land contours and narrow channels restrict the water's flow. In some cases, the difference between areas just a few miles apart can be several hours.

Because the factors which cause tides are constant and unalterable, man can accurately predict their occurrence and range long in advance. He knows that the tidal range differs from day to day according to the position of the sun and moon, and that under normal conditions the greatest range occurs when the moon and sun are pulling along the same line. Called "spring tides," they occur twice each month, at the time of the full and new moons. "Spring tides" normally move the greatest volumes of water, thus producing the strongest currents. "Neap tides," which take place one or two days after the first and third quarters of the moon, occur when the pull of the sun is at right angles to the pull of the moon. These tides normally produce the least variation in the rise and fall of the water. To clarify, these tidal extremes are not a sudden happening, they gradually build, reach a peak, and then diminish over a period of several days.

To this point we have focused on the duration of tides, what causes them, and systematic or normal variations. We have not discussed the most frequent and least systematic cause of tidal abnormalities. Along the East Coast, a strong easterly wind of considerable duration will create abnormally high tides. Usually, though not always, such winds accompany an intense coastal storm, and cause moderate to very severe flooding in shore areas. Blowing from this direction, the wind retards the falling tide and resultant currents, and at times in some locations, the tidal change will be barely discernible. In general, a strong northwesterly wind has the reverse effect. In either case, the wind's pushing or holding action interrupts the normal rhythm of the tides, and the harder and longer they blow, the more pronounced the abnormality will become. Such circumstances can be a mixed blessing for the surf fisherman, since they can spark a period of extremely productive activity, or spoil the fishing for several days.

The principal reason for tides having an impact upon fishing relates to the way in which they affect the availability of the predator's food supply. In some areas certain tide stages prevent or discourage game fish from venturing into locations where the bulk of the food supply is. This is the case along much of Long Island's south shore where most of the shoreline features a protective offshore sand bar with a somewhat deeper trough situated between. During the lower stages of the tide, the sand bar normally acts as a barrier to predators, and at such times the trough becomes a relatively safe haven for their prey. But as the water rises, game fish venture over the sand bar and begin prowling through the trough in search of food. In general, the most productive fishing in such areas occurs during the first three to four hours after high tide, and at some locations, the two prior hours should not be completely ignored.

In many cases there is no offshore bar, but rather a scattering of rocks, depressions, slight troughs, or marine vegetation within close proximity to the beach. To avoid predation, baitfish will often congregate in such areas around high tide. But as the tide begins to drop, the bait is gradually forced to retreat from these relatively safe areas. Under these conditions predators are most active during the last half of the falling tide, but may be present throughout this tidal stage. These circumstances prevail along much of the shoreline in Long Island Sound, Montauk's rocky south side, within many of the bays along both the north and south shores, and at many locations where fast moving currents develop during the falling tide.

While there are times when predators actively feed during the earliest stage of the tidal change, just after high or low water, in the majority of cases where swift currents develop, the latter half, or last three hours of the change are the most reliable. Normally, during the first hour or two the current builds slowly, and at some locations is not noticeable until the third hour. As the current grows stronger, baitfish within the area are swept from the ever-shrinking protective shallows and structures adjacent to the shore, while those passing through find it increasingly difficult to reach such locations. Eventually the bait is helplessly swept along. Upon reaching a rip, usually present when the current is forced over or around some structure, or when two currents meet, the resultant turbulence may cause the bait to lose all control, even to the point of being tossed and tumbled about. Such conditions offer easy pickings for the larger and more powerful predators, thus they will concentrate within the rip, shifting with the bait supply, across, up or down current, near or well below the surface, and usually remaining for as long as the food supply is sufficient to satisfy their appetites and thus, make their efforts worthwhile.

Wherever the action of tidal change forces a volume of water through a narrowing channel or opening, over a rocky or uneven bottom, or around an object which impedes or redirects the water's flow, a current will develop. Thus, swift moving water is encountered within and adjacent to inlets, certain harbor outlets and along irregularly shaped shorelines. That is also why under normal conditions, currents, or at least detectable ones, are seldom present along straight shorelines far removed from inlets.

As already pointed out, most locations produce best at a particular stage of the tide. In areas containing several potentially productive nearby locations, knowing which are the most reliable times for each can make a big difference in the angler's rate of success. In those cases where the prime time varies, the angler has the opportunity to work more than one location during the best stages of the tide, or if conditions don't seem quite right at the most favored spot, he can shift to another with a minimum loss of fishing time. The thinking fisherman forever searches, applying his knowledge to new areas, not just the more popular ones. Such ventures usually do not pay high dividends, but the few which do, make all the failures worthwhile.

From the past few paragraphs, it should be fairly evident that, in general, a falling tide (high to low) is the most productive—a point which I've delayed placing emphasis upon because there are a few exceptions. Perhaps the most notable being the rip beneath the Montauk Lighthouse, where the top of the incoming tide is clearly the best.

One final point with respect to the falling tide relates to the fact that it allows the angler to gain access to certain areas that are well beyond his range at high tide, or which would be too dangerous to venture to when the water level is rising. There are numerous locations around Long Island and elsewhere, where increased range becomes a very distinct advantage.

In addition to causing abnormal tidal conditions, wind

direction and velocity influence fishing in many other ways. As with tides, for all fishing locations there are wind conditions which enhance the likelihood of fish being present. In general, the outer beaches along both the north and south shores of Long Island are more productive when the wind is in the angler's face, and that is because an onshore wind tends to push the bait and pursuing predators closer to shore. Another plus is that an onshore wind usually produces white water along the beach and in shallower areas. The resultant turbulence stirs up the bait and provides concealment for wary game fish who might otherwise be reluctant to venture into shallow water. But too much of an onshore wind can interfere with casting, create a hopeless weed condition, or seriously reduce water clarity. Murky water is the upshot of an onshore wind, from one quarter or another, at many locations along beaches fronting on Long Island Sound. This problem relates to the composition of the bottom, which in many areas is extremely silty and/or spotted with exposed clay beds.

A wind blowing on the angler's back will ease casting, and perhaps produce very clear water conditions; but it may also push the bait and game fish beyond the surf angler's reach. If a chop or wave action normally improves the fishing in the area being fished, a prolonged wind from this direction is the least desirable as it will gradually flatten the surface, and the angler will be hard pressed to find any white water. At times, a strong north to northwesterly wind will cause extremely murky water along some stretches of the south shore by blowing fine sand into the surf zone. These light particles will remain suspended in the water until conditions moderate or change altogether.

A cross wind "might" improve water conditions and bait movement, or restrict either or both. It "will" create a belly or slack in the line which will reduce your ability to feel a fish strike and to set the hook in a timely fashion. This wind can also make casting an extremely frustrating experience. Anglers often use the term "set" to describe a condition which a strong cross or quartering wind frequently produces in the surf. In this situation a strong current, not a tidal current, develops as the wind pushes the water parallel to the beach. When this condition arises it becomes increasingly difficult to fish in an effective manner. Bottom fishermen have problems keeping their bait in one place as the sinker tends to "walk" or bounce along, and lures swing rapidly with the current. A belly in the line and deteriorating water clarity adds to the angler's woes. A strong "set" usually means very poor fishing!

The wind can also influence tidal currents. As previously pointed out, winds can alter the tidal range, thus increasing or decreasing the flow of water and resultant strength of currents. The wind can also cause a shift in the location of a rip by pushing it further out, closer in, or to one side or the other. The change may be very slight, but it can be critical in terms of the beach-bound angler's ability to reach the heaviest concentration of fish. In all cases, the effect of a wind from any direction is subject to variation, dependent upon its velocity, longevity, and the area under consideration.

Folks who spend a lot of time in or on the water know that wind has an impact on water temperature. In fact, at times the wind's influence in regulating water temperature will exceed that of the sun. The stronger the wind and the longer it blows, the more water it churns and pushes about. The churning tends to mix warmer surface with cooler sub-surface water, while the pushing action will move it from one place to another.

Sunny days and generally warm air temperatures can be very deceptive in terms of what one would expect their impacts to be. During the spring, such conditions combined with prevailing southerly winds, will produce a rather steady warming trend in the relatively shallow inshore waters, and this usually accelerates the northerly movement of migratory species such as striped bass and weakfish. But throw in a few days of strong northerly winds and the water temperature will decline and tend to retard the migratory process.

An added factor is the Gulf Stream, whose water temperature is substantially higher than the average for surrounding waters. While this amazing ocean current is an influencing factor throughout the year, its effects are most apparent to the fisherman during the late spring and early summer. Should the prevailing winds be from a southerly direction, the warmer water will gradually move inshore and displace the cooler water. If the prevailing wind is from the reverse direction, the warming of near-shore waters will be delayed. In that event, some migratory species are likely to arrive at a later date than normal, or in some cases, they may avoid the cooler waters by passing further offshore, or delaying their movement into inshore areas.

In the fall, southerly winds occurring more frequently than usual, are apt to maintain the water temperature at above normal levels, and slow the southward migration of baitfish and predators. Of course, northerly winds can have the reverse effect by hastening their departure. Changing water temperatures can improve or put a damper on the fishing at any time during the course of a season, not just along ocean beaches, but in Long Island Sound and smaller bodies of water as well. Even during the months of July and August a persistent northerly wind can noticeably lower the temperature of the water and alter the movement of bait and the feeding patterns of game fish.

The fact that the moon is largely responsible for tidal action has already been covered, but the earth's companion affects fishing in other ways as well. One recurring problem which often drives anglers "up a wall," is caused by phosphorus, or "fire" which appears in the water at night. If this condition is light to moderate it may not have too great an effect on fishing, and I have observed situations when it actually seemed to improve the action. But when the "fire" is heavy, fishing is nearly always the pits. The angler's line appears to be many times its actual diameter, and even the smallest lure when moving in the water, looks like a miniature comet, complete with an elongated tail. At such times, fish usually seem less active, are not very aggressive and if they are, will shy away from an unnatural appearing object. When this condition is extremely heavy, I've often found myself wondering if it interferes with the fish's vision? Since the slightest disturbance causes the dinoflagellates (the tiny creatures which produce this green light) to glow, does it blind or impair the fish's sight?

Moonlight offsets the effect of phosphorous simply by lessening the contrast between the glow and the dark of night. On that basis, the brighter the moon the less visible the glow will be. Of course, there will be dark nights when little or no "fire" is present, but on those occasions when it's heavy, moonlight can be a blessing.

Some surf anglers believe that a bright full moon on a clear night is the best of conditions and I will confess to having experienced two or three outstanding nights under those circumstances. But I have had many more nights with poor results, and from conversations with other surf fishermen, I'm not alone in that regard. It's true that anglers fishing from boats usually have some of their most productive moments on bright nights, while the beach crowd, not far away, bombs out. But I've seen this happen many times over the years, particularly at Montauk, and there is no mystery involved. The lads in the boats were not confined to fishing in the shallows where, because of the bright conditions, the game fish were reluctant to go. Nights when there is only partial moonlight, either due to hazy conditions or because it's a few days before or after the full moon, are preferred.

Fishing, and surf fishing in particular, is a game of chance, and that is certainly one of the attractions. But the more successful one is at it, the more enjoyable it becomes. To attain a reasonable degree of success, the angler must play the percentages. He must discover the best set of circumstances for many locations, and adjust his fishing efforts accordingly. This cannot be over-emphasized.

CHAPTER 7
Women in the Surf
by Joyce Daignault

Why not? Comfortable, accomplished lady surfcasters are rare, but I see no reason why there can't be more of us out there. The real question ought to focus on why women don't get involved in surfcasting more than they do. Certainly, in the past, role stereotypes have cast boys as Dad's companion as opposed to girls; but in today's world we see girls becoming engaged in traditional male professions and recreations.

No doubt, many females view themselves as not being capable of doing particular things and this apprehension deters the acquisition of new skills. In the case of fishing the beach, anxieties sometimes center on the mistaken notion that strength is involved. Take it from someone who had trouble opening a jar—it isn't. Good tackle compensates for a lot of shortcomings.

The first and most important step in becoming an effective angler is to have a good teacher. If you're married or have a boy friend, ask him for guidance. Most males would enjoy nothing more than to have their loved ones accompany them. If you don't have a significant male in your life who fishes, like a father, a brother, or a friend, go to a reputable tackle shop. In some areas, short term courses are offered by professionals in the form of clinics and are often advertised in periodicals. Learning to select the right tackle, fill a reel with line, tie necessary knots, and to attach the various lures or baits are techniques you will need to master in order to begin. Next, you need to learn how to cast. Patience and practice are the keys.

As you are exposed to this new world, don't hesitate to

ask questions: be an attentive, inquisitive, active learner. Once you are familiar with and can manage your tackle and cast, you then need to become familiar with a geographical area of interest. Talking to experienced locals, examining maps, and reading fishing books helps. But nothing teaches fishing better than fishing itself.

It is most necessary to think philosophically about

On some beaches a buggy is a big asset. The surf fishermen can cover more territory and intercept schools of quality fish such as this teen bluefish. Joyce Daignault Photo.

fishing—where to go, when, what to use. Just as an intelligent and thinking athlete succeeds more than one who lacks these skills, so an angler who ponders what she's doing will increase her chances for success. Reach out and try to locate fish. It is a satisfying delight to be out scouting with your "instructor" and to be able to detect the presence of your prey. An added treat is to be able to tell *him* what you're using and how you're using it. Discussions about the various elements of fishing will be enjoyable for you as well as informative. The exchanging of ideas and theories is one of the pleasurable pastimes of anglers everywhere. Participating in these talks will make you feel like a part of the whole scheme and your self-esteem will blossom.

My husband, Frank, and I converse constantly about this approach or that one. While we agree on most counts, there are times we disagree. For instance, he fishes with a conventional outfit; I prefer, even though it is considered to be less sophisticated, spinning tackle. While I recognize some of the advantages of his, I prefer the action and feel of my own tackle. Spinning tackle is supposed to appeal to the novice, but that doesn't faze me in the least. My own progress has brought me to the point where my choice neither makes me respond defensively, nor apologetically. As a result of my selection of gear, together with my very presence, I sometimes encounter reactions which can be insulting if taken too seriously. The time I took a 50 pound striper, one of the regulars comments, "A woman? ...with a spinner? ...I can't believe it!"

This kind of reaction is unusual. It does, nevertheless, represent a small group of men who do not, and will not, accept women. This same collection of males can be found where you work or play. My advice: don't let it get to you. Continue to fish and disregard those few who are prejudiced against you from the start. It is possible in time to win over some of them by proving that you are a worthy competitor. You're not going to do this if you sit in the car and let others do the locating, or if you wait until a school of fish is established as feeding in a certain spot and you cash in on the discovery. Anyone who wants to be a part of the scene in

Big bass roam the beaches in greater numbers at night and a surf fishermen should concentrate efforts on the night tides. Joyce Daignault Photo.

earnest has to pack his or her own gear—all the way around. What seems to turn men off is the pretty little thing with fake eyelashes whose husband casts the bait out for her. Do you own legwork.

One of the precautions I would strongly suggest is for you not to be sensitive to rough language. You may find yourself in a situation where a neighboring fisherman doesn't know you're there and uses an expletive you find offensive. I have found that men are usually embarrassed when they inadvertently employ "blue" words in my presence. However, I don't think that "we" should make others uncomfortable or overly-guarded because we're there. You command respect not by what you demand but by what you elicit according to your behavior.

Another "don't" would be not to play the female. By that I

For safety sake it's always a good idea to remove hooks with hook disgorgers or long nosed pliers when the game are big choppers. Joyce Daignault Photo.

mean avoid the "I can'ts." If there is anything that turns surfcasters off it is someone coming in seeking special treatment, seeking to exempt themselves from what has always been expected of men. They, after all, view the surf as a stronghold of rugged individualism where you go out on your own, choose your time, tide, method, lure, and style of retrieve and execute it yourself. They'll be polite, even tolerant of those who need hep, but deep-down they regard special treatment as just that. You will be accepted far more quickly on the angling front if you do things for yourself.

By and large, women are not only accepted in the surf, they are welcomed. There are a greater number of fishermen who would truly love to have their favorite women accompany them, not by sitting patiently with a book, but by participating eagerly. Many men have commented to my husband about their envy of him because his wife likes to fish. Involvement can be as limited or as complex as you choose, depending upon your level of interest and number of encumbrances.

I chose to fish because I came to realize that my husband would go anyway. He wanted me with him and so I tried to learn. Not always easy nor pleasant, there were times he was impatient and times when I was reluctant. But I've seen too many marriages fail, due at least in part to a sharp division and polarization of interests, to stay home alone. Somewhere along the line I came to love the surf.

Those joys cannot be overstated. While in search of game fish, you will behold sunrises so contemplative and peaceful that they are rivaled only by the moonlit nights. Moreover, you will become more aware of the natural world observing things like the continuity of tide, the influence of weather, and the drama of the seasons. To see birds working over a school of bait that is disturbed by a band of stalking fish will excite you more than you can possibly believe. Then to cast into the midst of that boiling water and to hook up to a sought-after species where you have to apply all the lessons you've attempted and to triumph in the ultimate culmination of your pursuit will fill you with a sense of achievement which is second to none.

CHAPTER 8

Starting or Joining a Surf Fishing Club
by Tom Fitzsimmons

There are many reasons why people join a surf fishing club. Most experienced fishermen join for the camaraderie, the sharing of fishing techniques, and also for the competition. For novices to the sport, these clubs can offer a wealth of information that can help them to learn and acquire skills to become more proficient at the sport. Others simply join for the involvement that a group of people sharing the same interest can provide.

There are only a few fishing clubs on Long Island that are devoted strictly to surf fishing. These clubs, over a period of years, have continued to promote this one style of saltwater fishing, whose skills are, by far, the most difficult type to acquire. So if your style of fishing is only related to the surf, whether it be a personal preference or for monetary reasons, I definitely feel your fishing can be better developed, sharpened and improved by joining a surf fishing club.

A few surf clubs have been around for many years; some that started in the 40s and 50s are still going strong. And, there are also a few new clubs which have formed over the past five or ten years. But, because fishing is not as good as it has been in the past, the number of clubs and individuals involved in surf fishing has declined over the years. Despite this decline, the main goal of all these clubs is to continue to develop and promote surf fishing, both as an interest and as an acquired skill.

Most clubs in the New York area have a very similar structure. The social aspect of these clubs is usually limited to their shared love of surf fishing. Most hold their meetings at VFW halls, or in private rooms of some commercial establishments around the Island.

Club activities, other than fishing, usually involve summer picnics, awards dinners and contests within their own club, and in some cases, contests against other clubs.

Membership dues vary from club to club, but usually range from $20 to $50 annually. The monies collected are usually divided between membership dues, which are used to defray the operating expenses of the club; i.e., mailings, newsletters, printing, rental of the meeting place, joining other organizations that promote the sport, etc., and contest fees, which cover the cost of trophies for their own club awards. Some clubs also employ other means of raising money, such as ticket raffles, to further help defray these costs and raise money to help support their award dinners.

The meetings themselves are usually held once a month at a designated time and place. Most meetings start with a prescribed order of club business and move on to "how-to" discussions on fishing techniques, making lures, equipment, etc., or have outside speakers give presentations on products, or describe different methods of fishing. At some meetings, open discussions are also held to help answer any questions other members may have. The Board of Directors, who govern the running and operation of any club, will usually have one other meeting a month to handle the "business end," help set policy for approval by the membership, and try to work out any possible points of disagreement within the club.

If you feel you may be interested in joining an established club, there are a number of ways to go about selecting the right one.

At several times during the year, most clubs post notices in The Long Island Fisherman or local newspapers inviting prospective members to attend open house meetings, or informing them that their membership rolls are open to any interested fishermen. Although you may not be familiar with any or all of the clubs advertising, the opportunity to attend an open house or a typical meeting will allow you to meet and talk to the members and judge for yourself if the club has goals and objectives that will be of interest and benefit to you.

Personal contact on the beach is another way of finding out about clubs. In talking to other fishermen, you may discover that you have similar interests and that they belong to certain clubs. This common interest can also act as a guide to the club that may best fill your needs. In contrast, this can also give you insight into clubs you may wish to avoid.

Once you have made your choice, it is a simple matter to contact the club membership committee and, by making application and agreeing to comply with that club's rules and regulations, you will then be able to participate in the club's functions and activities. If, on the other hand, you have found that none of these existing clubs has anything to offer you, whether it be based on your individual style, intensity of fishing or even personalities, then by all means, why not start your own club? There is definitely more than enough room for additional surf fishing clubs in the New York area.

The first step in forming a new club would be to get a few people together who, having similar interests to share, would be interested in helping you start one. With the help of three or four friends, you can sit down and set up a simple outline of how you think the club should be run, its goals, and a guide for the proposed objectives of the club.

Once this outline has been agreed upon, an ad should be placed in The Long Island Fisherman or a newspaper fishing column, informing anyone who might be interested that a new surf fishing club is being organized, stating your objectives, who to contact, where and how. Assuming that your ad receives a good response, the first meeting can be held and all prospective members can be informed of the proposed outline for the club. This is the time to formally elect officers of the club including a president, vice president, treasurer and secretary. At these early stages, depending upon the size of the club, several of these offices may be filled by one person.

After the initial meeting, these elected officers, with the help of input from all the members, should get together to draw up a more formal constitution (the constitution from another club may help to serve as a guide). A general list of categories within the constitution should include the following, with explanations of these topics to spell out all the requirements:

I. Club name
II. Objectives of the club
III. Membership
    A. who is eligible
    B. probationary periods (if any)
    C. method of voting
    D. membership quotas
IV. Dues
V. Attendance
    A. number of meetings a member is allowed to miss
    B. method of absence explanation
VI. Meetings
    A. set the schedule for monthly meetings
    B. the order of business to be conducted during the meeting
    C. special meeting requirements
    D. how meetings should be conducted (parliamentary procedure)
VII. Quorum
    A. minimum required for a vote
VIII. Club Management (brief explanation of duties and functions, how elections should be run, powers connected with each office, etc.)
    A. Board of Directors
    B. President
    C. Vice President
    D. Secretary
    E. Treasurer
IX. Amendments
    A. method and procedure of amending the constitution
    B. vote required
X. Code of Ethics for club members

Once the constitution has been formally drawn up, it should be presented to the membership for acceptance or modification.

When all the rough spots have been ironed out, and the membership has finally approved the constitution, your new club should then proceed to make application to the state to become a "not-for-profit corporation." This can help to protect the officers and members from any involvements in relation to legal actions brought against the club.

The application to the Attorney General's office can be prepared yourself. Copies of the legal forms and instructions by West McKinney may be obtained at your local public library. If, however, you find difficulty in filling out the application, the club could engage an attorney, for between $300 and $500, to process it for you. Obviously, doing this yourself can save the club a considerable amount of money, and it is quite possible that some local legal aid clinic may be able to help keep the costs to a minimum.

As the development of the club progresses, the membership should begin to set up functions within itself which will help round out the club's own goals, and develop an interaction between the members. Social functions can be organized—dances, picnics, possibly contests with other clubs, etc. Decisions can be made to join organizations which help to promote fishing and conservation, such as S.O.S., the New York Sport Fishing Federation, etc. The membership may also elect to participate in the New York Surf Fishing Contest. This is an important and extremely worthwhile contest. It was started to replace the Schaefer Fishing Contest and is limited strictly to promoting surf fishing by competing against other surf clubs with similar interests. It is a very meaningful contest that can aid in promoting unity and instilling pride in your own club.

Specific committees within your new club should also be set up. These committees help to get other members involved and promote activity within the club. The following is a brief list of possible committees, and a brief explanation of their possible functions:

1. *Fish Committee:* This group is responsible for the

yearly fishing rules and regulations and distribution of a fish call list for the club. (Call lists are made up of the names, addresses and phone numbers of the members, and are used to facilitate contact between members to inform them of some outstanding fishing that is taking place, or to notify members of important club-related items, etc.) Their duties should also include distributing fish blanks for recording contest entries, maintaining accurate record keeping for all the fish caught each season by the members, advising the membership of access to fishing locations, and generally keeping the members aware of what's going on and where.

2. *Conservation Committee:* This committee should keep the members aware of items that concern species conservation, and make them aware of any letters needed to help secure legislation that will benefit both fish and fishermen.

3. *Historian Committee:* They should keep a chronological record of the club and all its activities (keeping yearbooks of photos and newspaper clippings, etc.).

4. *"How-To-Do-It" Committee:* This group should develop presentations of interest to members, either by members themselves sharing their acquired knowledge and skills, or by arranging for demonstrations and lectures by fishing equipment manufacturers, etc.

5. *Social Affairs Committee:* This committee should arrange club functions, dinners, dances, cocktail parties, picnics, family fishing contests, kid's snapper derbies, etc.

6. *Newsletter Committee* (usually handled by the Secretary): They should distribute a monthly bulletin to the members informing them of club-related news, items of interest, meeting dates and times, etc.

As the club develops, I'm sure you will discover other areas of interest which your club will want to follow-up, and other committees may be instituted to handle these.

A specific meeting place should also be determined. As your club outgrows the basement, a more permanent, larger facility should be sought out. There are some bars, bowling alleys, etc., that have empty rooms during the week, and you may be able to convince them to allow your club to use the space rent free, in the interest of community service. Or you may elect to pay for the rental of a room for one night a month at a VFW hall or similar place having such space available.

As time progresses, advertisements and word-of-mouth on the beach should increase your membership.

So whatever your individual reasons may be for joining or starting a club—whether it be the social involvement or the challenge of the competition against fellow surf fishermen—a club can be a richly rewarding and educational experience, one which I am sure you will find to be most worthwhile, not only in what you can receive from others in the club, but in what *you* will be able to contribute as a member. This does not necessarily mean catching large quantities of fish, but more so in your participation as a contributing member of the club.

You should remember that in almost all clubs there are a few members who clearly are very successful in catching not only larger quantities, but also more consistently than others. Never let this inhibit or frustrate you as a member. You simply need to realize that experience, provided by many hours of hard fishing, is needed to gain this kind of success. And by listening, learning, and a lot of hard fishing and sleepless nights, you can also acquire this expertise. But above all, surf fishing should be fun, and something you enjoy doing. So, if fishing once a week or even once every two weeks is how you enjoy fishing, then that's what's important—so fish and enjoy!

PART TWO
Game Fish Approaches and Techniques

CHAPTER 9

The Big Three: Bass, Blues, and Weaks

by William A. Muller

Surf fishermen refer to them as the big three. We do so with affection. Although this concentration on only three species might seem to narrow the field and scope of the sport, it isn't an exclusive love affair. I haven't met the surf fishermen yet who didn't wet a line sooner or later in search of other species. Fish like flounder, fluke, blackfish, porgies, and mackerel are often as prized as a weakfish or a blue. So why the "Big Three?"

It is very hard to answer such a question since many of the answers are locked away in the minds and hearts of men long buried. However, it isn't hard to identify these three species as glamorous since they are large and hard-swimming fish. Yet, within this realm of glamour there is much room for variation. Some of you out there, for example, will remember the last cycle of weakfish abundance. The upswing began in the 1930s and, although diminished, persisted into the 1950s. There were weaks to be had from under the famed Montauk Lighthouse and weakfish also roamed the inlets and ocean beach troughs. In those days, there were those who pursued them to the exclusion of bass and blues, and they were often looked down upon by fellows who insisted that only striped bass and blues were worthy of intense effort. But these hardy surfmen continued to throw their worms, held off the bottom with floats, into the surf hoping for a tiderunner—a yellowfin of legend. In those days there were other opportunities for a good fish meal, too. There were the constant kingfish—a fish we almost never catch in the surf today. There were blowfish and even the stray channel bass. Many of these denizens were good eating, too.

There is a lesson in history for us. Today, even the purist surf fisherman chases after weakfish at one time or another, and we have to suspect that at least part of the reason is the decline of striped bass. One can be picky when there are plenty of bass to be caught. Gee, in the golden days bluefish,too, were looked upon with less than noble affection. Bass, bass, bass: it was the rallying cry in the surf. Well, things have changed and the bass are harder to find and thus almost equally hard to fool when you find them. We have been forced by necessity to chase other species of game fish once thought to be somewhat inferior to the bass. Whether we have matured to the point where we can appreciate weakfish and blues, or whether it's the lack of bass that has brought us to respect and fish for other species isn't the lesson. Instead, we should learn a little tolerance and appreciation for all the species of fish that are potentially available in the surf. We hope that man can find the collective wisdom to manage fish resources properly, but what if we don't? Bass are threatened by habitat destruction, pollution, and overharvest. Blues are threatened by large ocean purse seining, and weakfish, always threatened by overharvest, are cyclical and will come and go regardless. Throwing a worm to a blackfish may become an important activity some day. Take it from one who has done just that on many occasions; it's fun and challenging. Let's hope, though, that we can find a way to preserve good numbers of all marine species so that those of us who take up the challenge of other species such as porgies, blackfish, etc., will be able to enjoy much more than the limited sport of our fathers.

Each author, in his turn, covering bottom fishing techniques for other species will tell us about those fish. We will eagerly read through their descriptions and perceptions. But we mustn't break too far or too quickly from tradition lest we perish through the neglect of history and its concurrent skill.

STRIPED BASS:

Beyond the mention of the name, there is little more that a writer has to do to stimulate thoughts of respect, pride, and admiration. This is the glamour species of our area. In fact in recent years, since the introduction of stripers on the West Coast in the 1880s, bass have been introduced into many inland bodies of water and, thus, in a very real way have become the glamour species of the East Coast, West Coast, and may lake impoundments. Today, striped bass can be caught in 42 of the 48 contiguous states.

Striped bass *(Morone saxatilis)* is a very hardy species. Thus, it has adapted well to landlocked bodies of water. It is an anadromous fish; which means that the species spawns in freshwater and feeds in saltwater, thus there is an innate ability to tolerate freshwater. Two additional factors helped spell the success of bass in freshwater. One was the abundance of forage fish, such as gizzard shad in many

STRIPED BASS

lakes, and the second was the ability to spawn and rear the critters for dispersal in freshwater empoundments.

Although the distribution of bass in freshwater bodies of other states might seem a bit remote, a thoughtful examination might reveal that the development of hatchery and management regimes for the species could become very significant if the East Coast populations fall so low that it must man-influenced back to a fishable level.

That the species is a hardy one cannot be argued. Yet, we cannot be sure that the species will be able to withstand the numerous assaults man has made on its habitats, or the poisons we dump into the estuary that contaminate their reproductive organs and may kill the eggs and young. Finally, we cannot be certain that heavy harvests will not reduce stocks to a point so low that they cannot produce good or large year classes.

Federal and state attempts are well under way to protect bass from these threats. Securing management legislation has not been easy, but state by state it is coming forth. Habitat protection and the control of toxic waste dumping is even slower to come around, yet here and there chemicals are banned from use and governments order habitat clean-ups.

Striped bass begin their lives as semi-floating eggs drifting down sluggish moving rivers. The eggs hatch in hours and the young begin the process of adapting to the river habitat. Within a day or so they will lose the egg sack that nourished them fresh out of the egg and will begin feeding upon very small invertebrates. As they grow they eat larger and larger invertebrates and then fish and adult invertebrates. As they grow they also begin to dominate their habitat and take on many of the classic characteristics of a game fish. In the juvenile stages they are not easily distinguished from their close cousin, the white perch *(Morone americanus)* which are often found in the same river estuaries. Certainly this is the case in both the Hudson and the Chesapeake spawning areas.

The Chesapeake complex is by far the largest contributor to the East Coast stocks. In fact, about 90 percent of the East

Coast stock is spawned in that bay complex. The Hudson is believed to be the next largest contributor with percentages ranging from about 7 to 15 percent, depending upon the quality of the year classes produced from each major region. There are also minor contributions made by smaller river systems in almost every other coastal state from Maine to Florida. In fact, Nova Scotia is thought to make a minor contribution. These local spawning areas may positively impact on the fishing in the estuary immediately adjacent to the river, but they do not substantially affect the overall fishery.

The female bass remain in the river-estuary for their first two or three years. Only a few males leave after the second year. In fact, about 90 percent of the coastal migrants are females. This fact, some fisheries biologists suggest, should be seriously considered in the establishment of management plans. If plans do not account for the differential migration phenomena it is possible that harvests of small fish might be biased in favor of one sex or the other, depending upon location and fishing methods.

Bass migrate relatively close to shore. Typically, the fish is described as preferring the surf zone, although in recent years the fish seem to be cutting across the New York Bight. There are many possible reasons for this new behavior. It could be a question of available food or the shortcut might become necessary when unusual fall weather patterns delay the fall of water temperatures and then encourage a sudden precipitous departure. Others have suggested that smaller schools may mitigate this behavior. Whatever the reason, the fish has not been found migrating in abundance in the surf zone of New York waters in recent years.

During the northward migration, the fish travel rather rapidly. The first migrating schools leave the Bay complex in March (exact timing depends upon winter and early spring weather patterns) and arrive off New Jersey in early April. By mid and late April they are in the surf along Long Island's south shore ocean. In early May, the first catches of fish will be made at Montauk. Typically, the early migrators are school-size fish. By late May, the larger fish have begun to appear in our waters and by then school fish are already rushing baitfish in Rhode Island waters. By late May or early June, the bulk of the fish have reached Cape Cod where they settle in for the summer. During their northward move, some schools break off and take up residence in the waters of many Middle Atlantic and New England states. Pods of larger fish are not atypical summer residents along the south shore beaches and inlets of Long Island nor off Connecticut, Rhode Island, and Long Island in Long Island Sound. When the first cold fronts of autumn barrel across the northeast and water temperatures begin to fall, the bass schools begin to move south. We do not fully understand what initiates migration in some fish while failing to urge others, but it is clear that falling water temperatures get things going.

The large fish are first. October is prime time at Montauk and in some years, the fish linger into November. Throughout the late September through mid-November period, schools of fish move around Montauk and along the south shore beaches of Long Island. It used to be that the outward and southward migration of mullet turned on a migration feast for bass, but with fewer mullet and fewer bass the orgy isn't nearly as impressive when it occurs and often it doesn't happen at all.

By early December the small bass are pushing south so that by mid-month, in most years, all but the last few stragglers are well past us. They winter in a variety of places both in and close to the Chesapeake Bay complex. There has always been concern that commercial fishermen would find the comatose bass on their winter grounds and take too many of the spawning females. Indeed, this happened one year (1970-71) in North Carolina.

The Hudson population or stock moves a bit differently. They fan out into Long Island Sound and New York Bight in late April and early May. Scientists tell us that these fish don't migrate very far, but we suspect that how far they go depends upon available food and competition from northward-moving schools of Chesapeake fish. There has also been some talk that some Nova Scotia fish migrate south in winter and actually may winter-over in Long Island Sound. Interesting!

There is a big difference between the size and life span of male and female bass. Male bass are believed to rarely exceed 25 pounds and an age of about nine years, maybe ten. Females, on the other hand, have an enormous growth and age potential. A fish of about 42 pounds would be a female, about 12 years old, and likely be in the twilight of her spawning years. In fact, we now believe that females in the five to ten pound range may have the bulk of the spawning responsibility. Big cows may spawn only irregularly.

Female bass are believed to have the potential to reach weights in excess of 100 pounds. In the past, several fish in the 125 pound class were taken in nets. Rumors speak of fish in the 80s and 90s regularly found in haul seines. Trying to separate rumor from wishful thinking isn't easy.

Clearly, the great year classes of the late 1950s and 1960s are producing some huge fish and records in various line categories seem to tumble every year. The latest monster was taken by Albert McReynolds off the New Jersey shore in the fall of 1982. It weighed 78 pounds and 8 ounces!

Striped bass have seven or eight lateral stripes, a large full tail, broad head with powerful jaws, and a split dorsal fin. The front fin has nine to ten spiny rays, while the rear dorsal has 12 to 14 soft rays. Fresh out of the water these fish are very impressive combinations of gold, green, blue, silver, white, black, purple, and rust. The exact colors depend upon bottom colors, time of year, origin of the fish, and some say its state of mind when hooked and fought. There are those who insist a bass blushes rust prior to attacking a prey animal in an excited state.

Bass will eat almost anything from clams, to worms, to bunker, to mackerel, to blackfish and flounder. Anything they can fit in their mouths is fair game. However, the fish appear to prefer bunker, spearing, sand eels, squid, and sea worms. Smaller fish may prefer the smaller baits, but the cows like big bunker, squid, and eels among other large prey.

Clearly, striped bass are the smarter of the big three. Bass usually waste little energy in feeding. They will, for example, hide in the shadow line of a bridge and quietly pick off bunker or other large bait as the tide carries it down. They are so efficient that typically the baitfish school will not be disturbed by the taking of one of its members. The fish will lie behind rocks or in the hollow behind a bar or obstruction and wait for currents and tides to bring meals to them. When fish bait is lean, bass will nose into soft bottoms to collect crabs, clams, and worms. They are patient, clever, and smart. They are opportunists and they are the undisputed king of the coastal ocean. There are fish that fight harder, but the force of the fight is not what prompts the intense admiration alone. Sure, those first few runs from a cow are usually power-packed, but outsmarting the bass and finding her is where the satisfaction is. The challenge of the hunt, not the killing of the fish, is where the action is with this species.

WEAKFISH:

The weakfish *(Cynoscion regalis)* ranges from the Caribbean to Rhode Island. The bulk of the stock will be found from Chesapeake Bay to Narragansett Bay in Rhode Island.

This fish, rare in our waters only a little over a decade ago, returned in numbers around 1970. By now, everyone knows that the fish is called weakfish because of its tender mouth parts and not because it can't fight. Down south the fish is simply called "trout," along with its close relative the spotted or southern weakfish *(Cynoscion nebulosus)*.

The intense yet pastel colors of this fish have always impressed me, and prompted an instant love affair in an eight-year-old boy. That boy caught tiderunners in the dying embers of the last cycle of weaks that peaked in the 1930s and 1940s. I never forgot those shimmering yellow-orange, purple, blue, gray-topped fish and the first one I caught in 1970 brought tears to my eyes. The gray ghost has returned and we thought again about Montauk when the "Great Gray Hordes" were reputed to round the bend at

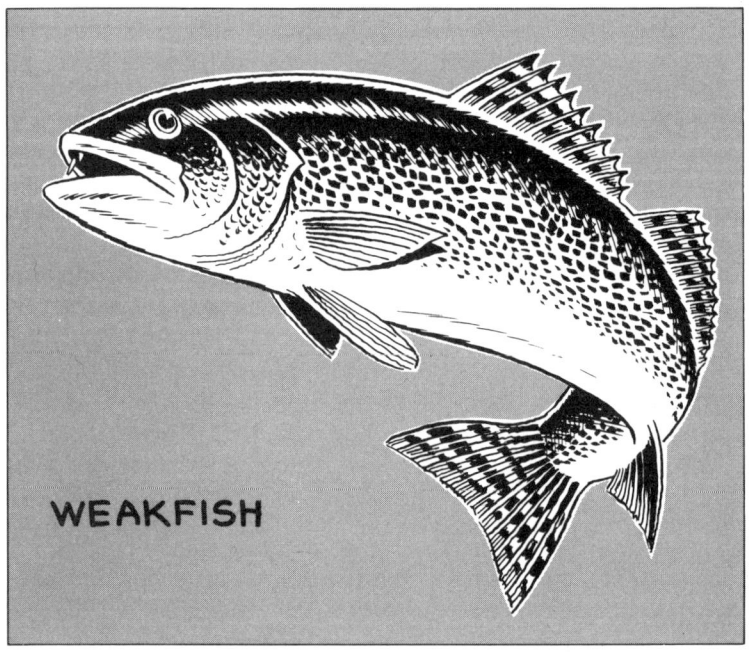

WEAKFISH

Montauk.

Weakfish spawn in the estuary and the young fish grow to about five to seven inches in the eel grass beds during the spring and summer of that first year. In autumn, they migrate south spending the winter in inshore waters of Virginia and the Carolinas. In spring, late spring, they migrate north again and find their way into our bays during July. The north-south migration pattern is repeated for several years, but once they reach a size of about five pounds the bulk of the school will migrate east onto the continental shelf where they winter in about 50 fathoms of water. Here they have been threatened by commercial fishing trawlers that sweep the bottoms during winter at that depth for butterfish and fluke. Occasional bonanzas have been made. The winter migration onto the continental shelf explains the more or less simultaneous arrival of the school of big tiderunners into our bays in late April and early May, as well as Long Island Sound, New Jersey, and

Rhode Island. If the fish migrated from the south the arrivals would be staggered.

The typical tiderunner weighs about seven or eight pounds and is caught in May or June. However, some places like Montauk, parts of Long Island Sound, and the south shore inlets may produce significant catches of weaks all summer and fall, too. The typical "summer-run" fish will be two or three pounds.

Weakfish are known to be able to reach a maximum weight of 30 pounds (all-tackle world's record), but few fish of this size have been seen, let alone caught by hook and line. However, there are enough fish of 12 to 15 pounds taken each year to make the active pursuit of teen weaks a worthwhile enterprise.

Typically few weaks feed upon first arrival. Instead, they spawn and then go on a feeding binge for several weeks. The fish are often sluggish until mid-May when waters begin to warm, and by late May or early June, the waters are warm enough to encourage large portions of the big schools to migrate out of the bays.

Unlike stripers, weaks prefer smaller baits (except for bigger tiderunners that often prefer live large bunker and snappers in some locales), such as sand eels, grass shrimp, spearing, and other small fish and invertebrates. It is this preference for small baits that often mitigates the choice of artificials. Although this is the topic of a later chapter, I must say here that lures like plastic shrimp, small Rebels and RedFins, as well as Whip-Tails and Eelworms top the list of favored lures in our area.

The abundance of weakfish is very cyclical and the cycle seems to run about 30 to 40 years. Therefore, the great fishing of the 1930s and 1940s gave way to a virtual absence of the species in our waters until about 1970. The top fishing from the peak of each cycle seems to last about ten years. Many reasons for the cyclical nature of the species have been offered. Some scientists blame the severe hurricane of the 1930s that destroyed millions of acres of eelgrass beds and eliminated many spawning and nursery grounds. Others suggest that periodically a fungal disease hits the eelgrass beds. *Labyrinthula macrocystis* is the suspected fungal agent and it turns the eelgrass plants to a mush. Still others suggest that overharvesting is the culprit. However, it does not appear likely that overharvesting could have decimated the weakfish stocks back in the 1930s and 40s because the size of commercial operations was far less than what it is today. It may be possible for overharvesting to impact that way today. Regardless, a reduced yearly harvest could spread the harvest out over a longer period of time and this might translate into a longer peak period of quality fishing.

Weakfish prefer to feed in one of two ways. Understanding their feeding habits can be of great assistance in improving one's catch from the beach. The first pattern, typical of night feeding on sand eels or shrimp, can best be described as the rise and slurp method. The fish cruise under shrimp drifting with the current or schools of sand eels roaming and squirming near the surface. Here and there, from time to time, a fish will rise towards the surface towards a shrimp or a sand eel. When the weakfish is close to its prey, it will turn its body and suck in water and shrimp. As the fish turns, it heads towards the bottom and the curved body, combined with the push towards the bottom, leaves an enormous boil in the water. The sudden opening of the mouth near the surface of the water that sucks in a shrimp or sand eel is what creates the characteristic slurping noise. The second feeding method is typical of weaks feeding on bunker, snappers, or squid. The weaks rush the bait with mouths open. When they close their mouths, the fangs on the upper surface of the jaw latch onto the prey, while the numerous abrasive and small teeth on the lower jaw hold the prey from the other side in much the same way that a towel or rag improves the hold of a hand trying to open a jar. Once the prey is held securely it must be turned in the mouth so that it can be swallowed head first. Thus, when weaks are feeding on small baits they should be hit as soon as the fisherman perceives that he has had a hit. However, when larger baits are used, the weakfish must be given time to maneuver the bait and swallow it. In fact, because the mouth of a weak is long and more pointed than bass or blues, a fisherman should give a weakfish a lot of time before striking back.

Perhaps the most famous characteristic of weakfish is their "weak" mouths for which they are named. Actually, the mouth of a weakfish is not as delicate as many people believe, but the jawbones are thin and the membrane between the bone elements is very thin. Thus, there is a greater likelihood of a hook pulling from the mouth of a weak than from a bass or a blue. However, I have known many fishermen to be reluctant to strike back at a weak because they are afraid a solid setting of the hook will pull it free. This fear is exaggerated and unwarranted. When a fish bites, the angler should set the hook in order to achieve a high hook-up percentage. It is possible that in the "old" days before fiberglass rods and stretchy monofilament lines, that a striking weak could be played very gently. With lines that do not stretch, the "hit" from the fish might well be enough to sink a hook into a weakfish. With today's tackle most experienced surf fishermen suggest sinking the hook well. However, drag settings could stand to be set a wee bit lighter than when fishing for bass and blues.

If a "weak" mouth is a characteristic of key importance for the species, we should not ignore the long, sleek shape, the delicately sloping head, and the rainbow colors of the species. Oddly enough, when the fish is seen in the water it appears a rather uniform dull gray. However, when seen from the side we are immediately impressed by the hues of pink, yellow, orange, purple, striking black, and bright white and silver belly. Indeed, these bright colors make a teen-sized weakfish an excellent trophy for a wall mount.

BLUEFISH:

Pomatomus saltatrix, the notorious wolves of the sea, choppers, slammers, gorillagators, and a host of other names are applied to this species—some with affection and some with dismay. Einstein said that everything is relative, and this statement appears very appropriate for bluefish. In the 1950s and the 1960 when bass were much more abundant, blues were often looked upon as a nuisance by experienced surf fishermen. Actually, two factors accounted for their attitude. First, as previously stated, bass, including big bass, were abundant. Stripers were and are the glamour species and since they were abundant, it was profitable to seek them out in preference to other species. The second reason was that there were few of the outsized blues that we see today available in those days to fishermen. The typical blue was two to eight pounds and a ten pounder was a happy surprise.

Today bass in quantity, and big fish especially, are not easy to come by. Meanwhile, folks regularly catch blues of 10 to 20 pounds from the beach. Why are bigger blues available today? Scientists do not have all the answers for this question, but several interesting facts are now known about the species that may help us to get a handle on possible reasons. Unlike weaks and bass, bluefish are distributed worldwide. They aren't found in every part of every ocean, but they do occur in every ocean with the exception of the colder Arctic and Antarctic Oceans. Such a wide distribution makes it likely that fish in one part of the world never breed with fish in another part of the world. Through time, differences between the fish genetically arise. In the science of evolution this is called speciation. This fact led scientists to take a close look at bluefish in north Atlantic waters. Through research they discovered some very interesting information. They found some significant differences. Although the evidence is not complete or conclusive, some scientists now suggest that there may be up to five subspecies of bluefish in the Atlantic off the coast of the United States. The North Atlantic is a big piece of water and some hypothesize that behavior caused schools of blues to avoid some areas and favor others. Again, the separation leads to genetic differences. The possible five subspecies of blues may be distinguished by their size among a variety of more subtle differences. Some have suggested one group that may only reach five pounds or so, another that may go to eight or nine pounds, a third that may grow to twelve pounds or so, a fourth that reaches into the mid-teens, and a fifth that may grow to twenty-five pounds. How these fish distribute themselves along the coast may very well be dependent on basically two factors. One, the relative abundance of the groups that is a result of the degree of successful spawning. Second, changes in bait distribution that is related to water temperatures and the relative success of baitfish spawning. Therefore, what may have happened is that during the last ten years, environmental factors have favored the success of larger blues over their smaller cousins in our region.

Other facts are held with greater confidence. For one, we now accept that there are two spawning areas and times in the ocean off our coastline. The first is on the edge of the Gulf Stream off the Virginia-Carolinas coast. This spawning occurs in April into May. The second spawning takes place closer to New York Bight and closer to the coast. This spawning takes place in May and June. The two spawning areas and times may reflect spawning of two of the subspecies that dominate our waters.

Bluefish apparently can grow even bigger than 20 or 25 pounds. Reports have come in from South Africa of blues reaching 45 to 50 pounds! Wouldn't we like to see schools of that subspecies pay us a visit once in awhile. Don't hold

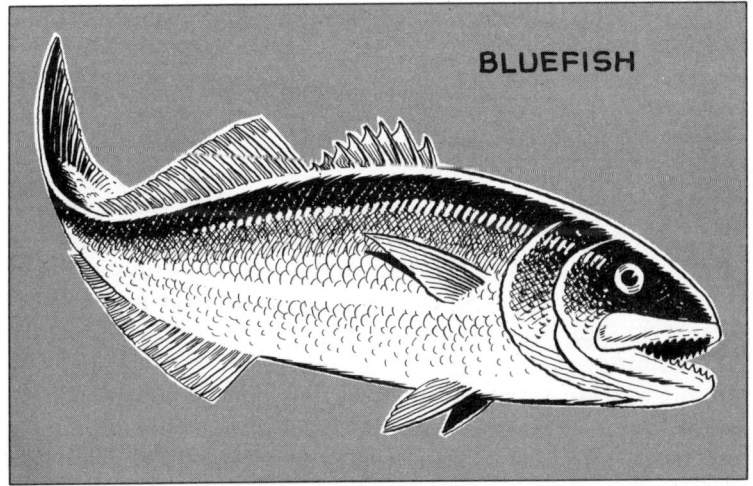

your breath, because migration to New York waters across the Equator is very, very unlikely. Blues of those sizes might make us forget about striped bass. Surely they would test the mettle of both tackle and men.

Another interesting fact about bluefish has been recently discovered. We've become used to calling fish "cold-blooded," which means that their body temperature will match that of the water. However, recent studies show that large blues can maintain an ambient body temperature of four degrees above the surrounding water. This fact may explain why large blues often linger into late November or even early December.

Unlike weaks and bass, blues are pelagic species. That means they are fish of the open ocean and less-so the shallow coastal waters. Bass are believed to remain within a mile or so of the coast and even spawn in brackish water river systems. Weaks perhaps have more of a tie to the open ocean since larger fish appear to prefer a winter seaward migration over a trip to shallow coastal southern waters. At least some significant portion of larger weakfish may prefer this, anyway. Blues spend a lot of time in the deep open ocean, they spawn there, too, and their movement into coastal estuaries seems to be related to feeding more so than a dependence on the conditions that exist there. Unfortunately this behavior is not well understood and it is still a guess whether the blues also seek escape from large sharks, tunas, and billfish.

Bluefish are sleek, torpedo-shaped fish with meager dorsal fins that are indicative of pelagic species. In fact, some pelagic species collapse their dorsal fins into grooves while swimming fast to minimize friction. The fish is blue or blue-green on its dorsal surface and this coloration blends to silver on the sides of the fish and then white towards the belly. The head of bluefish is a powerful and tough bony structure that has evolved to accommodate a complete set of triangular razor-sharp teeth. The teeth of the upper jaw are offset from those of the lower jaw so that when the fish bites down, the triangles mesh. This meshing accounts for the fish's ability to slice through even large fish with the ease and clean cut of a surgeon. The muscles of the head and face are large and short so that the fish can generate tremendous force when it bites. Thus, whatever isn't neatly severed will be crushed. The eyes of bluefish are large and they appear to hunt in clear water with their eyes. They also pick up vibrations with their lateral line, as do other fish, for long distance sensing and can "smell" the existence of prey as well. There is some reason to believe that the sense of smell in bluefish may not be as well developed in them as it is in other species such as striped bass, and this more limited sensing ability may be related to the pelagic origin of the species where vision in clear water can be a more valuable tool in predation.

Blues often travel in huge schools, even the large specimens. This is also typical of pelagic species. They are fast swimmers and can attain speeds of 40 miles per hour according to some reports. They are, therefore, easily able to run down most prey and their speed is a key asset in feeding along with powerful jaws and sharp teeth. Blues are thus rarely "clever." Instead, they overpower prey and the frantic swimming into, around, and out of schools of baits accounts for the frantic feeding frenzies that are known as typical of the species.

Blues will often feed with abandon and some have suggested that they become so caught up in the frenzy that they will regurgitate when sated and begin feeding anew. Whether this is true is not confirmed, but obviously their appetites are impressive and their killing capacity well documented.

Blues are the piranhas of the sea. They strike with devastating swiftness and when in a frenzy all must flee or be bitten—including human swimmers. As such, they perform a very valuable function. Similar to their animal brethren on land, the wolves, when a species becomes too abundant Nature sends in her executioners to help recreate a balance between those that eat flesh and those that eat plants.

CHAPTER 10
Artificials
by John Fritz

In the vernacular of sport fishermen, the purist is one who disdains the use of bait of any kind, preferring to seek his game fish with the aid of artificial lures only. There can be little argument with the assertion that there is a greater degree of satisfaction when enticing a wary game fish into striking an inanimate piece of metal, plastic, or wood. Certainly there are occasions when any object cast into a school of feeding fish will ensure a response but, in most instances, it requires much more expertise to attract a cautious predator. The angler must be proficient in the use of his tackle, able to perform many tasks even when fishing in inky blackness. He must also have a thorough understanding of the type, color, and size of the lure which should be used for each species, at what time of the season, knowledge of the prevalent species of bait and the effect of wind, tide and waves on the action of a particular lure. Even after acquiring this comprehensive wisdom and devising the most rational strategy there will be occasions when nothing but the most illogical methods will produce fish. Instances like this may be damaging to one's pride and confidence, but these occurrences contribute an additional unknown element to an already fascinating sport.

Artificial lures are designed mainly to imitate a particular bait even though some of the objects offered for sale today bear little resemblance to anything that swims, crawls, or even flies. "Matching the hatch," is a phrase whose origin dates back to antiquity. It is a fine theory, but one that is occasionally difficult to adhere to, or has little bearing on one's ability to catch fish. For instance, when large bluefish are feeding on sand eels by no stretch of the imagination could a bottle plug be mistaken for one of these slender baitfish. I am not suggesting that anyone should ignore this theory, only trying to make the observation that if one particular type of lure fails to produce, an angler should be willing to experiment with totally different lures and techniques.

Artificial lures, in my judgment, can be divided into three basic categories: tins, plugs, and lead-headed jigs. Again, there are theories which govern their use, but one should always be aware that exceptions abound. A few such principles, passed along the waterfront through the ages are: "dark nights, dark plugs" or "big bait, big fish." Then there is the advice to use tins and poppers only in daylight and wire leaders will spook striped bass, or if there is fire in the water, go home. Basically these maxims are correct and on this principle, the following comments are based.

Metal lures, more commonly referred to as tins, have evolved a long way since the forerunners of today's surf

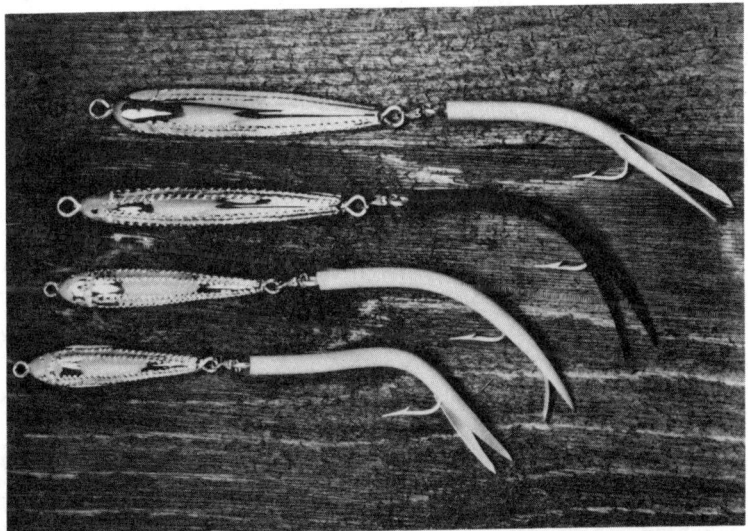

In recent years, due to the abundance of sand eels along local beaches, tins with tubes have been very effective during the fall run. Photo courtesy of Bead Chain Tackle Co.

caster polished his tin squid in the wet sand at the water's edge. These ancient tins were most often made of block tin which tarnished after exposure to the elements. They also featured a single hook which was molded into the body of the lure, a characteristic which resulted in many lost fish. The hooks on today's tins are frequently attached by means of a split ring, an innovation which provides for the simple exchange of hooks should replacement or additional decoration become necessary. There is an inherent trait in successful fishermen to try to improve the proficiency of any lure. In recent years the addition of a tube to the tail hook of a tin has added a new dimension to an already productive item. Many of the lures purchased today are already equipped with tubes in the most popular colors of green, red, or white. It should be noted that this added attraction will reduce the casting range which accounts for the reason they are usually only found on narrow bodied tins.

Tins can range in size from the tiniest 1/12 ounce Kastmaster to the newest 6 ounce Hopkins. For our purposes, sizes from 1/2 to 4 ounces are more appropriate, with shape and size determined by tackle weight, size of fish being sought, existing bait, weather and sea conditions, and bottom formation. The shapes of these tins can vary from the flat pancake-shaped Kastmaster to heavy, narrow lures such as the Ava jig. Basically the flatter tins will ride higher in the water and while they are ideal for fishing in areas where fouling the bottom is likely, they do not cast as well in a stiff onshore wind. The narrow, heavy-bodied tins, on the other hand, will slice through the wind providing the optimum in casting distance, plus they will quickly sink to the bottom in the roughest seas, should that trait be deemed desirable.

Many of the specialized tins in use today, reproductions of two late great surfmen, Charlie Graves and Charlie Pasquale, feature a keel which stabilizes the swimming action and, in some instances, forces the lure to ride at a shallower depth. Each of these past masters produced tins of many different shapes and weights for use in the surf, most of which are still available today. The Pasquale

Quiet back waters can be just the ticket for spring weaks. William Muller Photo.

Light tackle adds more fun to quiet water weakfishing, but watch out when the weak makes a last gasp escape attempt. Let the rod do the work. William Muller Photo.

collection of tins are offered in many tackle stores under the name of Diamond Feature Lures, just as they were years ago; while molds of the Graves tins were obtained by Ralph Votta of Levittown, New York.

In the early spring, when the fishing season is initiated by the influx of school bass along the Island's north shore, the smaller sized tins are more productive. The one ounce Kastmaster, the 1¼ ounce Hopkins NoEql, Tri-Fin's one ounce Spoon Jig or Luhr Jensen's 1¼ ounce Limpet have accounted for many bass, while the specialized tins such as Pasquale's V-8 and J-9 or Graves J-2 and J-5 are also ideal for this early season fishing. When weather conditions permit, it is more enjoyable to use light one-handed spinning rods. In many instances, the lighter weight lures, possibly the half ounce Hopkins or Kastmaster, necessary when using ultra-light tackle, will be more readily acceptable to these school bass. The loss of casting distance is often of little importance, for the stripers are normally close to shore feeding in the shallows.

Some of the beaches along Long Island Sound are littered with rocks and other obstacles which can snag any lure worked near the bottom. The flatter shaped tins are often preferred in these areas, but knowledgeable surfmen are aware that tins made of block tin have only half the weight of the standard chrome-plated lead alloy lures, a feature which is ideally suited for fishing rocky shorelines. A complete line of block tin lures are offered by The Diamond Feather Lure Company through your favorite tackle dealer.

As the season progresses, the arrival of blues along the south shore beaches provides the ocean beach rat the opportunity to sling medium weight tins at a willing game fish. The Hopkins Shorty and NoEql, J-8s, the Graves D-5 or the 3 ounce Kastmaster are all excellent lures for fishing the ocean beaches when encountering moderate sea conditions. After the weakfish have finished their spawning ritual in the interior bays they tend to congregate in the waters adjacent to south shore inlets, such as Jones or Fire Island, where they can be taken with these same tins; most often during the twilight hours. A technique, practiced by Fire Island

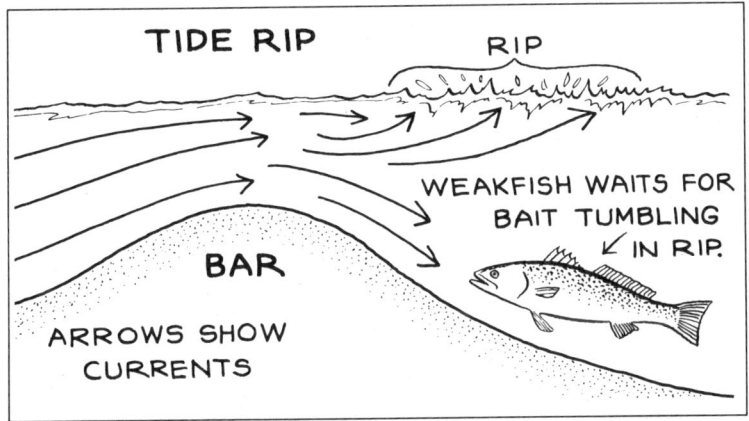

anglers, provides continuous action throughout the night on tin. They drag Hopkins 4H NoEqls along the sandy bottom from the inlet bars. A dynamite daylight lure for these same weakfish or their traveling companions of this period, hordes of smaller bluefish, is the Ava 007.

Except for locations where schools of small to medium bluefish take up residence, the summer months from August through early September offer little for surfmen casting tin. With the arrival of autumn and its accompanying stormy weather, larger tins are frequently needed to combat the more severe wind and surf. At a time when schools of decent sized bass, teen bluefish, and weakfish are preparing for their annual migration, lures capable of being cast beyond the breakers are often required. Diamond Feather's 3 ounce 8X or FT, or the 3½ ounce CB Jr. are possibilities, as are the Graves 3½ ounce PDQ and the 4½ ounce R/P. It is at this time of the year that the tin and tube combination receives its biggest play, although anglers fishing the eastern shores of the North Fork are convinced these same tubes, only in slightly smaller diameters, are excellent on departing monster bluefish and school bass.

Most of the tins found on the market today feature a thin layer of chrome plating over the lead alloy body, with a notable exception being the stainless steel Hopkins.

Unfortunately, after continued hard use this shiny finish loses its luster and becomes pitted and dull. Rather than discard these beat up tins, knowing surfmen refinish them with a coat of white or yellow paint and continue to catch fish. Painted tins are frequently used after dark, especially when weather and sea conditions hamper the use of plugs. It should be noted that when using any tin it should swing freely in the snap. Therefore, be certain that the loop of the snap is of sufficient size to permit unrestricted movement.

A type of metal lure ideally suited for use when snappers, butterfish, or small bunker are abundant along the shore are Diamond Feather's Butterfish, the Luhr Jensen 1¼ ounce Limpet, and spoon-shaped lures in weights adequate for casting, namely the Krocodile or Hopkins Hammered spoons.

Another style of lure used successfully in the surf is the lead-headed jig. Whether it is adorned with feathers,

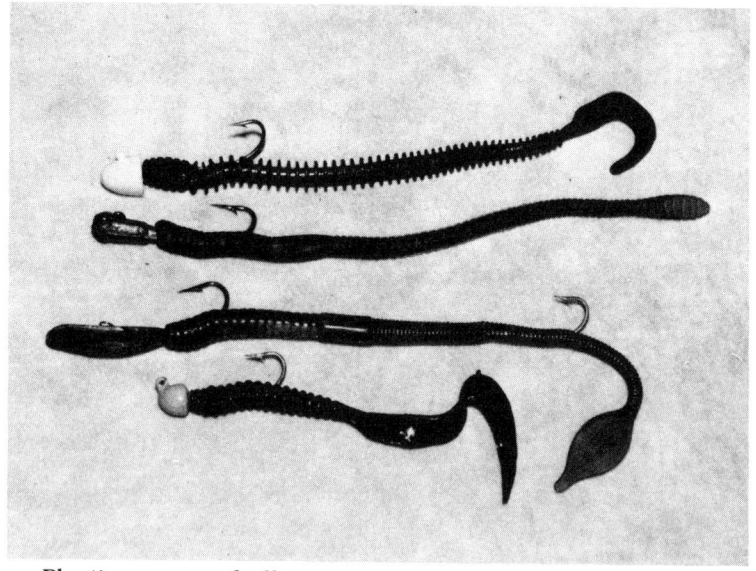

Plastic worms of all sizes, colors, and lengths have been important lures for spring weakfish. A variety of lead heads can be used to facilitate casting and even make the worm wiggle more. William Muller Photo.

ARTIFICIALS

bucktail, soft plastic, or rubber tubing, each is a necessary part of every surfman's bag of tricks, for given specific circumstances the use of these lures can mean the difference between success or failure. As a general rule, these lures are fished close to the bottom where they are retrieved slowly with an intermittent raising and lowering of the rod tip. It would seem that given this method of retrieve these lures would see little use in rocky areas, but 3 ounce bucktails are among the deadliest lures when seeking cow bass from the rocks under Montauk's famed Lighthouse. No, they are not retrieved at a brisk pace in order to keep them from snagging the weed-covered rocks, but at a leisurely rate of speed with the customary lowering and raising of the rod tip. Losses can be kept at a minimum by using new good quality line such as 20 lb. test Ande, but even so, extra bucktails should be on hand. Another instance where heavy bucktails are used successfully is in the south shore inlets where they are cast up-tide at a 45 degree angle and allowed to bounce along the bottom, with the tide in a wide arc; a method particularly productive when seeking striped bass and weakfish. The success of any bucktail is greatly enhanced by the addition of a strip of pork rind and if it is tied directly to the line without snaps or swivels. These two tips will ensure the best possible results from a lure which has caught untold fish over a period of many years.

As time passed, fishermen, true to form, started tampering with the standard bucktail by adding soft plastic or rubber tubing in place of the customary bucktail or feathers. Out of these experiments evolved one of the most successful weakfish lures of our time: the plastic shrimp tail. After its initial success, these lures fell into slight disuse, but they continue to take many weaks when used in swift flowing waterways such as the State Channel at Captree, Fire Island Inlet, or Shinnecock Canal.

Mickey Chiarenza, a top-notch local angler, experimented with rubber tubing on various metal heads and came up with two particularly successful lures in the Tri-Fin Whiptail and Eelworm. Both of these lures are extremely productive when fishing for striped bass and weakfish and used in a manner similar to that required for bucktails. While most anglers favor white tubing on the Whiptail, the Eelworm is often preferred in red, black or amber colors, although red probably yields the most consistent results. These lures are most frequently used along the north shore beaches or from the banks of the south shore inlets where they readily identify with the vast populations of sand eels present in these waters.

A novice angler introduced to the vast array of plugs found in today's tackle stores has reason to be bewildered since plugs are available in every conceivable color, shape, and size. By dividing these plugs into categories it might be possible to clarify their use with regard to time of day or season, sea conditions, species sought, and prevailing bait.

Plugs that are normally retrieved across the top of the

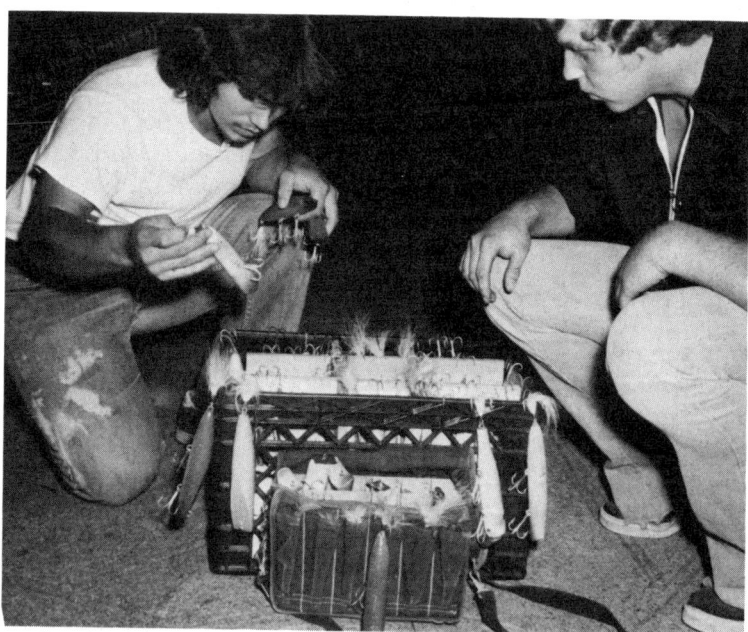

A good way to store extra plugs is in a plastic milk box that has been divided into sections. The box can be stored in a car, buggy, or garage for easy access. William Muller Photo.

ARTIFICIALS

water creating a series of splashes on the surface are called popping plugs. The Atom Striper Swiper is a prime example of such a plug, but this grouping should also include Pencil poppers, Polaris poppers and the Rabbit plug. Most of these plugs are retrieved at a rather rapid rate coupled with a rhythmic jerking of the rod tip to force the concave nose of the plug to create a splash. The Rabbit plug, more frequently used in the Massachusetts surf, is skipped across the surface with a fast retrieve. These particular plugs are shaped like a flattened piece of wood with little built-in action, but they cast like bullets in the strongest wind. On the opposite extreme are the Pencil poppers which are reeled in at a crawl, but given a violent jerking action by whipping the rod tip back and forth rapidly and forcefully, a practice which is extremely tiring when attempted with a stiff rod. For those anglers unfamiliar with the Gibbs

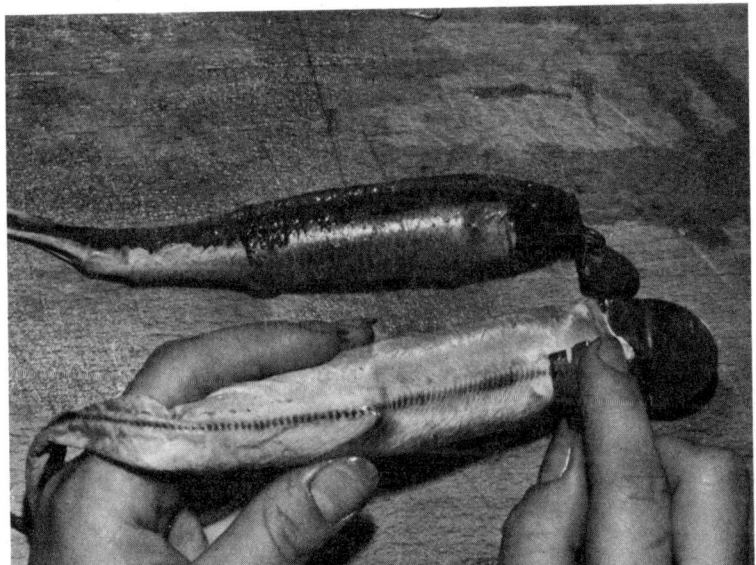

Eel skin plugs can be devastating lures especially for big bass. The use of "skin plugs" has been neglected in recent years. Atom 40s, Junior Atoms, Danny Plugs, and Super Strike swimmers are all good plugs to use a skin on. William Muller Photo.

Polaris, it is basically a standard popper, but in a shape and of weights that are ideal for using in rough sea conditions or a blustery onshore wind.

The choices of colors in these plugs is not as critical as is the case when using swimming type plugs, for their main attraction is offered by the commotion they create on the water's surface. There are occasions, though, when a particular color is more successful, with probably a chrome popper leading the list, especially when seeking bluefish in relatively calm waters. White or red and white poppers are universally accepted as productive colors, while yellow is favored by many anglers when the water is murky. During the early autumn south shore mullet run, a blue popper will often out-fish all other colors. A flame orange colored popper might not resemble anything that swims, but this color is often dynamite when seeking bluefish.

These popping plugs are most often used during the daylight hours and would be the first plug a surfman will choose when game fish are chasing bait on the surface. This is not to say that they cannot be used at night, especially under a bright moon, by slowing the retrieve or by swimming the plug slowly through the water. The Pencil popper is an ideal lure to use when trying to entice those lazy lunkers off the bottom, for this slow, tantalizing imitation of a crippled baitfish makes them hard to resist.

The metal lipped swimmers manufactured under the Atom, Super Strike, Creek Chub, or Danny Lupo labels are superior nighttime lures when retrieved painstakingly slow in sluggish water. In fast moving currents the exaggerated metal lip provides too much resistance giving the plug an unnatural motion. The balance and weight of these plugs makes them difficult to cast in an onshore wind, but then they are rarely used in rough sea conditions.

Plugs such as the 7¼ inch Atom 40 and the Super Strike swimmer are excellent fall lures when game fish are feeding on bunker or other large baitfish. During the late spring and summer months, especially along the north shore's rocky points, the 7/8 ounce Spin Atom is a superb lure for drawing bass out from the rocks. A fine feature of this line of plugs is

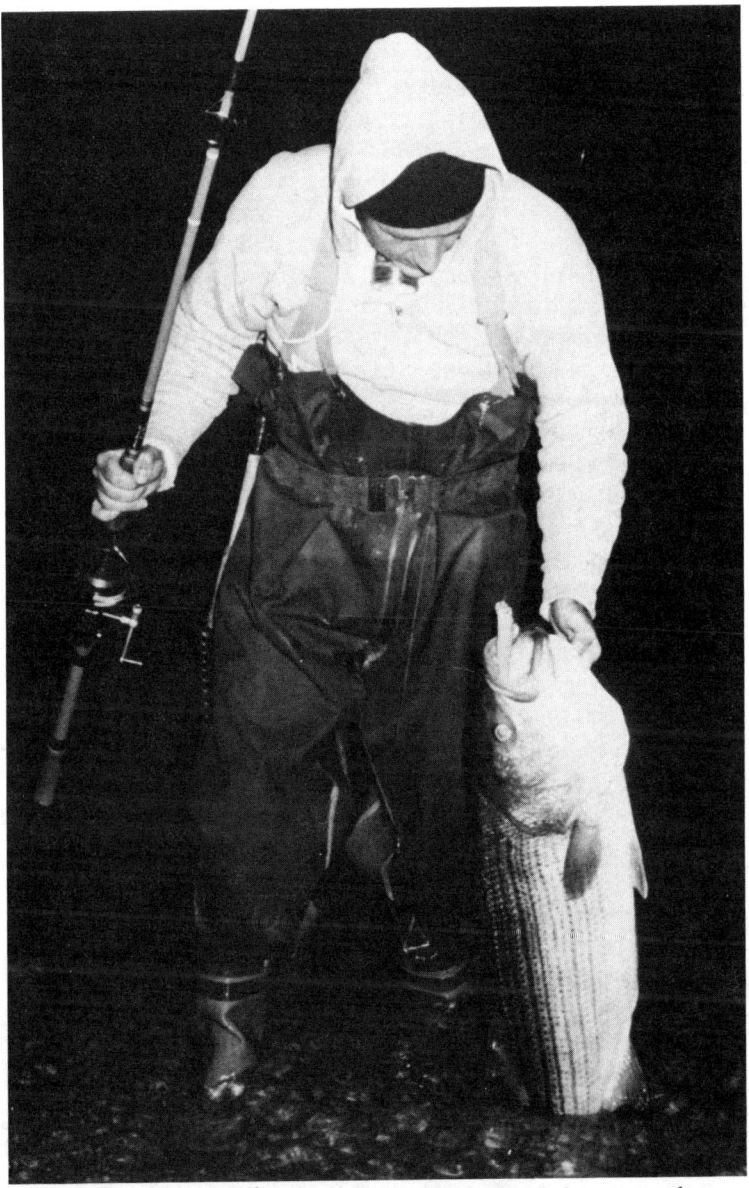

A small eel skin on a Spin Atom plug fooled this cow when worked slowly across the surface. William Muller Photo.

that the depth at which the lure swims can be varied by simply bending the eye in the nose of the plug. By bending the eye up, the plug will travel deeper; the opposite reaction will be gained by bending the eye at a downward angle. Wooden plugs of this type were used by veteran surfmen of the past, before the advent of the plastic style plug, to pull cow bass from the surf all along the Northeast Coast. Conventional reels were used to cast weighted Atom 40s and Creek Chub's Giant Jointed Pikies, which measure almost a foot in total length. Nowadays, a black, medium-sized Jointed Pikie is ideal for imitating baby blackfish—a bait eagerly sought by cow bass.

The second grouping of large swimming plugs include the bottle or casting swimmer and the darter. While it is true that the smaller versions of these plugs are occasionally used for school bass and weakfish, they are more commonly used in fast water during the fall run when searching for larger fish. At such legendary places as Montauk's Lighthouse and North Bar these lures are used almost exclusively by those surfmen seeking cow bass, large blues, and weakfish. At this time and place, yellow is by far the most favored color with white plugs a good second choice. When the night is exceptionally dark, blue or even black colored plugs will often produce better results. Reportedly these same plugs are used with much success from the piers and bulkheads of the Staten Island shore, in the vicinity of the Verrazano Bridge, among the rips of various north shore points and in the inlets of the south shore. Basically any area with deep, fast moving water is a good spot to try these lures. The nose of these plugs should bite into the water to achieve the best results. When the plug has a "bite," a rhythmic throbbing will be felt throughout the rod. If difficulty is encountered in getting the lip to dig in, one or two sharp jerks on the rod will start the plug working correctly, after which a slow retrieve is maintained; just enough to ensure that the plug continues to work.

The Rebel type plastic swimming plugs are relatively new to fishermen when compared to what surfmen used in the forties. The introduction of spinning gear, shortly after

Swedish style swimming plugs such as Rebels, RedFins, HellCats fool bass, blues, and weaks all season long. William Muller Photo.

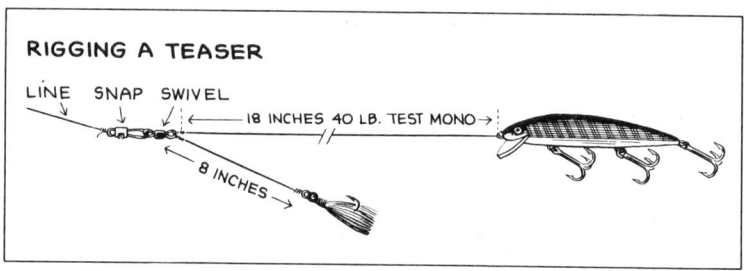

World War II, provided the means to get these lightweight lures to the fish. Whether you choose plastic Rebels, RedFins or Hellcats or the wooden Rapalas and Nils Master, these slim-bodied plugs are a season long favorite of surfmen working the more quiet waters. The north shore beaches or inside the south shore inlets and bays are ideally suited for slowly, I mean slowly, working these plugs throughout the nighttime hours. These plugs are adapted to the use of light tackle—a feature which provides more enjoyment, especially if the fish tend to run small. Do not be misled into thinking that these lures will only take small fish, for nothing could be further from the truth. The five inch versions of these plugs are known to be superb lures for taking cow bass even along the oceanfront when sea conditions are favorable.

The one drawback with these lightweight plugs, is the limited distance they can be cast. Experienced surfmen overcome this obstacle by injecting water into the hollow bodies of the Hellcats and RedFins. Plugs loaded with various small amounts of water will behave in a slightly different manner; on most occasions with an action more pleasing to the game fish. The seven inch loaded RedFin is a favorite plug of the wet suit clan who frequent the rocks at Montauk. At a time when striped bass are scarce, these hardy surfmen score impressive results using pearl-bodied RedFins with either a blue or yellow back.

During these times of increased sand eel populations, the use of a teaser can often mean the difference between catching fish or going home skunked. Whether a Red Gill or feathered teaser is preferred it can be used in conjunction with all types of lures, even tin, a feature which can lead to double-headers.

I'm sure there have been many lures which I have failed to cover. The Reverse Atom, the MirrOlure, Needlefish plugs and Super Strike's Little Neck Surface Swimmer to name a few. On specific occasions each of these lures is supreme and often the only plug which will take fish. Many instances could be recounted to emphasize this fact, only space limitations will not permit. Do not let the mere mention of these plugs imply that they are inferior lures. On the contrary, they should be a part of every surfman's repertoire.

Given the variety of lures on the market today and the contradictory nature of game fish, it can be seen why surfcasting can be one of the most perplexing pastimes. However, the feeling when all goes well, with the weight of those fish tugging at your stringer, makes all the fruitless effort worthwhile.

CHAPTER 11

Baitfishing
by John Fritz

I'm sure that the vast majority of surf fishermen would prefer to catch their fish with artificial lures. Unfortunately, this is not always possible and those plug casters who disdain the use of bait are ignoring an important and productive phase of surf fishing. One reason for this aversion is a general misconception that fishing bait is boring; a lazy man's way to fish. Some believe it is a technique which requires few skills other than to slink a chunk of bait into the wash and wait for a fish to swallow the offering, thereby hooking itself with a minimum amount of effort on the part of the angler. At times, this may be the case; but the consistently successful bottom fisherman uses all the natural forces to aid him, just as a plug caster does. Combined with an understanding of the external conditions, he also needs to have a detailed knowledge of the proper bait for each species, at what time of the season, plus a complete understanding of the type of hooks required and how they should be rigged to achieve the best results.

Many hard working bait fishermen can be seen fishing with two rods, particularly when the beach is not crowded and the fishing is slow. No, they are not necesarily meat fishermen, but rather smart surfmen who are trying to increase the odds by presenting more than one offering in one location. The usual practice is to cast one line as far as possible and the other just beyond the curl of the breakers. Another variation practiced is to try a different bait on each rod in an effort to determine the fish's preference at that particular time. In most instances, once the action picks up, the second rod will be put aside, to be used as a back-up should one become disabled. Two rods cannot be tended to properly when the fish are feeding actively. This practice of fishing with more than one rod can be carried to an extreme, especially when fishing in space-limited areas, which is frequently the case on Long Island. Still, I've seen lone fishermen with five to seven rods lined up on the beach like a picket fence. This practice is not conducive to paying proper attention to such details as drifting lines, rigs fouled with seaweed, light pickups, or if the bait is still presentable, whether washed out, stolen by crabs or the leader being fouled during the cast. It is a good practice to reel each rod in every 15 or 20 minutes to check the bait and, when using frozen bait, to replace it with a fresh piece.

When using cut bait that has been frozen, any attempt at a second cast with the same piece of bait injects the danger of the hook pulling free with the force of the cast. Once the bait has thawed, the flesh becomes soft with the likelihood that the hook will tear the flesh, enlarging the hole and allowing the hook to pull free. If fishing at night, this could result in fishing with a bare hook. No bait makes it extremely difficult for even the greatest fisherman to catch fish.

Fresh bait is always more effective than bait which has been previously frozen. A fine theory, but one that is troublesome to follow. Since few of us have the time to procure fresh bait before each trip, even if it was readily available, the practical way to approach this dilemma is to keep a supply of bait in the home freezer. If an edible fish is to be used as bait, a visit to the fish market a day or so before the planned trip should provide a supply of fresh bait. When freezing bait make sure the packages are sealed and only take to the beach the amount deemed necessary for that trip. Some anglers wrap the frozen bait in newspaper, trying to keep it frozen as long as possible and will only use twice frozen bait in an emergency.

Continuing along this same train of thought, let me now point out which baits are preferred for each species of the three surf fish with which we are concerned.

Starting with the number one game fish, the striped bass,

Live eels are great baits for both bass and blues. They can be fished with a bottom bait rig or cast out and retrieved as you would a lure. William Muller Photo.

this esteemed predator will eat anything available. With an appetite such as this it would seem that a striper would be among the least difficult fish to catch, but any angler who has pursued striped bass will attest to their contrary behavior. Naturally, some baits are more readily acceptable than others, with a live eel being the overall favorite. The list of other favored baits include, but are not limited to, bunker, mackerel, any of the three marine worms, skimmer clam, crabs, sand eels, snappers, butterfish, mullet, squid, blackfish, flounder and lastly lobster. I think, though, that we can disregard the latter, for anyone preferring to feed lobster tail to a bass rather than eating it himself has to be deemed suspect.

Several of these baits must be fished live in order to be effective. Sea worms, eels, blackfish, snappers or baby flounder should be either live-lined or used in conjunction with a fish finder rig. On the other hand, bunker, tinker mackerel, mullet or any of the smaller fish can be offered either live or dead.

Bluefish, even with their reputation for frenzied feeding binges, are slightly more selective in their feeding habits. Bunker, mackerel and live eels are the most commonly used baits, but actually any finfish placed on a hook will attract these toothy critters, even their smaller brethren. It seems that bluefish prefer to feed on anything that normally swims through the water. Therefore, worms, clam, or crabs are not used as bait when seeking bluefish.

The final species with which we are concerned is the weakfish, a species whose appetite is almost as extensive as the sea gull of the water: the striped bass. The most commonly used baits for enticing these spotted beauties are sandworms, mackerel, bunker, snappers or squid.

Given the extensive list of possible baits for each species, it can be correctly assumed that diverse methods and rigs are necessary in some instances. A detailed description of every possible use and technique is impractical. Therefore, only the most productive and commonly practiced methods will be explained.

The observation that striped bass are attracted to eels was

detected sometime in the distant past; an interest that continues today. Eels can be fished live, from a bottom rig, cast and retrieved in a manner similar to a swimming plug or peeled with the skin being used to adorn a plug such as the Spin Atom.

Most pin hookers travelling to Cape Cod during the autumn months make certain that they are well supplied with several dozen eels before they depart the Island. Serious surfmen, remaining on Long Island, should also ensure that they have an ample supply on hand rather than scurrying to the local bait shop before each trip to the beach.

A rag or handful of sand will help you get a grip on a slippery eel. William Muller Photo.

Several places around the Island sell eels by the pound at a cheaper price than when purchased three at a time. These eels can be kept in a freshwater filled plastic tub at home for an extended period of time. There will be little loss if a cheap aerator, normally used in tropical fish tanks, and a cover are used.

Live eels can be used for striped bass at any time during the season as long as bass over ten pounds have migrated northward. This usually occurs about the third week in May. Live eels are most frequently used in conjunction with a fish finder rig. Since it is desirable to have the bait appear

Check the eel frequently for vitality and damage from crabs or blues. William Muller Photo.

natural, small 4/0 to 6/0 bronze colored tuna hooks are favored by many local surfmen. These hooks are extremely strong, sufficient to subdue the largest fish, but there are some veteran anglers who prefer a lighter hook such as a stainless steel Siwash.

When fishing with eels in the surf there is no steadfast rule on how the eel should be placed on the hook. Eels can be hooked through the head, the middle of the back, or through the tail. All methods have their advocates, but anglers specifically seeking bass are inclined to place the hook in the head. Again, there is no precise rule in placing the hook other than that the hook should not pierce the center of the skull, thereby killing the eel. The more commonly followed procedures entail impaling both jaws from the bottom up, through both eye sockets or from underneath the jaw and out one eye.

Before continuing any further, let me point out that when fishing with any bait in the presence of bluefish, it is necessary to use a wire leader. This leader can be fashioned from either the more popular plastic coated wire or single strand stainless steel wire. If striped bass are the quarry, this presents a problem, for many anglers feel that the wary bass will shy away from the more visible wire leaders. This theory has been debated for many years with little conclusive evidence offered by either side to prove their case. In calm, clear water a wire leader could be a factor when fishing during the daylight hours, but at other times, I personally feel it will make little difference.

Besides using live eels, any small fish can be used as a bait for game fish. Baby blackfish are particularly deadly when seeking cow bass, while snappers, small bunker, or tinker mackerel are attractive baits for bass, blues, and also weakfish. All of these fish should be hooked high in the back near the dorsal fin, making sure that the hook does not pierce the spinal column. It should be noted that any bait or fish which is prevalent at any stage of the season can be used successfully, but such baits as eels, or clams are appropriate at any time.

Sandworms, bloodworms or ribbon worms are excellent

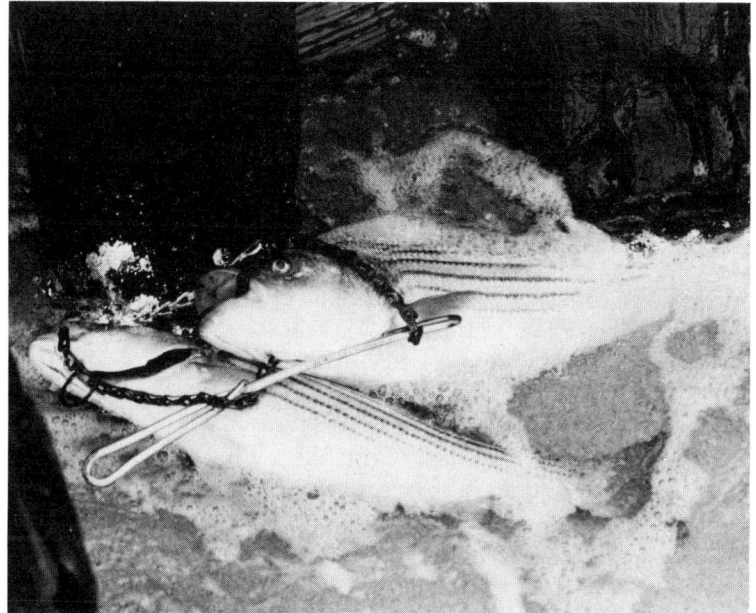

School bass, as well as cows now and then, have a decided liking for large sand worms fished on the bottom. William Muller Photo.

baits when seeking striped bass, most often during the spring and early summer months. One drawback when fishing with either sand or ribbon worms is that they tend to break apart during the cast. Ribbon worms, inaccurately called tape worms, are the most difficult to present in a lifelike manner for their bodies break apart almost under their own weight. The head portion is the only part that is worthwhile; even this should be bunched up on an Eagle Claw bait saver hook. Whereas bass will feed on any of the three species of sea worm, weakfish are partial to sandworms. When fishing worms for school bass or weakfish, hook sizes can range from 1/0 to possibly 4/0 with the smaller size significantly increasing the catch on many occasions.

The favorite sea worm for either striped bass or weakfish is without question the sandworm. Successful fishermen are careful to present these worms in a lifelike manner. When placing these worms on the hook the point should be forced into the worm's mouth exiting from the top of the head so that approximately one-quarter of an inch of the worm's body is impaled on the hook. The cartilage present in the worm's head will hold it in place during the cast and allow the major portion of the worm to float enticingly in the currents after the rig has settled to the bottom. It should be pointed out that fresh healthy sandworms are vital to successful bass fishing. Therefore, be choosy when purchasing the worms at the tackle store and care for them after they are in your possession. Keep them cool without freezing, with no additional moisture, but most of all, make sure they are kept out of the direct rays of a hot sun. The use of worms when seeking game fish requires an ample amount of bait with a minimum of two or three whole worms on each hook.

Cut bait is probably the most widely used bait in the Long Island surf. It is an excellent bait for all of the three species, having the added benefit that it can be packaged for the home freezer; available even if a last minute trip is decided upon. While some surfmen prefer to cut fillets from each side of the fish, many anglers achieve satisfactory results by cutting through the backbone and using an inch to an inch and a half cross-sections. Cutting fillets from fresh unfrozen fish presents little problems, for the flesh is firm and will remain intact. Freezing a bait breaks down the fleshy tissue which disintegrates rapidly, leaving only a washed out piece of skin on the hook. A cross-section of bait will have the skin of each side to keep the flesh from washing away. With either method the point of the hook should be exposed to ensure instant and positive penetration when the strike does occur. Hooks favored when fishing cut bait are either the Siwash or the offset Eagle Claw type with sizes ranging from 4/0 to 7/0 depending on the size of the baits being used and the game fish sought.

Skimmer clam bellies are a bait not often used in the present day and age, but their effectiveness is diminished only by the current scarcity of striped bass. This is another

Throwing chunks of mackerel and bunker into the troughs along south shore beaches has proven to be a productive technique for catching big bluefish during October and November. William Muller Photo.

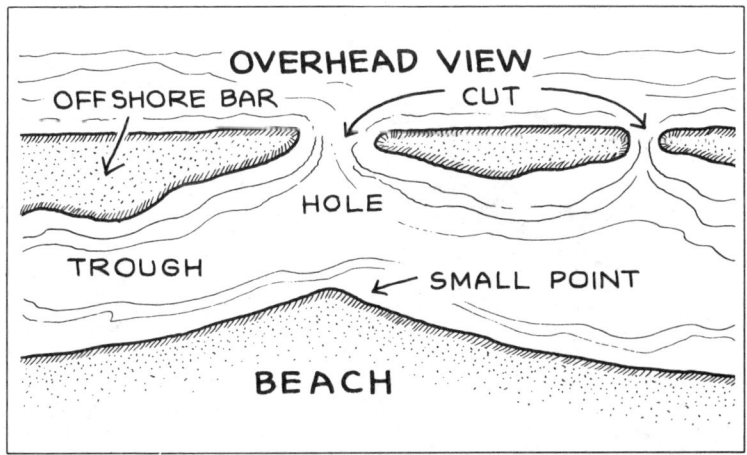

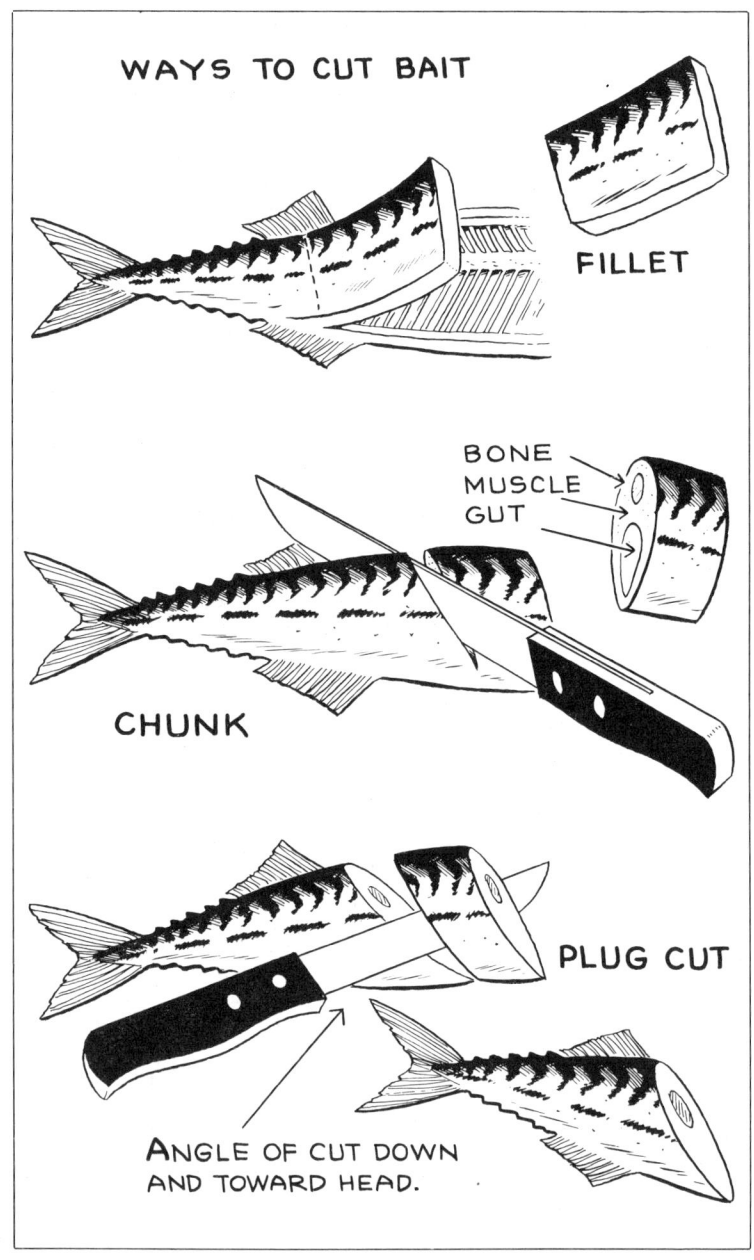

bait which lends itself to easy storage at home. Live clams can be shucked beforehand and frozen in plastic containers. Clam bellies, after they have thawed, have a tendency to fall off the hook during the cast. This difficulty can be partially overcome by adding Kosher salt before freezing to toughen the flesh or by carrying a spool of thread and tying the bait to the hook.

The tackle requirements for fishing bait along the various beaches of Long Island is not as varied as that necessary to partake in the diverse field of plug casting. It should be pointed out that the tackle deemed appropriate for the north shore frequently is totally inadequate when fishing the ocean beaches. North shore fishermen, mainly because they encounter less severe sea conditions, will find a 10 foot medium action spinning rod sufficient. A Penn 710Z would be satisfactory, but a reel similar to the Penn 704Z is more fitting, especially if teen-sized bluefish are sought. Under unusually calm conditions this outfit would suffice in the south shore surf, but in most instances, an 11 or possibly a 13 foot rod would be more appropriate. Large capacity heavy duty reels similar to the Crack 300, or the Penn 706Z are both able to withstand the abuse such fishing entails. Long casts are frequently mandatory in order to place the bait on the outside of a parallel bar or beyond a crashing surf. When seeking the larger bass or monster bluefish along the ocean's shore, 20 pound test line is preferred due to the size of the fish and the force needed to cast a large bait and a sinker; possibly weighing six ounces.

The terminal rig most commonly used when fishing bait is the fish finder or sliding sinker rig. This rig can be used with every type of bait, whether dead or alive. Since the sinker is not fastened directly to the line, a fish is able to seize the bait and make its run without detecting the weight of the sinker. This is a critical factor when fishing live eels or a large piece of cut bait. The predator will often seize the offering and swim away before attempting to swallow the bait. It is when the fish pauses in its run to ingest the bait that the hook is set.

When fishing with smaller baits for comparatively lesser

fish, such as school bass or weakfish, a pompano or double loop rig is often favored. This rig is ideal when using either worms or clam bellies, for it has the added advantage of offering two baited hooks rather than one. Leaderless 1/0 or 2/0 Eagle Claw bait saver hooks are secured to each dropper loop by simply threading the end of the loop through the eye of the hook, passing the hook back through the loop and pulling the line taut.

The surf rig, belying its name, is not frequently employed

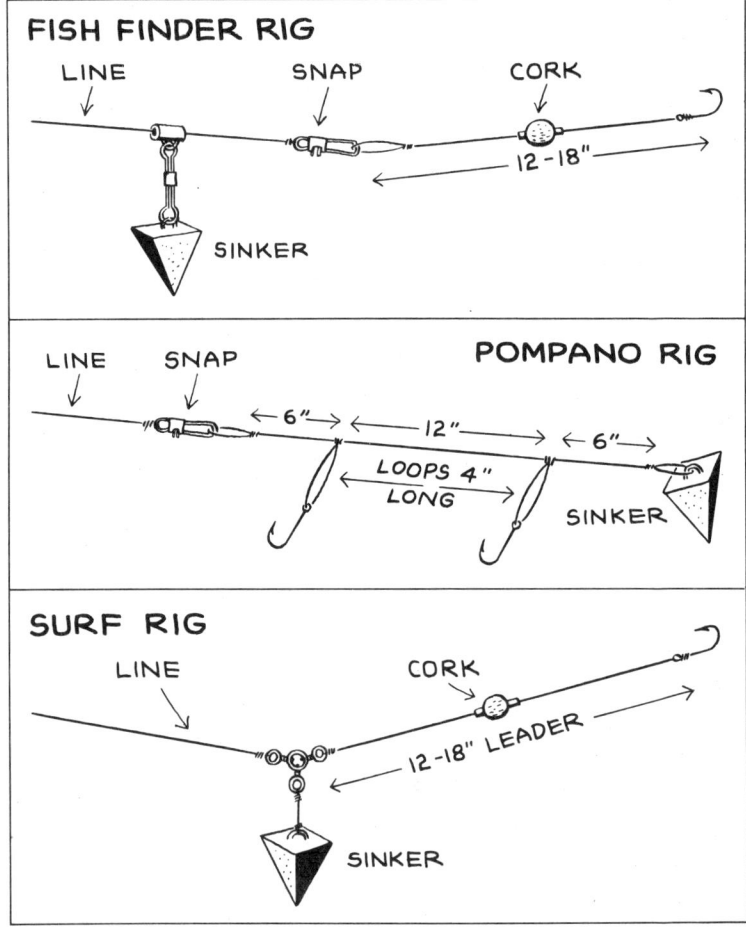

when fishing the open surf for game fish. It features a three-way swivel as its main component and can be a serviceable rig if baits other than live fish or eels are to be used. This terminal gear is used more often when fishing from a pier or bridge where the rig is lowered alongside the pilings, allowing the bait to float underneath the structure from a long leader which has been tied to one of the eyes of the swivel.

When fishing with any of these three rigs the addition of a cork float is vital if crabs continue to feed upon the bait. Live baits are little affected, but any stationary bait is susceptible to predation—the exception being live eels which are often attacked by crabs, but a cork is rarely used. The corks favored by most surfmen are equipped with a drawstring to be used to draw the line through the center hole of the cork. The basic sizes are the oval 2" X 1" for larger baits and the 1/2" X 1" long corks ideal for use with the pompano rig.

Sandspikes are an important item of a bait fisherman's equipment. In many instances the standard 18 to 28 inch spikes are adequate. There are occasions, though, when it is advantageous to have particular sandspike. For example, the thin walled aluminum spike is difficult to force into the gravel of some north shore beaches. On the opposite shore, a longer spike, say to 48 inches, is of assistance in holding the line above the ocean breakers. Depending on a person's height, of course, but any spike longer than four feet makes it difficult to remove the rod under the force exerted by a strong fish. In past years it was necessary to fashion these longer spikes at home out of a section of right angle metal or PVC pipe, but recently they have become available at the better stocked tackle stores. It should be pointed out that any rod left unattended should have the drag loosened, otherwise the rod can be dragged into the sea with the force of a large fish. Remember, we are seeking mighty striped bass and bluefish which have stolen more than one rod from a forgetful angler.

When fishing at night some kind of artificial light will be necessary. Aside from the standard necklight, many bottom fishermen will illuminate the entire area with a Coleman

DEFLECTING THE LIGHT FROM A COLEMAN LANTERN.

lantern. There is a belief among certain surfmen that a bright light will frighten the fish, especially in calm, shallow water areas. In an effort at blocking the beam from shining directly to the water, a plug bag or pail can be placed in front of the lantern. An idea that is more efficient is to scoop out a depression in the sand, placing the lantern in the hole, but tilted upward at an angle so that the beam is directed skyward at the rod tips where it is needed.

A practice, more commonly used at the Cape, which will eliminate the need for a lantern calls for attaching a small battery operated light to the rod tip. This dim light will permit the angler to detect the slightest movement of the tip which could signify that some unseen denizen of the deep is interested in the bait.

Bait fishing for any of the three great surf fish is a complex activity only lightly touched upon in these pages. Dissimilarity of terrain, unusual sea conditions or uncommon opportunities could necessitate the use of a method not described here. For instance, on the flats off of Great Kills in Staten Island, the appearance of snapper schools causes the local anglers to wade waist-deep where they cast live-lined snappers back to the lurking weakfish using a harness similar to that used by boatmen fishing live bunker for marauding bluefish. Experimentation is a key factor in becoming a successful surf fisherman, but the most important thought to remember is that more knowledge is acquired from observing and practicing the techniques of veteran surfmen while on the beach than from sitting at home reading about what should be done.

CHAPTER 12

Releasing Fish
by Fred Schwab

The deplorable waste inherent in nearly all methods of netting, and the "to hell with tomorrow" attitude of many practitioners of that mode of fishing has long bred contempt among sport fishermen for the netter. But there is a breed of angler whose thoughtless behavior and disregard for marine resources, also generates contempt among sportsmen.

These are the anglers who, regardless of size or species, keep everything caught, or, if they do release something, literally tear the poor critter apart during the unhooking process. Upon catching an unwanted species this type maims, tortures or deliberately kills the hapless creature. For want of food, a dogfish, crab, skate or whatever, tried to eat a piece of bait which was booby trapped with a hook. For the heinous crime of trying to satisfy hunger the poor creature is ruthlessly and needlessly destroyed by a species which is supposed to be intelligent and understanding. I have witnessed and/or seen evidence of this shameful behavior many times, and can only conclude that some *Homo sapiens* have a boundless capacity for brutality.

No matter how abundant a creature of the sea may appear to be, or how lowly esteemed it may be, killing it for the sake of killing is absolutely inexcusable. ALL marine species have an important role to play in the grand scheme of things, and may the fisherman—commercial or sport—who wastes a creature, leaving it to rot, be eternally damned.

It was not long ago that most folks believed that nearly all marine species were inexhaustible resources. To be sure, a few voiced concern for the future and advocated management, but they were ignored. However, during the

60s and 70s, the wisdom of their calls for restraint were repeatedly demonstrated as the population of various species precipitously declined.

Today's prevailing opinion is that most species are subjected to excessive fishing pressure, and management is an absolute need. Concurrently, there is increased understanding of the dependent relationships between species. That survival of the largest and the smallest, the most desirable and the lowliest, is intertwined. Oh, there are pockets of resistance to change: Self-interest groups who hold to simplistic views on why a species has declined and who claim that so-called "traditional rights" justify their unregulated use, and resultant abuse of these limited resources. These bastions of ignorance delay needed regulatory programs, but fortunately, the commitment to manage these precious resources is strong and growing stronger.

Long before this age of enlightenment, some anglers routinely practiced conservation of marine resources by carefully releasing much of what they caught. Some even participated in fish tagging programs. In recent years, the ranks of the conservation-minded have swelled, with many sportsmen's organizations, as well as individuals, encouraging the release of fish. There are even fishing contests which stress this aspect of sport fishing. Awards are given for releasing fish, with the recipient being determined by the pounds or number released. To make the contribution to conservation, and the resultant awards more meaningful, entries may be governed by minimum sizes, thus, small fish whose release is customary do not qualify. This encourages the release of larger, sexually mature fish, which might otherwise have been kept and consequently removed from the fishery, and unavailable to participate in the spawning process.

Various factors motivate anglers to release fish. Some do not eat the critters or, in the case of certain species, most notably the striped bass, contamination of the fish's flesh with Polychlorinated Biphenyls (PCBs), Dioxin, and Lord knows what, has convinced the angler to be cautious. Some find it morally unacceptable to take a life, or consider a good game fish far too valuable a resource to be killed. Others keep some for home consumption, and holding to a strong conviction that it is unethical for sport fishermen to engage in the sale of fish, release the excess. But, in the final analysis, most who regularly practice restraint are influenced by the desire to preserve the fisheries, and they know that collectively anglers who take such action are making a meaningful contribution towards that goal.

The magnitude of that contribution is suggested in the detailed records of one small Long Island surf fishing club. In 1982, this group of less than 25 anglers, released 413 striped bass, bluefish and weakfish ranging from 5 to 47 pounds, and having an aggregate weight of over 3,950 pounds. Along with the many smaller fish and other species, this group released well in excess of two tons of fish. These are fish returned to the fishery for someone else—perhaps you—to experience the pleasure of catching on another day, and more importantly, some may survive to spawn once and perhaps several times.

Releasing a fish is seldom a complicated and time consuming matter, and you have cleared the toughest hurdle when you make the commitment to do so. Since the purpose is to reduce fishing mortality by returning the fish to the fishery, the objective is to achieve a successful release. That requires patience and a lot of TLC or, tender loving care.

Being hooked and landed is an exhausting experience for any fish, and stress and shock differ, even between fish of the same species. The conditions under which a fish is fought and landed are another variable, and a fish which bounced all over the beach may be harder to revive than one which appeared to be halfway to fish heaven. But, if little or no damage has been done to vital organs and it has not been out of the water for an inordinate period of time, a bit of TLC can revive even the most exhausted fish.

The most critical factors with respect to a fish surviving relate to how it's hooked, what the resultant damage is, and how it's handled. Bleeding does not necessarily mean that a fish is doomed; in fact, a spot or trickle of blood is not unusual. But profuse bleeding around or from a gill, and one which is torn or broken is another matter. The gills are the fish's lungs, and the vital organ most frequently damaged by the hook or by a careless angler during the unhooking process. A damaged gill can mean death, but there are fish swimming around with deformed gills, thus slight damage is not a certainty that the fish will die.

Because so many fishing lures have two and three sets of swinging treble hooks, it's not uncommon for a hook to become embedded in or very near an eye socket. Over the years I've caught several one-eyed fish, which judging from appearance had sustained the injury long before. There was one bass in particular, a strong chunky fish of about 12 pounds who, despite its handicap, obviously had no trouble feeding itself, and when released it swam away with absolutely no hesitation. Removing a hook from around or in an eye socket requires a lot of TLC to minimize damage.

Obviously, during the unhooking process the angler must avoid damage to himself. Becoming the hookee can be a painful and costly experience. If the intention is to release the fish, there is the added concern of minimizing the damage to it. Some anglers effectively deal with both problems by flattening or filing away the barbs on the hooks. A barbless hook is comparatively easy to back out, and if done with care will not tear flesh—human or fish. The absence of a barb also increases hook penetration, a distinct advantage if it's set in bone or the tough tissue surrounding the mouth, and in the case of lures with multiple hooks, the likelihood of the fish being held by more than one hook is increased. Though it is easier for a fish to shake a barbless hook, those who regularly use them maintain that there is little chance of that happening if the angler remembers to maintain a tight line.

Whether you beach the fish or remain in the water, if you intend to release it, using your gaff is out of the question, unless you can lip-gaff the fish. The first step is to locate the hook or hooks and guided by the physical characteristics of the fish, determine the safest and surest way to hold it.

Certainly not a complicated matter if the fish is beached, but tricky business when standing in the water at night. If the fish is small, obviously weighing much less than the pound-test of your line, lift him out by it, and with your other hand, rod under armpit, get a grip on the fish. But if it's large, and you are not experienced, you should beach it.

When standing in a strong current and using large lures, such as an Atom 40, big Darter or Bottle plug, there's another method. But before describing it, I want to make it abundantly clear that it's definitely not recommended for the beginner. In this case, you lift the fish partly or completely out of the water by grasping the head of the plug VERY firmly. This is accomplished by grabbing the line, after the fish is played out, and draw the fish in to determine where the forward or head hooks are. The next step is to run your hand down the line, and with a vise-like grip, grab the head of the plug and quickly lift the fish. Needless to say, with this insane method, one mistake and you are in big trouble. Never try this with a green fish, and don't try grabbing the plug if he's not on the surface and very still. The current helps by keeping an exhausted fish on or very near the surface and generally, headed in one direction. Try to anticipate the fish's moves, and until you have lifted him, be prepared to pull your hand away in an instant. When I was younger and more reckless, this system worked for me on countless occasions; but I had many very close calls, lots of luck, and must confess that a slow down of my reflexes now limits my use of this method.

If the location of the hooks permit, the least harmful, and certainly most secure method of holding a toothless specimen such as a bass, is by the lower jaw, thumb in mouth. Incidentally, this is the only safe hold for a sea robin. Needless to say, using this hold on a toothy fish such as a bergall, blackfish or fluke is out of the question, and you can kiss part of your anatomy goodbye if you try this with a bluefish.

A good hold for species with no sharp spines on the dorsal fin, is to spread the palm of your hand across the top of the head and insert thumb and middle finger in the top of the gill slits. This works well with weakfish and, dependent upon the size of your hand, bluefish up to about 13 pounds. Don't try this with a bass or bergall; their dorsal spines will do a number on your hand.

Another hold, applicable to most fish, is by the bony septum just forward of the belly, below the gill covers. Perhaps less desirable for the fish's sake, but secure and sometimes the best option, is to slip two or more fingers under a gill cover with the thumb outside. Remember to be gentle whenever you start poking your fingers around the gills.

Of course, beaching the fish makes the whole operation

Treble hooks can be a problem when releasing fish. Hooks can become embedded in gill plates and the body. Often the fish can still be released and little damage done to the fish if the hooks are backed out carefully. William Muller Photo.

much simpler, and a lot safer. On terra firma the angler has the option of merely restricting the movements of the fish by holding it down; but don't use a foot or knee. Just steady him with your hand and avoid putting pressure on the stomach. Since you will be working the hook out at the front end, that's where you should be controlling the fish's movements.

Patience and TLC during the unhooking process reduces damage to the fish, and usually the consumption of time. Never grab the shank of the hook and just pull; you will tear the surrounding tissue, probably cause irreparable damage, or drive the hook deeper. Since the object is to widen the puncture and back the hook out through the hole it made on the way in, firmly grasp the shank with thumb and forefinger and gently twist the hook with a backward motion. If it is a toothless species, don't be afraid of sticking your fingers inside the mouth. On occasion, removing the hook may necessitate "gently" putting your fingers through a gill slit. Once free, slowly pull it out through the mouth. Doing it quickly will almost certainly result in the hook being embedded again.

Sometimes a fish caught on bait will swallow or take the hook so deeply that any attempt to remove it will almost certainly mean death. If it's an illegal fish or you are determined to release it, snip off as much of the snell and shank as is possible. If it's not a rust resistant hook, there is the chance that the fish will survive and eventually the hook will disintegrate. That's one reason why stainless steel hooks are seldom used by some anglers. (Snipping the snell or line is also the best approach to freeing a stingray; it being inadvisable to even beach this critter whose tail is its defense mechanism. They are a gentle but powerful animal, and even with someone's help a big one is hard to control. Respect these giants and allow them to return to their natural environment unharmed.)

Having removed the hook, place the fish upright in the water, loosely grasping him just forward of the tail. If he immediately swims briskly away, the job is done. But if he wobbles about, turns over, or shows little sign of life, it's time for a bit of artificial respiration. Using the previously mentioned "loose" hold, gently move the fish back and forth, six to twelve inches is fine, or if conditions permit, slowly walk the fish. If the mouth is not opening and it's a toothless species, gently holding it open with your other hand should help. This works well with bass and weakfish,

but obviously keep your fingers away from the business end of a bluefish. The objective is to flush water through the mouth and past the gills, thus restoring oxygen to the blood and vitality to the muscles and other organs.

Normally this treatment produces a quick revival with the fish breaking free of your hold with a forceful kick of the tail. But no two fish are alike. He may spurt away only to reappear and wobble or roll over a few feet away. This does not mean that the fish is dying, but rather that he's still weak or in shock and needs further attention. If you do not repeat the revival process he's likely to drift away, belly up and die. Something which often works for me is, with slight wrist action, impart a lazy side to side motion while slowly moving the fish back and forth. Perhaps it helps because the resultant movement of the fish's body is similar to the way he normally moves and it stimulates him into doing what comes naturally.

The aforementioned procedure is ideal when the surface of the water is calm, but it may be impossible to employ in a rough surf or when fishing from an elevated structure. Under such conditions, a successful release is still likely if the fish has not been out of the water for an inordinate length of time and is not seriously injured. In both cases, the best bet is to gently toss the fish back. In the surf, time the release between the waves. This gives the fish precious moments to adjust and work his way beneath, and possibly beyond the breakers.

In discussing the question of releasing fish with a biologist who has tagged and released many, he observed that small fish often revive instantly when tossed back. I've tried it and it works, if the fish is uninjured and only a minute or two has elapsed since it was landed. Presumably the impact does the trick. A sort of shock treatment? But don't slam the fish on the surface, just gently toss it a few feet.

Reviving a large fish usually requires a bit more effort than it takes to revive a small one. That's probably because the ordeal of being landed takes longer, thus, the jumbos expend a greater percentage of their energy in the struggle to get free, and perhaps younger fish simply have more vitality. I really don't know why, but those seem to be reasonable explanations.

Once you develop the release habit, you begin to experience a very deep feeling of satisfaction each time you grant some critter a lease on life. In fact, just watching a fish, especially a big one such as a 30 or 40 pound bass, amble off to continue spending her time where she was meant to be, is as much of a thrill as when she was caught. Her release was a forfeited opportunity to experience an ego inflating moment waving her lifeless carcass before friends and neighbors. But the lasting good feeling that you get from knowing that she remains alive and may create more of her magnificent kind, far surpasses that fleeting moment which would have been yours...at the cost of her life.

CHAPTER 13

How to Catch Flounder and Fluke

by Gerald Hahn

FLOUNDER

Flounder and fluke are members of the flatfish family, which includes various small soles and the 600 pound halibut. Anatomically, the flatfish goes through a bizarre metamorphosis during the first months of its life. The fish begins life as a normal, upright individual, but soon turns on its side as one eye travels around the head (sometimes, through it) to meet the other. Now laterally compressed and with eyes together on top of the head, the fish settles down on the bottom—fluke facing left and flounder right. Pointing in opposite directions is a sign that the two fish may have different destinies. They have. In the first place, flounder are taken primarily in spring and fall, whereas fluke are strictly summer residents; hence, their distinction in some regions as winter and summer flounder. An examination of their mouths, moreover, reveals that the flounder is a sucker and the fluke a biter. One has a small, toothless mouth, whereas the other's is large and generously equipped with razor sharp teeth. There is a significant difference in size, too. A 5 pound sea flounder or snowshoe would be considered a prize by any fisherman, but it would take a fluke twice that size to attain doormat status. Indeed, 20 pound specimens have been taken in New York. Thus, the flounder is strictly a bottom fish, while the fluke is an aggressive predator. And fishermen must use entirely different methods to catch them. Let's begin, then, with flounder.

The first fish undoubtedly taken every season by the vast

majority of surf anglers is the blackback flounder. Its relative, the yellowtail, is more abundant up north. How early are flounder taken? A warm day in February will attract a surprising number of fishermen to such popular flounder haunts as the Shinnecock Canal and the Cross Bay Bridge. The earliest flounder I ever caught was on New Year's Day. Most surf anglers, nonetheless, start fishing for flounder soon after boatmen unofficially open the season on St. Patrick's Day, the peak of the spring run extending to mid-May. At this time, the fish, though thin, are plentiful. From September through November, depending on the weather, flounder are taken again in the same places as in spring. These fish, though harder to catch, are heavier now. Substantial numbers of flounder actually remain in local waters throughout the summer, but by then, anglers are pursuing other quarry, including summer fluke.

Where are flounder typically found? I know a creek that passes under Montauk Highway and drains into the north side of Moriches Bay. In the winter it is frozen over in a milky light, but sometime before the lowly skunk cabbage sends forth purple and brown shoots and the smell of rotting meat, the creek comes to life. Melting ice and rainstorms scour particles rich in organic content from the swollen creek's banks, and soon a host of living microorganisms, including infant shrimp and mollusks, amphipods, copepods, fish larvae and various seaworms, spice the chilled drifting soup. The creek doesn't move rapidly; it doesn't have to. A one knot current is sufficient to shift its fine gravel and silt bottom. Now laden with suspended matter, the creek slowly meanders into the bay where it cuts a channel and then spreads out to form an intertidal flat. Here, the creek unloads its gift of nutrients, and the result is a rich mud bottom.

Fishermen welcome mud in the spring, as well as in the fall, for they know that in this delicate ecosystem they are bound to find flounder. The flounder, you see, is perfectly designed for an indolent life in a muddy terrain from which it will not have to range very far. Among other things, the fish is a poor swimmer. It can bury itself in the mud, however, and scan the waters above for glistening tidbits trickling down to the bottom. It can hop about in short spurts. It can change the color and pattern of its dark brown back to blend with the surroundings, the kind of bottom into which our typical creek drains. And consequently, the flounder is found in almost every back bay and harbor on the South Shore, North Shore and East End, along the mouths of estuaries, in canals, and even in brackish water. For these shallow waters warm quickly in the spring and obtain the same temperatures again in the fall. Flounder, too, welcome mud.

The flounder we have been describing are generally a small fish, ranging from the size of a postage stamp to about a pound. In some places, however, such as the Atlantic surf, the East End bays and the eastern sector of Long Island Sound, larger specimens over two pounds are occasionally taken.

Most of the time, fishermen use light tackle, even freshwater gear, for flounder. Outfits range from a five foot ultra-light rod and reel spooled with four pound test to a seven foot spinning rod and a small matching reel with a capacity of 200 yards of eight pound test. Freshwater spincast outfits spooled with six pound test are popular as well. Where obstructions occur on the bottom, or when fishing from an elevated position such as a town pier or a bridge, a stronger eight foot rod and a medium-sized spinning reel with ten pound test should be considered.

The most popular hook for flounder is a No. 10 or No. 12 Chestertown. Its long shank facilitates hook removal and its angular bend turns the offset point inward, making it a perfect match for the flounder's small twisted mouth. Nonetheless, I find a No. 4 or No. 6 beak hook, with its rolled-in point and barbs on the shank, more effective. The beak's short barbed shank prevents the bait from sliding down to the bend in an unsightly manner and, therefore, makes a better presentation. In any case, either of these excellent hooks should be snelled to a 12 inch leader of 20 or 30 pound test, depending on the flounder's size and mood. Some fishermen use baited hooks adorned with a yellow plastic corn kernel or yellow hair, and these eye-catchers are effective as well.

A two-hook, tandem-tied rig is undoubtedly everyone's favorite, since flounder are often taken in pairs. In this arrangement, the looped end of one snell is tied to the middle of the other snell, and the hooks are then simply placed on a snap swivel together with the sinker. The swivel is tied beforehand to the end of the fishing line with an improved clinch knot or a Uni-knot. The two hooks may also be secured to a dropper loop on the fishing line about one or two inches above an end loop for the sinker, thereby eliminating the hardware. In this regard, hardware in the form of spreader bars and other metal contraptions make casting difficult, attract vegetation, inhibit the flounder's fight, and should therefore be avoided. Because large flounder are known to rise slightly off the bottom in pursuit

Sometimes surf fishermen forget that good-sized and good eating flounder can be good sport on light tackle. Gerald Hahn Photo.

of a meal, some people add a third hook to the rig. A dropper loop at least a snell's length above the bottom hooks secures it. Sinkers for these rigs range from split shot on a gossamer line above the hooks when fishing in an estuary, to one to three ounce banks where the current moves quicker. Since flounder are not rig shy, many fishermen paint the sinker fluorescent yellow or red.

Toothless flounder enjoy a soft meal, including bloodworms, sandworms, even earthworms, skimmer clams and bank mussels. Worms are cut in small pieces about an inch long, one of which is threaded on the hook point and pushed up the shank. A morsel should dangle below the point for added attraction. Clams are cut in thin strips, the firm part impaled and twisted several times on the hook, with a small amount of the soft part trailing below the point as well. Veteran fishermen often dye their clams yellow or red-violet, with artificial food coloring, again for eye-catching appeal. Mussels, though difficult to work with, can be deadly in the spring. I once observed a surf angler at Cedar Beach catching sea flounder-after-sea flounder with mussels he was drying out in the sun. The soft bait is toughened this way and can then be impaled in the same manner as clams, starting with the tough tongue and ending with the soft lip. To be sure, many fishermen use at least two different baits, including corn kernels, and try various combinations on separate hooks and even on the same hook. For there are days when finicky flounder want nothing less than a combination platter.

When flounder are feeding close to shore, additional food in the form of chum will hold them there. A mixture of crushed mussels or clams, to which is added corn, cat food, rice, sand, or even broken eggshells, is tossed to the upcurrent side of the fishing spot. The chum, catching the light, trickles down to the baited rig and mimics the suspended matter on which flounder feed. A chum pot attached to a long line and stuffed with the same goodies is equally effective.

Flounder are notoriously lethargic when the water is cold, and the only way to fish for them is with a dead stick. The

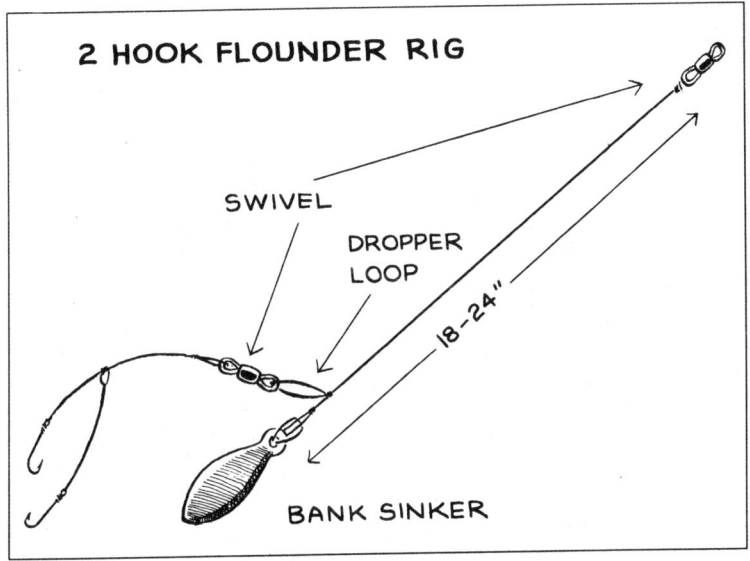

rig is cast and the bait is held motionless on the bottom. When the fish are active, however, as happens later in the spring and in fall, anglers move the bait slowly, dragging it along the bottom, with long pauses, and even raising and quickly lowering the sinker so that it bounces. This stirs the mud somewhat and dislodges particles with a "puff of smoke," once again attracting the fish. Flounder, seeing these morsels momentarily suspended, will hop 20 feet along the bottom. Sluggish fish, however, often inhale the bait like a vacuum cleaner and then fall asleep on the bottom, and only a raised rod tip will awaken them. Then again, I have seen aggressive flounder jerk a rod out of a sand spike and set the hook themselves. Generally, the angler merely has to flick his wrist to hook a flounder; this method also hooks a fish that is toying with the bait. The flounder, seeing the prey attempting to escape, will make a short leap off the bottom and grab it. Leaving the hooked fish on the bottom for awhile is recommended, because another flounder may soon come along and grab the remaining bait. On light tackle, the average flounder provides good sport, its downward surges stretching the thin line like a rubber band. A 1½ pounder, in fact, will fight harder than a fluke of comparable size. Postage stamp specimens should be released, however, unless you intend to do some serious fishing for stripers. In that case, save a few flounder fry for bait. Bass love them.

Fishing for flounder in various places, of course, requires an understanding of the locale. For example, at the Shinnecock Canal experienced anglers line up on the south side of the locks and wait for them to close. At other times, the current is so swift that no flounder are caught. Simple enough to remember. Fishing a back bay inlet, however, may require more detailed study. I am reminded of one on Gardiner's Bay, a small inlet that leads to a rather wide creek harboring a marina. The inlet itself is often dredged, and here swift currents and shifting sand make for poor bottom fishing. At the back of the inlet, however, where it widens into the creek, the bottom reverts to mud which, in places, is higher than the aforementioned sand bottom. The current is slowed around the mud bars, and the accompanying dropoffs hold flounder. Continuing with other potential flounder spots, estuaries may be vastly different from one another; but the juncture of the smaller body of water and the greater is always worth trying. In these places, moreover, the bottom should be checked at low slack for sloughs. Undoubtedly, flounder will holeup here when the water starts coming in. Last, but certainly not least, when looking for snowshoe flounder at the beaches between Mattituck and Orient Point, look for strong currents, not sluggish water, and remember to use that high hook. The large fish here are accustomed to leaping for their meals. Flounder are easy to catch once you know how to find them.

Flounder are taken around tidal changes, as well as in any running current. In estuaries, the incoming tide is generally better since the water may be too shallow for productive fishing at other times. Backwater inlets, however, are often productive on the outgoing tide, particularly at the entrance where flounder wait for tidbits to be swept out.

There is no need to rush to your favorite flounder hole at

the crack of dawn. In cold weather the fish are more active later in the day. Periods of high winds and rainstorms should be avoided, however; the water becomes too murky for good bottom fishing.

The first fish I ever caught in the salt was a blackback flounder, and I return every season for more. This humble bottom feeder is easy to catch and its excellent flavor is acclaimed everywhere. If you're a raw beginner, consider the flounder as your first best bet.

FLUKE

Fluke are flatfish of a different order from flounder; not mud grubbers, but stowaways in sand. Their favorite hideouts are at the base of sandy slopes formed along the edges of channels and sand bars. Here they wait for swift, turbulent currents to bring helpless baitfish, fish fry, various crustaceans and squid to them. Fluke are rapid swimmers, too, and can easily overtake the prey in sand flats and thin water.

So the first thing to consider when fishing for fluke, as opposed to fishing for flounder, is a bait that moves either on

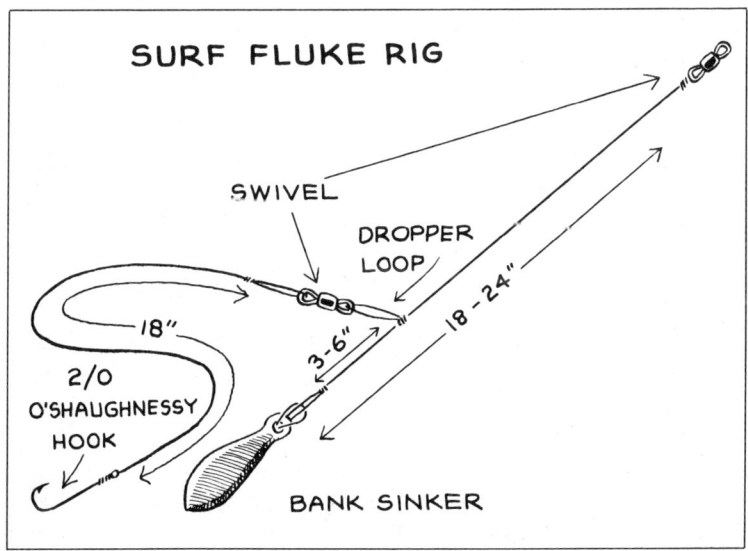

its own or through the action imparted by the angler. In many places, such as along the North and South Shore inlets, swift currents will cause the bait to drift along the bottom, and here, even a bottom rig, properly weighted, will drift. The rig begins with a 2/0 beak or O'Shaughnessy hook snelled on an 18 inch leader of 30 pound test. The long leader enhances the bait's movement. An end loop for a bank sinker and a dropper loop on the fishing line about three to six inches above makes an effective rig in strong currents. If the rig seems to settle on the bottom, try a lighter sinker. A slow retrieve will activate the rig as well.

In sand flats, however, where snags are not likely to occur, a Florida rig is better for drifting. This rig is mounted with an egg or a worm sinker, its hole through the center for threading onto the fishing line. A barrel swivel is then tied to the end of the line with an improved clinch knot, and the snelled hook is attached to the remaining eye of the swivel. This arrangement prevents the sliding sinker from bumping into the hook. A fluke, moreover, will not feel the sinker's resistance when it engulfs the bait. Rolling along the bottom, this rig is excellent for fishing the flats, hence the name Florida rig. An effective variant of a Florida rig may be fashioned with a small in-line trolling sinker which comes with two eyelets: one for connecting to the fishing line and the other for attaching the snelled hook.

Boatmen often use high-low rigs for fluke, but they seldom catch any fish on the top hook. Fluke like their action lower down. The surfcaster will also find the extra hook not worth its snagging potential. Then again, a high hook may attract a stray weakfish or blue, so the choice is yours. This rig simply involves a second dropper loop at least 20 inches above the first and another snelled hook. Actually, a stronger high-low rig, with less of a tendency to tangle, is fashioned with a long leader of 30 pound test and a three-way swivel. The fishing line is tied to one eyelet with an improved clinch knot; the leader goes to the second eye with the same knot; and the third eye receives the top snelled hook. The other hook and the sinker are tied, as before.

Some boatmen also use fluke hooks adorned with bright red beads and flashing blades, and there are days when these attractors are effective from the surf as well. The hook, in this case, is a 3/0 or 4/0 Carlisle, a long-shanked pattern that was highly popular at one time when large fluke (2½ to

Fluke fishing can be great daytime family fun. William Muller Photo.

5 pounds) were commonly taken. Then, during the 1950s, marine biologists discovered that fluke, migrating to their summer nursery grounds in the South Shore bays, were being overharvested by commercial fishermen and sport fishermen alike. So, today we have a legal minimum size limit of 14 inches for fluke—one of the few saltwater fishing restrictions in the Northeast. And today's smaller fluke require smaller hooks.

Over the years the bait for fluke has changed, too. A decade ago, spearing were used everywhere, but today sand eels, the most abundant bait in our waters, have replaced them. Both of these fragile, silvery baitfish come frozen and must be handled gently. Pass the hook point through the baitfish's eyes or through the mouth and out the gill cover, and then impale it near the tail. Another excellent baitfish in frozen form is the smelt, a small relative of the herring, with a yellowish tinge and a silver band on the side. All these baitfish, of course, should first be thawed out and the remainder stored in a shady place, unless you want to fish with mush.

Since fluke also like their offerings alive, a killy (mummichog), a plump little baitfish with a dark green color, can be the deadliest of all. Invest in a floating bait box on a long line, and you can keep killies alive for a long time. The killy should be rigged lightly through the lips so that it can thrash its tail about freely.

Another deadly bait that is often fished alive is the snapper (young bluefish), which is easily acquired by the angler in August and September. Bring along an ulra-light outfit and a small metal lure (half ounce), catch a snapper and immediately transfer it to the fluke rig, hooking the fish in the shoulder just ahead of the dorsal fin. Fluke have large mouths and can easily swallow an eight inch snapper. Indeed, some of the largest doormats have been taken with this bait, which can also be fished dead.

Most of the baitfish mentioned are given extra visibility with the addition of a strip of squid. To be sure, fluke are so fond of squid that the bait can be used by itself. Remove the speckled skin to uncover the squid's snow white flesh, then

Bank and pier surf fishermen have their innings too. This fluke was taken on a snapper. Gerald Hahn Photo.

cut the squid into pennant shapes from the mantle, about three inches long by half an inch wide, and impale the strip once or twice near the wide end. When drifted, alone or in combination with a baitfish, the squid strip undulates in the current in the most tantalizing manner, an irresistible offering to fluke. So does a strip cut from the belly of a fluke itself, or a winter flounder, or even a sea robin.

Artificial lures will also attract predatory fluke. In fact, I once caught a fluke at night, under a lighted bridge, with a tin squid. Metal lures should be no larger than an ounce and are most effective when sweetened with a strip of squid. So are 3/8 to 5/8 ounce, all-white leadhead bucktails. Either of the lures is tied directly to the fishing line with an improved clinch knot, and then is dragged slowly along the bottom.

Tackle for fluke, of course, varies with the fishing conditions. From the banks of a South Shore bay or a North Shore harbor, a light spinning outfit consisting of a seven foot rod and a small matching reel spooled with 10 pound test is adequate. At the inlets, however, an eight foot jetty stick and a light surf spinning reel filled with 15 or 20 pound test is better for fishing in rough currents near treacherous bottom formations. And a nine foot surf rod should be considered for Long Island Sound's open beaches where long casts to outer bars are required.

One of the best fluke fishing days I ever encountered took place about eight years ago at Shinnecock Inlet. On this midsummer day, when the fish should have been scattered, the west jetty was lined with 50 people and fluke were all over the place. Precisely; they were on the west or ocean side of the jetty. As generally happens when there is a run, almost any bait is effective, and some people were using sand eels or spearing or killies, while others simply resorted to squid. It didn't seem to matter, since the fluke were eating whatever they could sink their teeth into, including a few lures. Short casts were in order, the rigs momentarily sinking before drifting out to sea at the beginning of the ebb tide, and soon a fish would be hooked. I had never seen so many fluke caught from shore and I have grave doubts that I will ever see it again. Today, fluke fishing requires patience

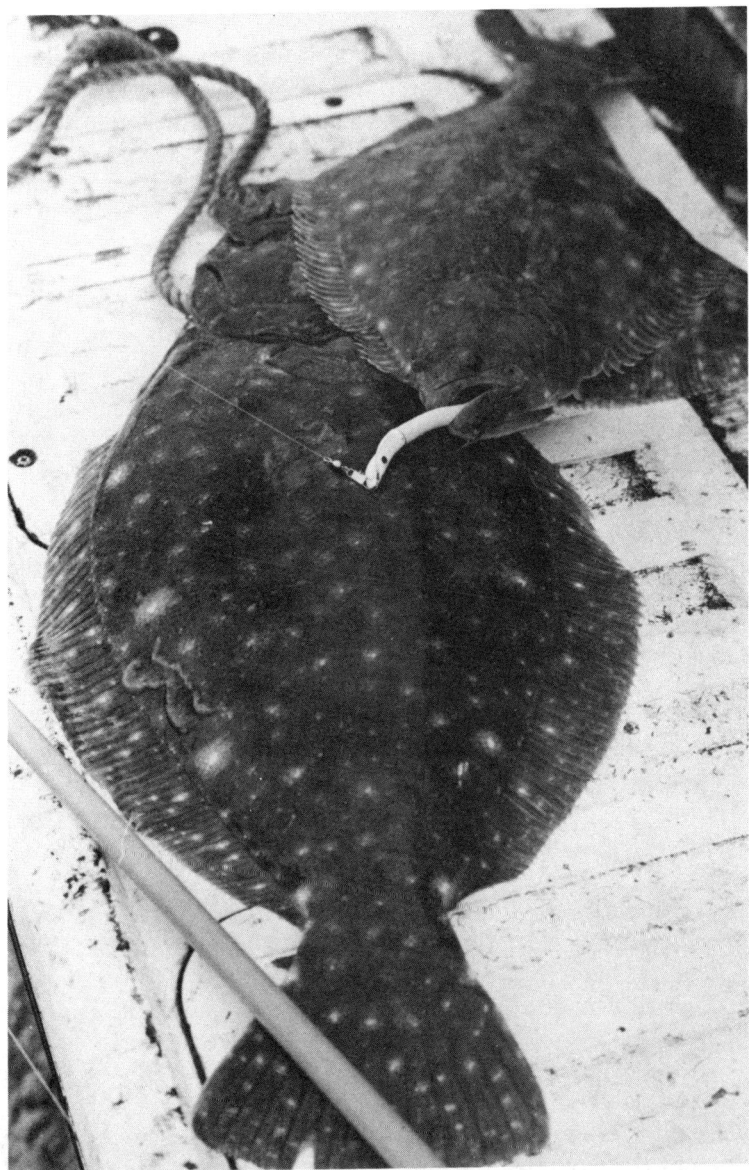

Doormat fluke are sometimes taken on artificials worked close to the bottom in south shore inlets. These weighed eight and five pounds. William Muller Photo.

and a delicate touch.

Many of the small fluke that predominate today are short strikers, hitchhikers who like to grab hold of the end of the bait and hang on for a free ride. A faint weight is felt on the line, and nothing more. These fish are best attended to by lowering the rod tip, even releasing some line, and then waiting for the heavier tugs before setting the hook.

Even so, fluke fishing is frequently productive, especially at any of the South Shore inlets in June and September. For these months mark the beginning and end of the fluke's inshore migration, and it is through these narrow passageways that the species comes and goes. The fish are more abundant at the beginning of the season, till mid-July, but the chance of landing a doormat is better at the end. By then, those fluke that have survived heavy fishing pressure from boatmen will be larger and heavier.

Each South Shore inlet must be studied individually. For instance, if Shinnecock's fluke are generally taken at the mouth of the inlet or on the ocean side, Moriches' are taken in back. Here, turbulent shoal water empties into a deep pocket on the south side where fluke lie in wait for a meal. Then again, if Shinnecock's fluke are in front and Moriches' in back, the fluke at Jones Inlet are right in the middle, halfway between the ocean and the bay. At this spot near the radio shack, a sand bar is accessible during the ebb tide, enabling anglers to reach the edge of the deep channel. More complex than these inlets, however, is Fire Island Inlet, since it is irregularly formed. Consequently, there are several places to try for fluke, including the jetties and sand bars at Democrat Point and the Sore Thumb and the mini-inlet that is formed around Captree Island's fishing piers.

Fishing for fluke elsewhere along the South Shore bays generally occurs along sand flats or deep channels. By example, Heckscher State Park in Great South Bay contains an extensive sand flat close to shore. In this kind of terrain, look also for sand patches between eelgrass or seaweed beds in very thin water. Remember, even a large fluke can use its flat shape to move about easily in the shallows. An an example, a fisherman in a boat once caught a 19 pounder in

Moriches Bay in water less than six feet deep. Deep channels, however, are usually reached where a bay such as Moriches becomes narrow. Under the Smith Point Bridge, for instance, it is possible to cast to the main channel and work its edges from either side.

North Shore and East End fluke fishermen favor sandy points. At Lloyd Neck, Cedar Beach, Shagwong and Culloden, the points form entrances to harbors, coves and bays. They also become peninsulas during the outgoing tide, enabling anglers to gain casting distance to outer bars. Similarly, the North Shore jetties, inlets and breakwaters, such as at Garvey Point, Shoreham and Mattituck provide several hundred feet of access to channels and bars.

At all these places, a moving current on one tide or another is the best time to fish for fluke. The water must be clean, however; so avoid windy days and roiled water.

On both shores, too, summer fluke and winter flounder are often mixed with yet another relative: the windowpane flounder. This fish faces left like the fluke, but its dentures, like the flounder's, are of no consequence. This fish is so thin, however, it transmits light when held up to the sun. Windowpanes, nonetheless, are even more aggressive than fluke. They will readily attack almost any bait, as well as metal/teaser combinations and bucktails. Lots of fun to catch, though too thin to eat, windowpanes hang around from May through November.

Flatfish, as you can see, are very different soles. And they require entirely different methods. Yet one June day on the Sound, I managed to catch a winter flounder, a summer fluke and a windowpane flounder in succession—a full house of flatfish on, believe it or not, a sandworm. I was, of course, trying for weakfish. At such times flatfishng can be wonderful.

CHAPTER 14

How to Catch Porgies and Blackfish
by Gerald Hahn

PORGIES

At a certain time of the year the bottom of Long Island Sound is paved with mother-of-pearl. These rainbow hues do not come from the overturned shells of dead oysters, but from the glistening sides of porgies on the move. Having fattened up since spring, the fish start heading back in the fall to the Continental Shelf's gentle slopes. It would take a scuba diver to actually see this extraordinary iridescence on the sea floor, but fishermen sense it nonetheless. Their vibrating rod tips inform of the bustle below.

Porgies, nonetheless, are members of the Sparid family, relatives of the tropical sea bream, southern pinfish and mid-Atlantic sheepshead. If only the porgy grew to the size of a mutton snapper, to which its taste has often been compared, anglers would then experience some real tackle busting action. Alas, a three pounder is considered a trophy and the majority are panfish size.

Yet the pip-squeak porgy is a scrappy battler, stronger, some people say, than a weakfish of comparable weight. Its lightning jibs and zigzag movements, as though it were running an obstacle course, have impressed countless light tackle enthusiasts. This aggressive school fish, moreover, is a professional pickpocket, an educated bait-stealer. Porgies seem immune to warm temperatures, and many are taken throughout the summer. So with suntans and scup going hand-in-hand, no wonder the fish is so popular among the bottom fishing clan!

Scup? Up North, this is the fish's name, which is derived from the Narragansett Indian *muscuppanog*. Somewhere along the line, New Englanders simplified it to *scuppaug* and finally, to today's *scup*. From New York to Florida, however, the fish is a porgy.

Porgies favor a littered terrain, the kind one finds not only on the North Shore, but in the Peconics and Gardiner's Bay. The porgy uses its narrow body to slip between the rubble, while its sharp dorsal spines are for defense, as many fishermen with bruised fingers will verify. The fish's small mouth, moreover, is filled with strong incisors—excellent for rooting out tiny invertebrates and other prey that hide in rock crevices, mussel beds and broken shells, or that burrow in sand.

Porgies, though small, come in three classifications: 1/2 pound sand porgies, 1 pound bay porgies and 1½ to more than 3 pound sea porgies or humpbacks. When the fish

Double headers of porgies are not uncommon during the summer fishing from many north shore beaches. Gerald Hahn Photo.

grows large, it develops a distinctive hump on its shoulder. Humpbacks are usually taken in the fall, or offshore, although they also enter the East End bays briefly in late-May or early-June. I once believed that porgies, like scrappy youngsters, buddied up only with those their own size, but this is not always the case. So be prepared for the sudden jolt of a sea porgy when tackling the sands.

Fishing from various shore points over relatively unobstructed bottom, such as from a town dock, the end of a north side jetty or the banks of a bay can be performed with light tackle consisting of a seven foot spinning rod and a small matching reel with a capacity of 200 yards of eight pound test. When the bottom is littered, however, with rig snaring stuff, and where casting requirements are greater, an eight or nine foot spinning rod matched with a light surf reel spooled with 20 pound test should be considered.

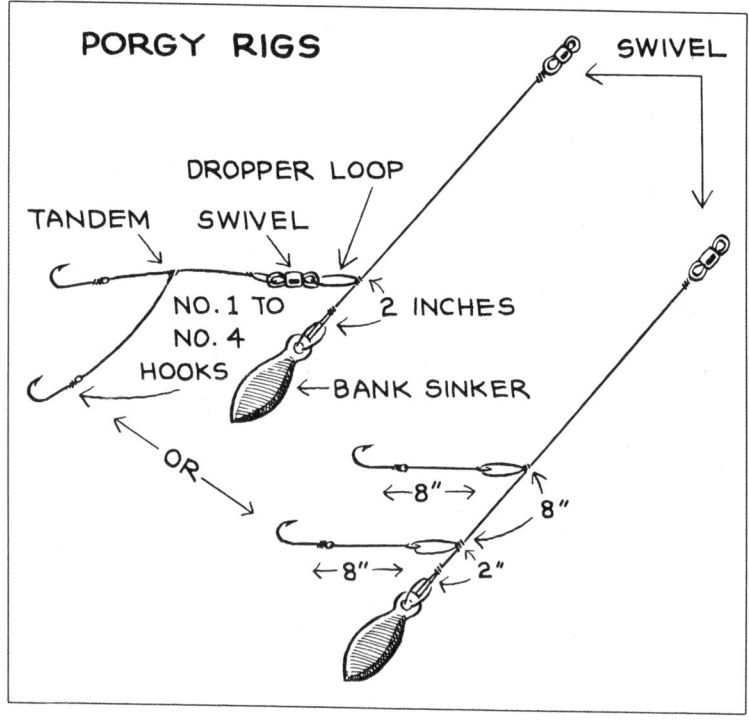

Although tackle for porgies may vary, the hook remains essentially the same no matter whether the quarry is a runt or a bruiser. A #1 beak or claw hook, with barbs on the shank and snelled on a 12 inch leader of 30 pound test is the largest you will need. Indeed, some fishermen favor a #4 size and a 20 pound test leader. This forged hook, with a strong hollow point and a reversed bend, is perfectly matched for the porgy's small mouth.

Rigs, like the tackle one uses, vary considerably, however. Where small fish congregate over sand patches, the same kind of two-hook rig one uses for flounder is excellent for porgies, since double-headers commonly occur. Tie the hooks in tandem, as described in previous chapters. Bank sinkers are favored everywhere and range from one ounce in the bays to four ounces on a rough day in the Sound.

When fishing amid dense bottom structures, as from a North Shore beach, many anglers favor a high-low rig. This involves tying the hooks above each other at least a snell's length apart, beginning with the bottom hook about two inches above an end loop for the sinker. In this arrangement, shorter eight inch snells are sometimes employed. Large porgies will rise off the bottom and attack the top hook, which remains in their feeding zone. In littered terrain, moreover, the top hook may be the only one that is not soon covered with vegetation.

Offshore porgies are fond of clams and squid, but inshore porgies dine on sandworms, bloodworms and even earthworms. Not always, of course, which is why veteran anglers bring several different kinds of bait. In any case, the worm should be cut into one inch pieces, one of which is carefully threaded onto the point and over the barbs on the shank. Clams and squid should be cut in thin strips about an inch long as well, but twisted and impaled several times on the hook. Letting the tiniest morsel trail below the point adds attraction, but carelessly slapping the bait on the hook in a feverish rush to get a line out is an invitation to disaster when fishing for porgies. The fish will strip if off the hook before you can close the bail. Some fishermen use two different baits on the hooks or combine them on one hook.

For example, a piece of skimmer clam tipped with a sandworm morsel makes an effective combination platter, and bringing along several baits, moreover, allows the porgy to decide which one will have feature billing on today's menu.

Porgies may create rainbows on the sea floor in anticipation of their fall departure, but earlier in the season the fish are scattered, and it may take awhile to locate them. One way is to wait them out with a dead stick, the bait held still on the bottom. Another method is to make the rig crawl like the New York subway in rush hour. Among other things, a long pause at each station, with snail-like retrieves in-between, finds the fish that feed close to shore. This is especially true on jetties, since deep water is already close by. When porgies are few and far between, however, I instruct the rig to go find fish in the current. This method I discovered quite by accident one day when I couldn't catch a porgy to save my life. The dead stick method had only brought deathly silence and the subway method a snarl. Then a stiff breeze came out of the north, and joining the incoming tide, made the rig drift toward shore. Suddenly, the rig stopped and I was into a fish, my first of the day. Others soon succumbed to this method, for where one porgy lurks, others are sure to follow. Although porgies are primarily bottom feeders, they will attack a moving bait with gusto, as many boat men have discovered. The fish, moreover, strike a moving bait harder than a stationary bait, and drifting close to the bottom is one way to overcome their bait stealing antics.

For, in every respect, attention must be paid to the rod tip when fishing for cunning porgies. Several taps on the line, followed by deathly quiet, is a signal to bait up again. This is one advantage to fishing as light as possible. Another is that the porgy, once hooked, seldom gets away, yet it will put a fine bend in the wand as it tries.

Likely porgy spots on the Sound are near submerged boulders, mussel beds and sand patches between the rock piles. Try fishing the beaches with two rods set in sand spikes to cover more territory, and give each spot a thorough workout for at least twenty minutes before moving on. Parking restrictions make fishing here difficult in the summer, but several State Parks are available, including Sunken Meadow and Wildwood. Both places are known to hold good concentrations of porgies. Here, and in the East End bays, the tips of jetties and the entrances to inlets can be particularly rewarding. In the summer, the best fishing occurs at first light after the water has cooled overnight. By then, the fish are ravenous and head inshore to feed. Consequently, dusk is also a good time to fish when the weather is warm. Superb porgy fishing, nonetheless, begins with a westerly or northwesterly breeze stirring the north side waters in late summer, and fish can then be taken almost any time of the day. Tidal changes are best, however, and my preference is the tail end of the flood tide, through the slack, and into the beginning of the ebb. Between the end tides, the current is too swift and few porgies are caught from shore.

Porgies are bony fish, difficult to fillet, and their large scales fly like projectiles. Whenever possible, clean the fish at the beach. It's certainly worth the effort, for porgies are superb table fare, as any Oriental chef or gourmet will inform you. Then again, if you simply enjoy the sport, release the fish so that the bottom of the Sound will be covered with mother-of-pearl for years to come.

BLACKFISH

One of the first times blackfish ever aroused my curiosity, I was casting my arm out for scarce bluefish while an old Swede was standing near me on a rock pile facing the Atlantic and flipping his rig only ten feet out. "He should retire his gear and try checkers," I was about to mutter, when his nine foot surf rod suddenly took a downward turn, and he yanked a hunk of black leather out of the rock pile below. The leather hide was a five pound blackfish. Two hours later, while I was still anticipating my first blue, the Swede's stringer had turned black with 15 of the critters.

Ever since that memorable day, I became a devoted fan of this most ungainly looking bottom dweller. Among other things, I discovered that blackfish can be taken in the same North Shore places that harbor porgies. The two species are entirely different, however. For one, the hyperactive porgy and the lumbering blackfish are about as closely matched as the hare and the tortoise. Blackfish, moreover, are homebodies, their primary range being restricted to south Massachusetts and Delaware Bay and their winters spent in a lethargic state slightly offshore; nor do they range very far even from the inshore habitats they establish in spring and fall. Yet another distinction is size. Humpback porgies are no match for bulldog blackfish weighing over 10 pounds. The two species may have small mouths and human-like dentures in common, but the blackfish's mouth is guarded on both sides—by rubbery lips up front and an extra set of teeth in back of the throat. These pharyngeal teeth or crushers are lined with a granular surface that can grind the exoskeletons of various crustaceans, mollusks and bivalves to the consistency of talcum powder. Finally, the blackfish's leathery hide, unlike the porgy's, glistens not with mother-of-pearl, but with a thick coat of slime. The fish is as slippery as an eel. The blackfish, or tautog (pronounced *t'tog* in New England) is not a Sparid then; it is a member of the Wrasse family, cousin to such warm water species as the crimson hogfish, the California sheepshead, as well as our own pesky bergall (cunner), with whom it is often associated.

As one can imagine, a stocky, slow swimmer, with a slippery hide and rubbery lips and rock hard crushers is bound to set up shop wherever rock piles, shipwrecks, artificial reefs, bridge supports and weathered pilings are found. For in these marine junkyards the fish can easily slip through the rip-rap, pick off mussels, clams and barnacles and pulverize snails, lobsters, shrimp and assorted crabs. It can even suck out an occasional worm.

Fishing in this kind of bottom structure, whether along the North Shore beaches or the South Shore jetties, requires an outfit that is more substantial than one used for porgies. A stout eight foot jetty stick or a nine foot surf rod with a strong tip is required. So is a strong intermediate-sized spinning reel spooled with at least 20 pound test. A high

Blackfish such as this one are abundant close to jetties along south shore inlets. Gerald Hahn Photo.

speed surf reel isn't necessary for blackfish; a smooth drag system is.

Because snags are a nightmare in blackfish country, anglers come prepared with a cool temper and many hooks and sinkers. Their rigs, moreover, are formed as simply as possible, generally with only one hook. The rig often begins with a short leader of 30 pound test connected to the fishing line with a barrel swivel and two improved clinch knots. When a hopeless snag occurs in t'tog terrain, the line breaks at the swivel, not at the rod tip. An end loop at the bottom of the leader secures a bank sinker weighing three to five ounces, and a dropper loop three to six inches above holds the hook, which is snelled on a 12 inch leader of 40 pound test. Almost everyone favors the Virginia hook, a blackfish specialty item that comes with a short bite and a small bend and an offset point. On dark bottom the blued hook is nearly invisible. Although many fishermen favor the larger #4 hook for the bruisers; I prefer the smaller #6. I have taken eight pound specimens with this hook and it has never straightened. In rig snaring terrain, moreover, it is less likely to foul. And since this hook is small it often snags bonus catches of porgies or flounder. In either size, the Virginia is custom-made for the blackfish's favorite meal: crabs.

Of all crabs, veteran blackfish anglers say that the green

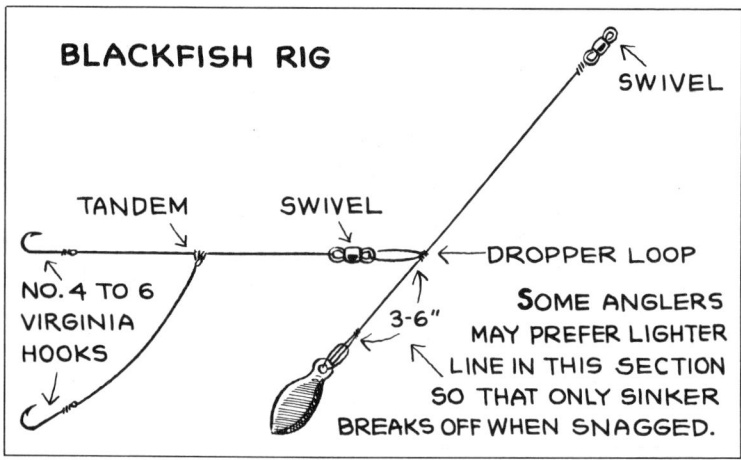

crab makes the best bait. This crab certainly is the largest bait. It is cut in half from head to tail and sometimes quartered. Some anglers simply impale one of the pieces as is; others remove all the legs and claws, as well as the outer shell, and what remains is a luminous chunk of white meat and gristle. The hook is inserted through one claw socket and out another or buried wherever it will hold. Small specimens are favored by many people, since they can be fished alive, simply by impaling one through the tail end of the shell and exposing the point but not the barb. Small green crabs may also be crushed slightly to release their juices, and breaking off a few legs provides other hold-fasts for the hook. It also prevents the crab from scurrying into a hole and hanging you up on the rocks. In this respect, blackfish are more than enough to contend with.

Another popular crab bait is the smallest of them all: the fiddler. This frisky little crab, no larger than a thumbnail, is always fished alive. One or two are simply impaled through the rear of the carapace. The male, however, has the large fiddler claw, and most fishermen remove it. The hook may then be inserted in the socket and out the rear, once again exposing the point ever so slightly and using the barb as a wedge. Close inspection of the fiddler crab reveals not only its beautiful china-back markings, but various colors from dark brown to pale cream. The fiddler has a biological clock that enables it to change colors in the day and night, and to match its environment at various stages of the tide. Curiously, the crabs, imported from warmer climates, continue changing colors according to the tides of their origin. Thus, it makes sense to select fiddlers not just by size but by color. Light-colored fiddlers, for example, make good contrast with dark bottom structures.

In the East End of the North Fork, where some of the largest blackfish have been taken, local anglers swear by yet another crustacean: the hermit crab. This expensive bait requires more preparation than the others, but when properly done, it is deadly. The hermit crab has a soft appendage, a spongy sac that resembles a tail but is actually its abdomen, and this is the part that blackfish (as well as

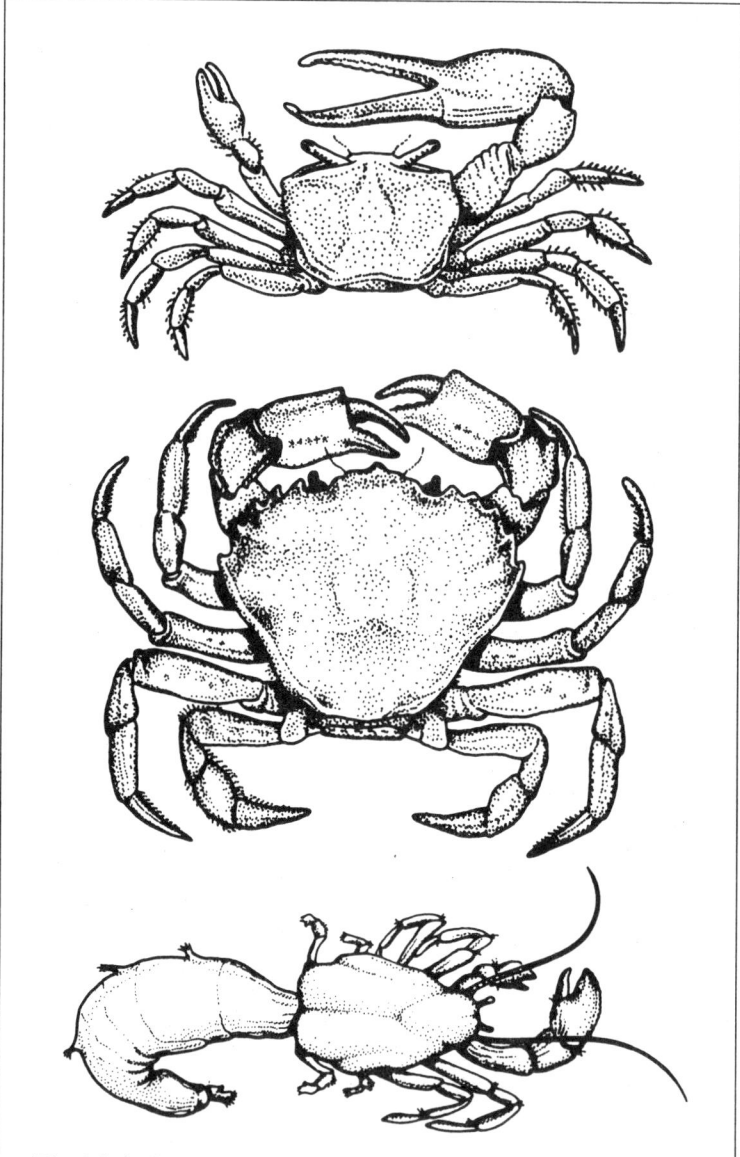

Blackfish baits: (top to bottom) fiddler crab, green crab, hermit crab. Illustration by Dan Connor.

porgies and large flounder) relish most. Consequently, because the hermit is so vulnerable, it must seek shelter in a discarded shell like a squatter. Its soft sac fits snugly inside the shell's innermost chambers, while its two large claws seal the entrance. So the only way to evict the critter is to become a mean landlord. Break the shell carefully with the flat side of a diamond sinker or a block of wood. Once the hermit is evicted, its large claws are removed, and the hook is impaled through the belly side of the hard forepart so that the point enters the soft sac. Some anglers discard the hard section altogether and rig the sac like a worm. Blackfish like to give their crushers a rest at times, and dine on a soft meal, as anglers in the spring have discovered. Then, the fish can also be taken on a slice of skimmer clam or a generous sandworm.

Blackfish head inshore when the water temperature is in the mid-50s, although the Swede insisted on a temperature of 61 degrees. At any rate, there are, as a result, two blackfish runs: one in May and June, and the other from about Labor Day to Thanksgiving. In a mild winter, some blackfish anglers celebrate Christmas at the shore. The fall run is generally considered the better, perhaps because a greater number of large specimens are taken. Then again, by late fall the glamour species have long departed.

No matter when you try for them, catching blackfish can be a frustrating experience requiring the patience of a Saint and the concentration of an airline pilot. There are two fishing methods for tautog: the southern and the northern. The southern method takes place along the South Shore jetties at the ocean entrances to such inlets as Shinnecock, Moriches, Fire Island and Jones. Here, the beginner whose casting range is no better than the Swede's will find being a third-rate fly caster is perfectly adequate, for the fish are not *out there*, but close to the rocks. Working the rock piles without snagging, however, takes perseverance and, of course, experience. After flipping out the bait a short distance, tighten the line and engage the reel, and hold the bait absolutely still. Blackfish are not fond of chasing their meals. The first sign of life is a series of staccato taps on the

Larger blackfish can be real bulldogs providing quite a fight on light and medium tackle. Gerald Hahn Photo.

line, somewhat like a porgy's or a bergall's. At the inlets, it could also be the crashing surf. If nothing ensues, retrieve the rig and bait up again, for blackfish are as cunning as a cunner. Should the drum beat develop into a resounding thud, however, raise the rod instantly, while at the same time cranking the reel, otherwise the fish will surely foul the line on his rocky real estate. Once hooked, the blackfish is relatively easy to bring in; indeed, more fish are lost after they are brought on the jetty than in the water. Therefore, a wet sack or a stringer should be handy, for blackfish have a tendency to overturn a bucket and slide into unreachable crevices. Though frustrating to catch, South Shore blackfish require no scouting. Either they're at the inlets or not.

The big bruisers are on the North Shore, anywhere between the New York City line and Orient Point, and here the northern method must be put in service. First, fishing the open beaches requires much legwork, for blackfish are not hiding behind every boulder or in every mussel bed, and sometimes they are reached only with a tournament caster's arm. Here, the methods used for catching porgies will also catch blackfish, except perhaps for drifting the bait. Large blackfish dispense with the drum roll preliminaries. The fish gingerly picks the bait off the bottom and a slow, downward surge on the line is felt, the fish practically setting the hook himself. A king-sized blackfish will not make fancy runs—it certainly will not leap out of the water—but it will put its broad, powerful shoulders to work towards the bottom while you are trying to gain leverage with the rod held high. A tautog-of-war soon develops and if you lose, your rig will become another adornment on the jagged boulders the blackfish calls home. Regular-sized specimens, of course, are also taken on the Sound, on the same littered bottom that attracts porgies.

On both shores, too, the best period for catching blackfish is the same as for porgies, and that is around a tidal change. Consequently, relatively cool waters stirred by westerly or northwesterly breezes on the North Shore and relatively calm seas on the South Shore are best.

It is not surprising that a fish that dines on lobsters and crabs should taste so good, whether filleted or pan fried. Scaling a blackfish, however, is impossible, and its skin is inedible, so skin it like a catfish. That memorable day, the Swede also told me he simply wraps the fish in foil and the skin adheres to it. He knew everything about blackfish. So the next time you're scanning the distant horizon for gamesters, pay attention to that odd fellow who can't seem to cast.

CHAPTER 15

How to Catch Mackerel, Whiting, Kingfish, etc.

by Gerald Hahn

MACKEREL

Can you imagine a school of fish the length and breadth of Long Island? Old-timers say that mackerel schools were once this size, a continuous stream of fish moving east along the South Shore and west along the Sound, like lights racing around a theatre marquee. Then commercial fishermen pulled the plug and the mackerel stocks dwindled. But mackerel are prolific breeders—a female can shed a half a million eggs a season—and immense schools still appear in our waters every spring.

Indeed, if fishermen had their way they would gladly celebrate May Day as Mack Day, in honor of an extraordinary migration that began in February somewhere in the mid-Atlantic. Gorging on plankton along the way, the mackerel arrive at Cape Hatteras in March. From here, they take the northerly route, reaching the Chesapeake Bay region in early April and the Jersey coast two weeks later. On May 1st, give or take a few days, mackerel converge on the New York Bight like grid-locked cars in mid-Manhattan. Not for long, though, for their northerly migration is not over. Three weeks later they are found in New England, and throughout the summer they form a long column between Massachusetts and the Maritime Provinces, inshore as well as on the offshore banks. The mackerel return in the fall, only this time they take the offshore route. For surf anglers, then, mackerel fishing is a rite of spring.

The mackerel, like its cousin the giant tuna, certainly gets around. Actually, the poor fish has little choice in the matter, since it has no air bladder and would otherwise sink. So, in every respect this fish is designed for speed. The mackerel is a streamlined fish with a muscular body and densely packed blood vessels which function both as fuel and exhaust systems. Oxygenated blood and wastes are transported along these vessels like delivery trucks on a network of super highways. A deeply forked tail provides accelerated power, while keels on the sides of the peduncle help steer a steady course. The elongated mackerel slices through water easier than a sharp knife cuts through soft butter, for it has the tiniest scales in the rear and none up front. Other notable features are the mackerel's two rows of finlets just ahead of the tail and wonderful worm-like markings spilling down its back and quickly fading into silvery white. Mackerel average 15 to 18 inches and 1½ pounds.

Mackerel form dense schools and their abundance makes fishing a great pleasure. Many fish are taken in a short period. Mackerel fishermen also find pleasure in dispensing with bait. Indeed, the fish can be finicky when offered a natural bait, but they are always eager to pursue metal spoons and diamond jigs weighing 3/4 to 1½ ounces. Although the mackerel's diet consists largely of planktonic organisms—its oblique mouth is designed for slurping the stuff from below—it also feeds on squid, seaworms, young crustaceans and small baitfish. Consequently, experienced fishermen add a teaser hook above the metal lure. This hook, a #1 or 1/0 long-shanked Beak, O'Shaughnessy, Carlisle, Pacific Bass, or Limerick, adorned with a brightly colored tinker tube (thin surgical tubing), resembles a small fry being pursued by a larger baitfish. Sensing competition, mackerel pounce on the teaser. Favored colors for the teaser are red and yellow, although mackerel will agree to almost any color. Almost any material, too, as those who employ a red streamer fly with mylar piping, or even aluminum foil wrapped around the hook shank have discovered. The metal lure is most effective when tied directly to the fishing line with an improved clinch knot, and the leaderless teaser hook should be connected directly, as well, to a dropper loop 10 inches above.

Light tackle fishermen favor the North Shore where mackerel are more consistently found in shallow water. These fish have broken away from the main schools on the South Shore. The jetties at Mattituck and Shoreham, or breakwaters, or beach points on the Sound, hold concentrations of mackerel. I often fish the jetties and breakwaters with a light seven foot spinning rod and a small matching reel with a capacity of 200 yards of eight pound test. From the beaches, however, I find that an eight foot rod matched with a light surf-spinning reel spooled with 10 pound test is better. Mackerel occasionally move within casting range on the South Shore and around Montauk. Here, an eight foot jetty stick or a nine foot surf rod and an intermediate surf-spinning reel spooled with 10 or 12 pound test should be considered. Although mackerel have small teeth they can cut a light line, and consequently, many

Mackerel are common visitors to north shore beaches in the spring. They'll hit metal lures as well as Eelworms and other small tube lures. Gerald Hahn Photo.

fishermen tie a shocker of 12 or 15 pound test to the main line with a blood knot.

Mackerel move quickly, and so should the lure. Most metal spoons are so well designed that even an ordinary retrieve yields a frantic darting action. Diamond jigs, however, are like junked cars—dead hunks of metal which the beginner must bring to life. This is achieved by raising and lowering the rod periodically, or quickly twitching the rod tip, or simply changing the speed of the retrieve. Mackerel swimming just beneath the surface are attracted to a quick, jerky retrieve that begins as soon as the lure strikes the water. This method mimics a small baitfish frantically dodging a larger one. Another method involves sinking the lure, then retrieving it with long sweeps of the rod while taking in the slack. Best performed in deep water from an elevated jetty, this method simulates the jigging method employed by boatmen. Mackerel feeding in midwater hit the lure on the fluttering downstroke.

In some respects, mackerel fishing is similar to fishing for school blues. Indeed, comparisons are inevitable since both species are highly attracted to metal lures and are known to raid the beaches for brief periods. Fishing for either species is fast and furious. The mackerel lacks the blue's angry power and head-shaking antics, but it makes up for it with speed. Lightning runs in every direction, sometimes toward the angler, are typical when fishing for mackerel.

In New York, the peak of the mackerel run occurs during the first two weeks in May, although north side stragglers, especially those in the West End, sometimes hang around through June. Everywhere the best fishing occurs at dawn in a slightly rippled sea, regardless of the tide. Consequently, on the North Shore the favored winds are from the west or northwest. For easterly winds create havoc here; they bring a garden of vegetation inshore. On the other hand, southerly breezes are blocked by the North Shore cliffs, and the Sound's as lifeless and flat as stale beer.

Mackerel are oily fish, excellent eating when freshly broiled or smoked, but poor table fare if kept in the freezer too long. Save a few for bait for fall blues and bass. And remember, although mackerel are still abundant, the season is brief. Follow their schedule, and you will surely celebrate mackerel fishing every spring.

WHITING

The first time I ever went surf fishing for whiting I lasted 15 minutes. Three eager friends convinced me on the spur of the moment to join them on a cold winter's night at Coney Island's Steeplechase Pier, a well-known haunt for urban anglers. Of course, we hadn't given the slightest thought to dressing properly for the auspicious occasion. We figured that a prelude at Nathan's would warm us instead. Having fortified ourselves with the dog, we were raring to go, and quickly crossing the beach under icy stars, we mounted the pier which extends for several hundred feet into the Atlantic and joined six bundled-up anglers doing a slow pick on whiting and herring. We flipped our baits over the frosty rail, but Nathan's frankfurters soon wore off. We started shivering. A concession stand at the back of the pier seemed inviting; so we headed there. It was warm and cheery inside: the coffee urn bubbling, the counter heaped with pastries, the kind of atmosphere that lends itself to exchanging fishing yarns. It seemed that there was no end to these stories, however; for as soon as one of us suggested heading back to the pier, another would pick up the refrain: "Did I ever tell you about that 15 pound blue I lost last year?" And so it continued through the night—a night in which I didn't catch a single whiting, but managed to put on five pounds.

Fulfilling in one way though not very productive, that night also made me understand why so many surf anglers stow away their gear in the fall. Nevertheless, for those hardy souls who come prepared (we hadn't) with thermal underwear, a down jacket, waterproof gloves and foul weather gear, the winter sea is neither unbearable nor barren. Indeed, when the whiting are biting it is a hotbed of activity.

The whiting, also known as frost fish, winter trout and winter weakfish, is actually the cod's odd cousin, a silver

HOW TO CATCH MACKEREL, WHITING, KINGFISH, ETC.

hake. Most of the codfish family, including pollock, haddock and other hakes, are stout, if not pot-bellied. The whiting is streamlined. In other respects, too, the whiting seems best known for what it lacks: the cod's chin barbel, third dorsal fin and massive head. Then again, the whiting has large nocturnal eyes, a generous mouth equipped with sharp recurving teeth, and scallop-shaped fins on both the posterior dorsal and anal sides. The name *whiting* undoubtedly refers to its color: gray on the dorsal side blending quickly into white. Its other name, *frost fish*, presumably originated in those plentiful years when schools of whiting pursued baitfish right onto the beach and became stranded. Fishermen would gather the glistening frozen fish in the moonlight.

Such voracious predation leads one to believe that whiting are not strictly groundfish. They aren't. Like pollock, they will rise off the bottom in eager pursuit of prey, and like many other species averaging 1½ pounds

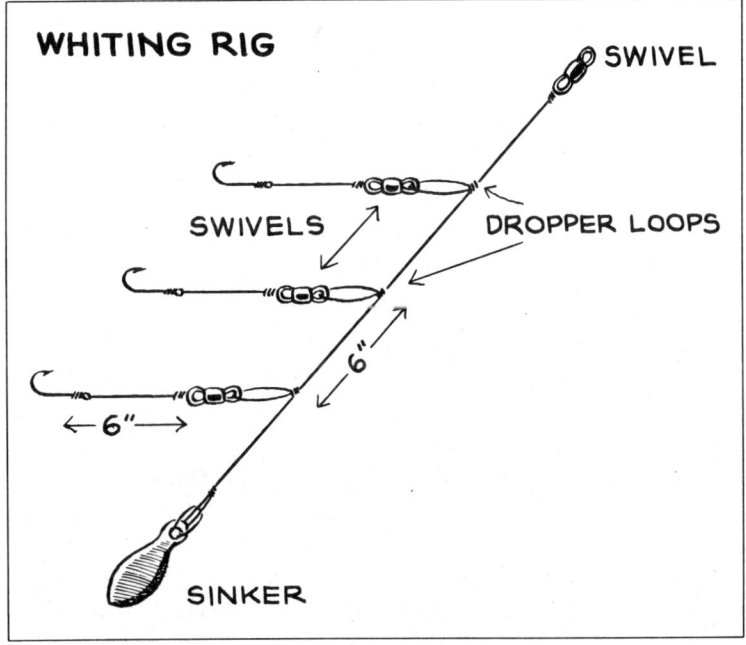

(mackerel, for instance), whiting swim in large schools spaced with mathematical precision. Thus, they are the mainstay of the winter party boat fleets in the New York Bight and Montauk. To be sure, resourceful surf anglers find appropriate shore points in these vicinities.

Aside from my first failed encounter with the nocturnal whiting, the majority of surf anglers catch them at this time. Night fishing is performed exclusively with bait, and the rig that is employed resembles a mackerel tree. Large dropper loops, about 10 inches apart, secure three or four leaderless hooks, and an end loop below holds a bank sinker of suitable weight. Instead of tinker tubing, however, whiting fishermen adorn their hooks with natural baits. Other people favor two or three snelled hooks on six to twelve inch leaders of 30 or 40 pound test, also mounted in series, but at least a snell's length apart. Since whiting have large mouths, there is considerable leeway in the choice of hook sizes and patterns. The largest hook I ever caught a whiting on was a 10/0 Siwash covered with a bright red surgical tube. For most purposes, a 3/0 Carlisle, Beak, O'Shaughnessy, Pacific Bass, Aberdeen or Sproat is the largest hook you will need. Long-shanked patterns are favored since they are easy to remove from the whiting's bridgework.

A long leader of 30 pound test is recommended for all the rigs mentioned. The stiff leader reduces tangles around the main line when snelled hooks are ganged up. Connect a dark barrel swivel to the main line and the leader with two improved clinch knots, and use the leader for attaching the hooks and sinker.

Whiting will nibble at seaworms, skimmer clams, whole sand eels and spearing, but mostly they relish strips cut from squid, herring, or mackerel. The strip should be long and narrow, about 1/2 x 4 inches. For firmness, leave the skin on when filleting a fish strip; but for greater visibility, remove it from squid.

Of all strip baits, however, anglers favor the whiting itself. Cannibalistic whiting are known to feed on their young and will eagerly make short shrift of their brethren in strip form.

After catching a whiting with one of the other baits, cut the belly into strips and impale them near one end. The fresh, tough strips last longer than the other baits. Indeed, four or five whiting can be taken before replacing the strip, an important consideration on a finger-numbing night. Veteran fishermen will also squeeze a freshly caught whiting to retrieve disgorged baitfish on which it has fed. Thus, even in winter, matching the hatch goes on.

Curiously, tackle for a fish that is no larger than a mackerel is heavier than one would expect. Whiting are not the problem; the terrain is. For people fishing from piers as high as Steeplechase's or from treacherous rock jetties facing the Atlantic require a fairly stiff eight or nine foot rod and a medium-sized surf-spinning reel spooled with 15 or 20 pound test. In addition, sinkers may go to more than four ounces at these places. Elsewhere, as will be seen, a lighter eight foot oufit and 10 pound test will do.

Whiting are often accompanied by their relatives, the lings, also known as red or squirrel hake. The ling is easily identified by its long "feelers," actually modifications of the ventral fins, and by its pot belly. The fish grows larger than whiting, but not by much. Since ling are strictly bottom feeders, moreover, a whiting rig usually begins with the bottom hook no more than six inches above the sinker. The reds will go for this hook, while the whites attend to the others.

As happened that night at Steeplechase, whiting are occasionally mixed with herring. At such times, it is advisable to exchange the larger hooks for smaller #6s, and to bait up with the tiniest morsels of squid or fish strips. Herring have small mouths and are primarily vegetarians. Averaging a pound and glistening with a spectrum of hues, a freshly caught herring showers its scales like a fireworks display on the Fourth of July.

Nighttime whiting anglers fish whenever possible near overhead lights. Some people bring a Coleman lantern or a strong flashlight. Playing the Pied Piper, the light attracts curious baitfish which, in turn, attract the whiting. The rest is relatively simple. The baited rig is cast and allowed to settle to the bottom. Then a slow retrieve ensues, the rod pumped up and down intermittently, as when jigging for mackerel.

By no means are whiting taken only at night. Some anglers catch whiting at dawn and dusk with the same rigs and methods used at night. But the majority of daytime fishermen favor artificials: tin spoons and diamond jigs weighing an ounce; lighter leadhead jigs dressed with bucktail, shrimp-tails, or eelworms, tipped with squid; small three or four inch floating and diving plugs. Rigging a teaser above most of these lures, as when fishing for mackerel, also attracts whiting. The teaser, adorned with tinker tubing or a strip of squid, may be leaderless or on a short snell. At times, ling will also go for a metal lure, provided it is tipped with squid. And daytime herring are fond of artificials, too: shad darts, mackerel tree rigs, foil-wrapped hooks.

When fishing for whiting with a lure, use a slower retrieve than for mackerel. The lure may also be jigged from an elevated position in the same manner as for mackerel, but closer to the bottom. Whiting are not as strong as mackerel, although they are more aggressive than ling or herring. Perhaps the cold water has something to do with this.

For whiting are most active in water temperatures between 38 and 48 degrees. Beyond this margin, the fish move to deep water out of casting range. In the New York region, these temperatures are attained primarily in November and December, and consequently, whiting can also be taken in early spring and sometimes throughout a mild winter.

Whiting may seem indifferent to tides, but they always prefer clean water. Thus, the old adage, "Fishing's best with winds from the west," certainly applies to whiting. A westerly or northwesterly wind creates a flat sea on the South Shore. On Montauk's north side, so will a wind out of the southwest.

In the New York Bight, any jetties, piers or inlets facing the ocean between Coney Island and Jones Inlet should put you in touch with whiting. Montauk's whiting grounds are off Culloden Point which forms the eastern entrance to Fort

Pond Bay. Deep water runs fairly close to the beach, a good place to flip a plug with moderate tackle. The jetties at Montauk Inlet, just east, are also worth trying. New Jersey's sector of the Bight attracts numerous whiting fans as well, perhaps more than in New York. The beaches, piers and jetties between Sandy Hook and Island Beach State Park are all known to harbor whiting. A favorite whiting haunt is New Jersey's version of Steeplechase—the Long Branch Pier.

Whiting are not nearly as abundant as they once were. The fish are not as prolific as mackerel, and cyclical patterns, overharvesting by commercial fleets and inshore pollution have taken their toll. On the other hand, whiting take up the slack during the dead winter months, and sometimes buckets overflow. Later that winter mine did, for this time I was prepared. I also lost the five pounds I had gained, for among other things, whiting are the leanest fish in the sea.

KINGFISH

Whenever I mention kingfish, anglers invariably think I'm describing king mackerel, those regal game fish of the Gulf Stream. But the kingfish I'm referring to is an inshore runt and a poor contender for the throne.

Then again, this half-pint's curious name may be appropriate after all. Wasn't little David a powerhouse when he brought down the giant Goliath? Didn't the pip-squeak Napoleon overrun Europe? Where would the Big Apple have been without LaGuardia, "the little flower," to clean it up? If big things come in small packages, then the kingfish's nasty disposition is tailor-made for its scale. For anglers say that a surf run kingfish packs more clout than a striper twice its size.

Regrettably, most fishermen cannot make this claim, for today there are few kingfish in our waters. Although there were good runs in the early 50s and 60s, my last decent kingfishing occurred in the early 70s, and even then, I never fished for them exclusively. I caught some kings in June while fishing for flounder and school weaks, and later on while pursuing porgies and small blues off various jetties on Gardiner's Bay. One day I'd catch six, the next day none. In those times, one pound kingfish were also found in all the South Shore bays and in the Peconics, and three pound specimens were occasionally taken in the Atlantic surf. Kingfish may be scarce today, but patterns change and we should see a return of these magnificent little fighters.

Actually, the kingfish's extraordinary ferocity comes not from a mean streak, but a missing air bladder. The kingfish, like the mackerel, must snatch its prey on the move or else it will sink like a stone. The fish is not a mackerel, however; nor is it a whiting or a mullet as some Southerners claim. The kingfish is a member of the drum family, including weakfish. It has the weak's robust anterior and gradual tapering in the rear, but it also has unique characteristics: a long spine on the front dorsal fin; a tail both pointed and round; the cod's chin barbel; and a small mouth filled with a healthy set of dentures. The kingfish's back, moreover, is a melody in viridian and olive greens accented with dark moon-shaped bars. These gradually fading colors and markings extend to the greater portion of the sides, revealing only a hint of the fish's silvery white belly.

Kingfish, though small, have large appetites, so the choice of baits is wide. Sandworms, bloodworms, skimmer clams, mussels, and small sand eels or spearing will attract kings. Hooks should be small, #6 to 1/0 O'Shaughnessy, Beak, Sproat, or even a Chestertown snelled on a 12 inch leader of 20 or 30 pound test. A fair amount of any bait mentioned should dangle below the exposed point and sway in the current.

Tandem-tied rigs, high-low rigs, and Florida rigs, covered in previous chapters, are all employed for kingfish. Generally, the hooks in two-hook rigs begin about three inches above the sinker. For bay fishing, a one or two ounce bank sinker is adequate; for surf fishing a three or four ounce pyramid sinker is better.

Since kingfishing can take place in the roaring surf as well as in a calm bay, tackle varies considerably. The South Shore surf angler will need an eight foot jetty stick or a surf rod at least nine feet long, and a light surf-spinning reel spooled with 15 pound test. Bay fishermen will find a light six or seven foot spinning rod and a small reel filled with eight pound test adequate. In fact, bay fishermen can use freshwater gear.

Kingfish are located along south side piers, docks, banks or bridges. The backside of an inlet or any surf point with a deep gully close by is also worth exploring. Incoming water is favored everywhere. The angler, after casting to a likely spot, should retrieve the bait slowly, as when fishing for fluke or weaks. A bait lying motionless on the bottom is also effective, since kings often look for snacks between meals, by grubbing in a mixture of sand and mud.

Then again, ravenous kingfish have been known to attack a lure, particularly if it is sweetened with a small strip of squid. Snapper fishermen are sometimes surprised by a kingfish smashing one of their tiny metal spoons; so are weakfish anglers who employ a small (¼ to ½ ounce)

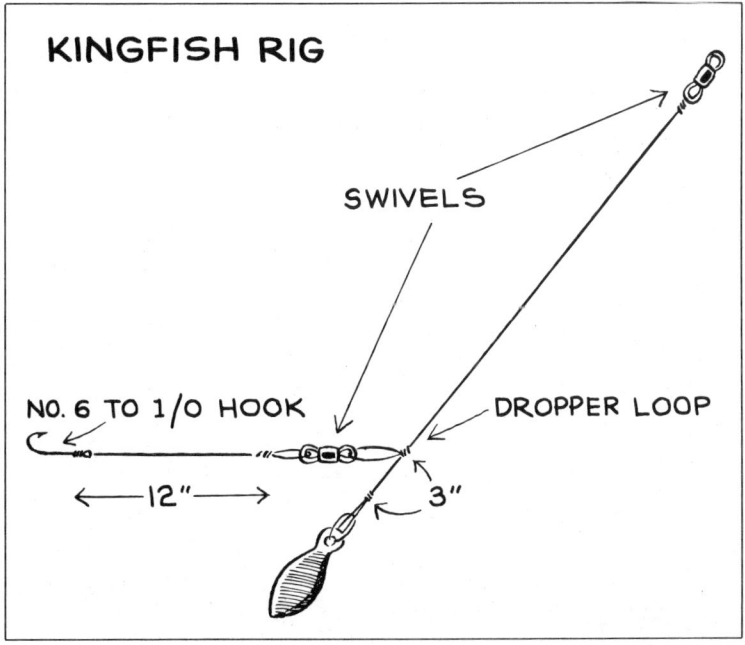

leadhead jig with a soft plastic shrimp-tail in red or white. Lures should be tied directly to the fishing line with an improved clinch knot and twitched slowly along the bottom wherever shoal water meets a dropoff, channel or gully. Resourceful anglers concentrate on kingfish between Memorial Day and Labor Day.

Kingfish are not the only species to have come and gone repeatedly. Blues and fluke, now abundant, have been scarce a number of times in the past. So when the little king decides to return, anglers undoubtedly will spread out the red carpet. I know I will. How about you?

PART THREE
Regional Game Fish

CHAPTER 16

Montauk

by Fred Schwab

Montauk does not appeal to every surf angler. In fact, it's probably true that for every newcomer who enjoys his first Montauk experience, there's another who finds its fish producing appearance to be a shattering illusion.

It's been said that fishing at Montauk Point often demands more from the angler and his gear than any other location along the East Coast. At Montauk, one must regularly contend with crowded conditions, rocks, swift currents, poor footing, a wet rear end, and more often than not, wind and a booming surf. A mix of circumstances seldom encountered elsewhere and requiring a great deal of getting used to. But there are fish to be caught and the place has an appeal which draws many anglers back year after year.

Perhaps the newcomer's most common mistake is to devote most or all fishing effort to the more publicized and, consequently, most heavily fished locations. Then he attempts to fish within the crowd which, especially during night tides, will include Montauk regulars. These are hard fishermen who have worked these areas for years, and who know what they are doing. Most have learned to discipline themselves, and have developed a degree of endurance which few newcomers can match. In his prime, a Montauk "sharpie" is the hardest, most competitive and often the most reckless surf fisherman to be found, a fact which visiting anglers from other states have noted. They have learned to adapt to the worst conditions, accepting the rips, rocks, mauling surf and a bone-weary existence as challenges to be overcome by mind and body. Here, where the wet suit was adapted to surf fishing, the Montauk veteran's effort to catch fish often takes on the appearance of a struggle to survive.

In general, the best advice for the newcomer is to start slowly with limited expectations. Explore the area in daylight. If your goal is to fish "up front," walk the beach from the Lighthouse to North Bar. Familiarize yourself with the various formations. Note how the waves break and the

Many Montauk regulars favor the use of the wetsuit while fishing spots such as North Bar, Jones Reef, as well as many south side areas. William Muller Photo.

currents flow. Watch the regulars, observe and learn, ask questions, but don't press for more information than they are willing to give. To avoid what could be an unpleasant and perhaps disastrous experience, gain an understanding of your physical capabilities. When others are wallowing in a rough surf or fast current, be sure that you do not overextend yourself. They may have no problem dealing with the situation or may be pushing themselves to their physical limits, and beyond yours.

Anglers in wet suits are part of the Montauk scene and while not all are highly aggressive fishermen, most are. In addition to doing what the angler in waders can do with greater safety, the wet suiter can push further out in the water, swim to an offshore rock and if he chooses to, he can avoid the impact of a passing wave by simply ducking under it.

The wet suit does not appeal to all anglers; in fact, many regulars never use it. Newcomers who opt to try this gear are forewarned that it can produce a false sense of security. Because the wet suit has a degree of buoyancy which eases one's movements in the water, an angler can unknowingly place himself in harm's way. Never forget that you become more buoyant as the water depth increases, thus, your ability to maintain a firm foothold decreases. With the combined forces of waves and swift current at work, too much buoyancy can lead to serious problems for the careless angler.

If you acquire a wet suit, it's advisable to try it out first. Do so under controlled conditions, where the water is calm and there is no current. Get used to how it feels, how you can and can't move, and most importantly, find the most effective method of swimming with the gear you normally would use when fishing. The writer can attest to the wisdom of that advice. In 1967, I was swept off a massive sand bar, which waves and current prevented a return to. This resulted in a lousy swimmer being roughly 1,000 feet from terra firma. That, and the knowledge that sharks were frequent visitors to this area, led to senseless thrashing about. Fortunately, that behavior subsided quickly but only

Jack "The Painter" Murray demonstrates a good reason to use a wetsuit while fishing atop a south side rock. John Fritz Photo.

because I'd swum in the suit before and realized that if I allowed its buoyancy to take over, my gear and I could make it to the beach with a minimum of effort.

Whether you use waders or a wet suit, if you intend to fish Montauk's rocky areas, felt soles are a must. When available, some tackle shops, including Johnny's at Montauk, will carry sandals specifically designed for this purpose, or felt sole kits with or without the needed cement. Some anglers buy a top grade of hard felt, cut it to size and adhere it with Contact cement or a similar product.

Spinning gear isn't a must, but it's strongly recommended if you plan to throw artificials in the rips and rocky areas. The reel should have a smooth drag and ample line capacity. The big Penn is fine, but if you can get one, the Crack is ideal. Use a good quality monofilament line testing at 15 to 20 pounds. Ande has stood the test of time and is probably the most widely used in the Montauk surf. Long casts are often required, thus it's advisable to use a rod of 11 feet or more. Some regulars go to a 13 footer in the fall, and during summer months most bring along a one-handed outfit.

As elsewhere, access to Montauk's beaches and the angler's freedom of movement have diminished during the past two decades. But it remains as New York's only area where, with a minimum of shifting about one can fish under nearly every condition imaginable. Swift currents, rocky shorelines and sandy beaches can be found in a high surf or the calmer waters of Block Island Sound, and it's one of the few areas where even under very adverse conditions one can usually find a fishable location.

Tidal action continuously moves immense volumes of water back and forth between the mighty Atlantic and Block Island Sound, thus, swift currents prevail along much of the Montauk peninsula. This, and other errosive forces, yielding only to the rocks, have carved out an irregular shoreline and variable water depths. The best of the resultant currents and rips, in terms of the surfcaster's

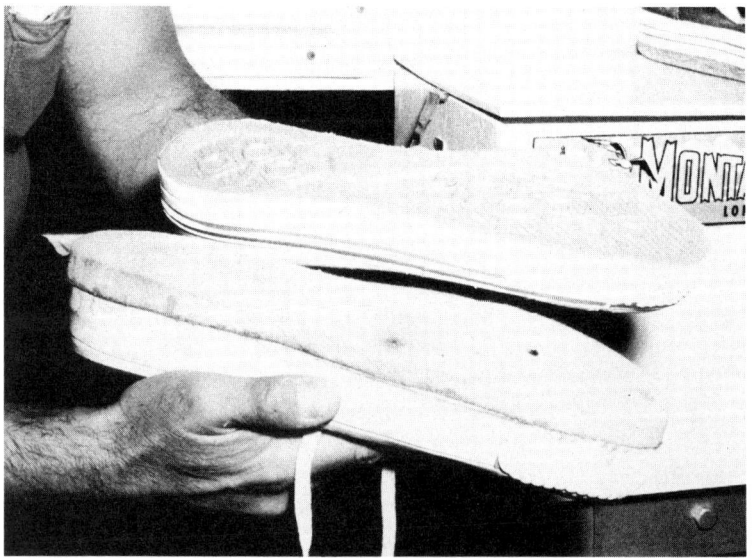

Felt soled sneakers and waders are helpful at Montauk because most areas feature bottom made up of small round slippery rocks. William Muller Photo.

range, are situated from the Lighthouse back along the northern shore. Along this rugged beach one will find Weakfish Rock, Jones Reef, Evans Rock, False Bar, North Bar, and off in the distance, Shagwong Point. All but the rip under the Lighthouse, are most productive on the outgoing tide, and all but Shagwong are within the boundaries of the State Park and accessible by foot from the parking fields near the Lighthouse.

While crowded conditions generally prevail during the fall months,that is when productive fishing can be widespread, more consistent, and most likely to be rewarding to the newcomer. For that reason, the following is largely focused on the fall fishing, it being noted that there are generalities applicable throughout the year.

While bottom fishing can produce fish throughout the season, newcomers are advised not to employ that method at the aforementioned locations during prime time, which is best defined as being on the most productive tide with emphasis on night hours. Conditions at these locations are such that bottom fishing is impractical, and definitely incompatible with the way others fish these rips. Casting artificials is the accepted and far more effective method. What's more, there are many nearby areas where the baitfisherman can fish without interfering with others.

With the exception of the rip beneath the Lighthouse, all of the aforementioned locations and the areas between, are normally fished by wading well out from the beach. The objective is to increase the potential of getting a strike. Since the rip is where the lure works best, and the greatest concentration of feeding fish will normally be, it's advantageous to maximize the time that your plug is moving through potentially productive water. The direction of your cast should be up-current. In general, at a 45 degree angle, or if the current is moving from left to right, cast between ten and eleven o'clock, if right to left, between one and two, and unless you know that the fish are close, cast for distance. This procedure allows the lure to move down and across current, which combined with the retrieval process imparts movements similar to a baitfish swimming or being swept along. Under crowded conditions this procedure will also save you and those around you a lot of grief, as others will be casting in this manner and any significant variance will produce repeated tangles.

Another variance which nearly always causes problems occurs when the majority of anglers present are fishing with heavy gear and big plugs, and a minority insists on using light tackle and small lures. This results in a substantial difference in the distance of casts, and as the lures swing with the current, lines are constantly being crossed and picked up on the retrieve. The upshot of this situation is aggravation for all concerned.

In tight quarters avoid casting at the same time as those closest to you. If it becomes obvious that the fish are not in close, don't let the plug swing too far. When it's moved out of the rip, crank it in and cast again. This increases the time that your plug is where the fish are, reduces tangles, and if someone connects with a fish there is less chance of a foul-up. Obviously when someone near you, or up-curent from your position has a fish on, you should refrain from casting until the fish is close and under control. A hooked fish invariably runs with the current, if it's a strong fish the angler should move with it, and the courteous thing to do is to give him plenty of room.

Newcomers are cautioned to pause and check for other anglers before making a cast at these rips. Now this advice may seem pretty basic, but on a dark night, one or two lads neck deep in a rough surf or clinging to distant rocks may not be readily seen. More than one newcomer, after several casts, has found himself the target of a charging regular angrily emerging from what had appeared to be a deserted stretch of water. If others are already there and out beyond where you are willing to tread, remember that if you fish up-current and to their rear your lure will sweep toward them, and should you hit a fish, it will run towards them. If you fish too close and hook someone, you may find yourself the recipient of a deserved punch in the nose. If the early birds are not out as far as you had planned to fish, remember that the first to arrive establishes the distance off the beach from which the fishing will be done. But it's a two-way street; the early birds must compromise. If no fish are being caught or the hits are at the end of the cast, it's reasonable to assume that edging further out may improve the results.

The same assortment of tins and surface lures used elsewhere, are applicable to the Montauk surf during the day, but it's wise to carry a few swimmers. Most Montauk sharpies seldom fish during daylight, conserving their energy for the normally more productive night tides when striped bass, bluefish, and weakfish move in and out of the surf zone most frequently. But it's advised that the newcomer's initial efforts be focused on daytime fishing until he becomes familiar with the area. As already pointed out, the regulars already know how to handle themselves among the rocks and swift currents, even under the cloak of darkness.

The stretch of beach between the Lake Montauk jetty and Shagwong Point often produces good catches of weaks, bass, and fluke during the period from late June into mid July. William Muller Photo.

At one time or another nearly all swimming plugs have produced during the night tides, but the most consistent producers are the darter, bottle plug, Atom and Rebel types. During summer months, the smaller versions are most effective, with the reverse generally being the case during the fall.

It's probably true that over the years the darter has accounted for more fish at night from the Montauk fall surf, than all others combined. In relatively shallow and swift currents where long casts are usually needed, it's a natural. The bottle plug is another favorite which casts well. When working properly the darter, as its name implies, darts in an erratic back and forth, up and down fashion, while the bottle plug tends to run deeper, with a repetitive wobble. When there is little or no current, or extremely rough conditions prevail, the darter tends to run on or near the surface with little or no swimming action. On such occasions you should switch to the bottle plug, and vary the speed of the retrieve until you feel it throbbing.

The Atom swimmer, other makes of similar design, and the Rebel types do not cast nearly as well as the darter or bottle plug, but they do catch fish. Their built-in action can make a big difference when the fish are in close or there's little or no current, and while they work well in a rip they are a must at night when fishing most of the rocky areas south and west of the Lighthouse. The wise angler always carries a variety in his plug bag.

To achieve a reasonable consistent degree of success requires more than just routinely casting and reeling in. The objective is to obtain as much swimming action as possible, and normally that's accomplished with a slow retrieve. When the aforementioned lures are working, they transmit a throbbing action to the fishing rod, and the stronger the current the more pronounced it will be. Because conditions change from one day to the next, and at various stages of a tide, the speed of the retrieve is not always the same. With experience you develop a sort of sixth sense, usually adjusting to the proper speed without giving the matter much thought, but always remember that the unusual is a

During the fall run crowds gather on the rocks under the Montauk Lighthouse both day and night catching bass, blues, and weaks. William Muller Photo.

Landing and releasing a fish while perched on one of these rocks can be a tricky business so approach the task with caution. William Muller Photo.

possibility and that experimentation is often the key to success.

As elsewhere, the depressed bass fishery and changed composition of baitfish has reduced the quality of fishing at Montauk. The area from North Bar to Jones Reef still produces fish, but not in the quantity or quality that it did prior to the middle 70's. Fishing from Weakfish Rock continues to yield some outstanding catches, but that's probably because it's fished more consistently, and during the past decade the surrounding water depth has undergone significant change. Always having the edge in yielding large fish and traditionally the most heavily fished, the rip below the Lighthouse has been the most productive in recent years.

While the Light can produce fish during various stages of the tide, unlike the other rips, incoming or rising water, with emphasis on the last two to three hours, is clearly the best. Prior to the middle 60's one normally fished from the rocks scattered about in the water, but scouring action has increased the water's depth. Today's anglers are forced to fish from the "balcony", that jumbled wall of rocks protecting the cliff from the ravages of the sea. Since one stands high above the water and it's usually too rough to scramble down below, long handled gaffs have become standard equipment here. The left or northerly half of the wall is where the rip forms, and that's where you want to fish. Some anglers arrive early to stake out a favored spot and there are times when the tardy find that there is no room for them. In that event try Scott's, which is the stretch of beach leading to the wall (see map).

Surfcasting opportunities at Montauk are most definitely not confined to fishing in fast currents and locations adjacent to the Lighthouse. In fact, that area consists of just a small percentage of Montauk's beaches. The shoreline south and west of the Lighthouse is extremely rocky and highly irregular for several miles. High cliffs, from which centuries of erosion have freed great boulders, add to the rugged beauty of this area. While fishing along these beaches can be difficult, especially in a heavy surf, it can be

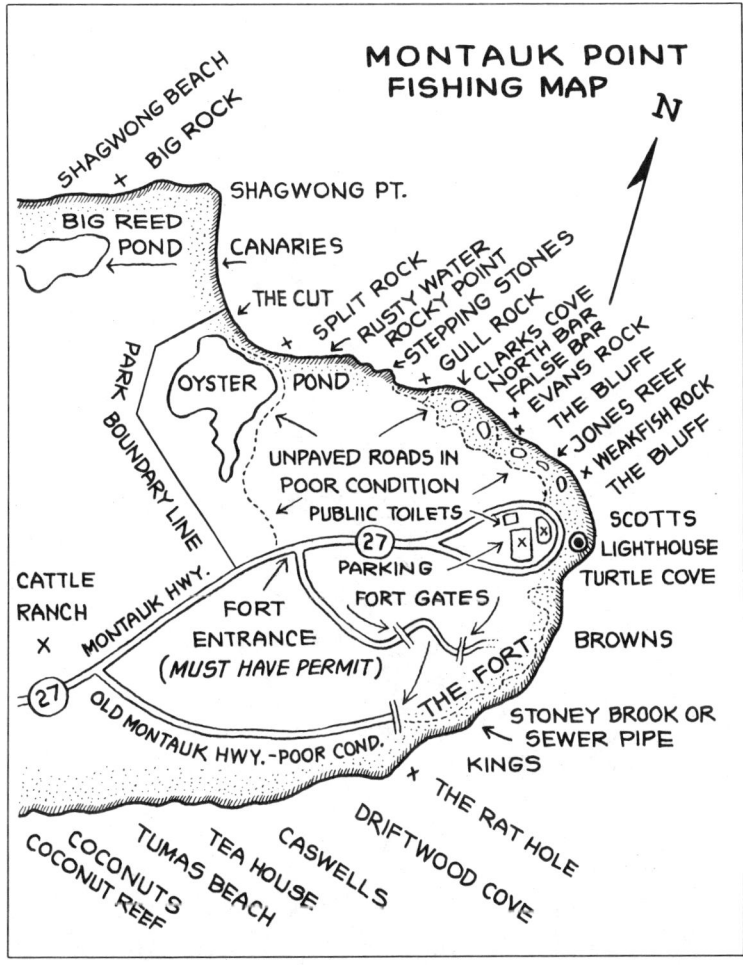

an extremely rewarding experience. There's plenty of room and there are a countless number of potentially productive spots to choose from.

There are two ways in which to work this area with artificials. With experience one discovers locations which, under certain conditions, are more productive than others, thus the regulars usually work particular areas, casting from favored rocks. For those unfamiliar with the area, a

The stuff that dreams are made of. Kenny Kassan with a good bass under the Montauk Lighthouse. John Fritz Photo.

better approach is to slowly move from one place to another, pausing to cast at productive looking locations and keeping a sharp watch for spraying baitfish, swirls, breaks, and gulls who show a lingering interest in a particular spot. With this method you have a good chance of spotting some fish, and there's always the possibility of walking into a blitz with the likelihood of having it all to yourself. By following this procedure you accumulate knowledge and come upon isolated spots where excellent bottom fishing opportunities exist. Because access to this area has grown increasingly difficult, the best advice is to walk in from the Lighthouse, or in the fall, one can park in the Ditch Plains area and work to the east.

Stretching from Ditch Plains to the west are miles of sand beach which can be very productive when fished with bait as well as lures. Vast schools of bluefish hit these beaches every year during the fall and from time to time during the summer. During late September and through October a blitz with bass and bluefish mixed, is likely to occur at any time and has been known to last for several days. During the fall, anglers with four-wheel drive vehicles can often keep pace with moving schools of fish, that is if a gill netter or haul seiner doesn't wipe them out somewhere along the way. Normally a dropping tide is best along the south side.

Bottom fishing in the Montauk surf can be very rewarding and there are times when the only fish being caught are by this method. Sandworms, which can be dug at several locations along the north side, are the most popular bait, but what works elsewhere will also work at Montauk. Most anglers use a fishfinder rig with a small cork positioned a few inches above the hook to minimize the loss of bait to crabs. Pyramid sinkers are fine for the sandy beaches, but definitely out of the question in the rocky sections where bank or pencil sinkers are a must.

A very sizeable population of blackfish inhabits the rocky areas throughout the season and, if one puts in the time, specimens of five pounds and up are not unusual. At several locations along the north side, throughout the spring and fall, one can enjoy some excellent fishing for winter flounder, and there have been summers when fluke were available in a few areas.

While weather related conditions do effect surf fishing at Montauk, the resultant impacts are subject to many variables. For instance, an easterly wind tends to move baitfish and predators closer to the beach and often ignites fast action, but it may also create a heavy surf and inhibit tidal flow and the resultant currents and rips. In the fall, if there is an abundant supply of bait north and west of the Point, and there are game fish in the vicinity, a northwest wind can be a blessing. On the other hand, if there's little or no bait to be pushed along and there has been a "pick" of fish from the rips along the north side, this wind could spoil the fishing, or make it difficult. A southerly wind sometimes improves the fishing at some locations, but if it blows too hard casting becomes a problem on the south side; and if it lasts for several days, the north side usually becomes increasingly unproductive. One must always remember that Montauk is a peninsula and thus, a productive situation in one location may be unproductive in another. The effects of wind are so unpredictable and so variable that it is often a mistake to draw conclusions. Unless you are there and fishing, you just can't be sure.

Montauk is probably the only area along the South Shore of Long Island where rain can have a significant impact on surf fishing. The problem stems from the erosion which occurs along the face of the cliffs. If it rains heavily for an extended period of time, the water along the south side becomes discolored. Tidal action gradually carries this coffee-colored water around the Lighthouse and into Block Island Sound resulting in the Point being surrounded by a stain which can extend out from the beach for several hundred yards. How long this stain lasts and how it affects the fishing is largely dependent upon the velocity and direction of the wind after the storm passes. There are times when a strong northwesterly wind and one or two tide changes quickly restore the water to a fishable condition, but there have been occasions when it took several days for that to happen. When that circumstance arises, it's advisable to seek areas to the west of the Point where the water clarity is better.

The information in this chapter represents only a fraction of what can be said about surf fishing at Montauk. With literally hundreds of potentially productive locations to choose from, and countless variables to be considered, there can be no substitute for experience. Believing that the newcomer would be better prepared for that first Montauk experience, negative as well as positive aspects were touched upon. It is believed that enough information is furnished to point the newcomer in the right direction and increase the likelihood that he will one day be a Montauk regular.

CHAPTER 17

South Shore Ocean
by John Fritz

One of Nature's most awesome features is a sea riled by a ferocious wind. In our area it is Long Island's south shore beaches which bear the brunt of the ocean's fury. This sandy shore is constantly in a state of reformation, being gouged out by the winter gales and refurbished by the gentle, southerly breezes of summer. The area to be covered in this chapter is a resilient shore where a productive location of one season could lose its appeal after a single serious storm. Fortunately for surf fishermen, general areas will continue to produce fish year after year; it only remains for the angler to rediscover the most potent locations.

Successful surfmen fishing from these sandy beaches are able to determine the more productive locations and concentrate their efforts in areas most likely to harbor game fish. Certain beaches, even after severe coastal storms, tend to remain flat, gently sloping shores, while other sections of the coast become disfigured with steep embankments and parallel bars which are furrowed and sculptured by the sea to form sluiceways, troughs, and shallow sand bars. Deep water pockets and troughs are usually identified by water of a darker color with a minimum of wave action, and are areas that are usually favored by bottom fishermen. Plug casters, on the other hand, because of their greater mobility, are more apt to search both the shallow, white water locations as well as the deep holes when attempting to locate elusive game fish.

Available beach access is an ensuing dilemma with additional areas being closed and tighter restrictions placed on those beaches that remain open. Governmental agencies exercise control over a major portion of the accessible shoreline; especially in the western section of Long Island. Access to shore fronts under the jurisdiction of the Federal and State Governments pose little difficulty for bona fide fishermen who obtain the necessary permits beforehand. It is when control of the waterfront falls under the supervision of the county and town agencies that non-residents experience problems in gaining access. It should be noted that a surfman's main concern is in gaining nighttime access, for many parks and beaches are open to outsiders, usually for a fee, even in the summer season during the daylight hours. It seems that vandalism and general rowdiness have forced all levels of government to severely restrict usage of our parks and beaches in an effort to control this senseless destruction. A few towns in western Suffolk issue fishing permits to their residents, a plan of action strictly adhered to in the summer months, but which is loosely enforced upon the close of the bathing season. Each area differs in their enforcement, with changes in policy fluctuating year by year, so that no rigid guidelines can be summarized here.

In a sector by sector itinerary along the south shore we find that surfmen residing in New York City are fortunate to have two fine fishing areas with guaranteed access. The beaches at Fort Tilden and Breezy Point are part of Gateway National Park, therefore under the control of the Federal Government. Beach vehicle access to the oceanfront adjacent to the Breezy Point jetty and parking facilities for walk-on access to Fort Tilden's shore require the angler to stop at the Ranger Station inside the Fort and obtain a permit.

Excellent fishing can be found in this area starting in the latter part of May when schools of bluefish invade the surf. These fish can be taken in the daylight by surfmen casting tins, standard popping plugs, or pencil poppers; especially when overcast skies are coupled with a moderate onshore wind. After the sun sets and darkness descends upon the shore, bait fishermen using cut bait will continue to take fish throughout the night. Towards the middle of June a change in bait to sand worms will reward persistent anglers with striped bass, occasionally into the twenties, along with some weakfish.

Determined fishermen can achieve some measure of success working the shoreline of Fort Tilden throughout the summer months with either bait or swimming plugs. As the month of August draws to a close, a flurry of bass activity usually takes place in the Breezy area with Rebel type plugs and metal lipped swimmers accounting for some nice sized stripers. The fall run is generally typical of the action which has taken place further east, the only difference being that the run usually starts later and continues after the East End surfmen have stowed their gear.

The complex at Jones Beach State Park provides three areas for fishermen, two of which we as surf fishermen are concerned with. The fishing piers at Parking Field No. 10 should not be ignored completely because it is a prime location for snagging bunker and occasionally provides for some hot fishing when the bluefish and weakfish prey on these schools of bunker. Parking Field No. 6 and West End II are valuable pieces of real estate for those fishing the surf. West End II provides ready access to a very productive shoreline, the section just east of the Jones Inlet jetty, as well as the jetty itself and the eastern shore of the Inlet. Parking Field No. 6 is the nearest approach to an area which remains in the hearts and minds of many older surfmen: Parking Field No. 9. Unfortunately, Field No. 9 has been washed away by violent coastal storms—a serious blow to local surfmen, for this was one of the better locations on the entire shore. Ambitious anglers can still reach this famed part of the beach by walking in an easterly direction from Parking Field No. 6, a trek which is often unnecessary, for good fishing can be had from the left side of Field No. 6 itself.

The principal attraction at West End is the inlet jetty which is a major obstacle in the movement of baitfish along the shore. The east side of the jetty forms a natural pocket which corrals the bait as these schools try to follow the shore. This is especially true during the fall migration when the bait, followed closely by the predator game fish, travel the traditional east to west route only to be temporarily hampered by the obstructing rock wall.

Further east along Ocean Parkway lies the Town of Oyster Bay's oceanfront beach, Tobay. Off-season access for non-residents is often possible from the parking lot on the north side of the Parkway.

The attractive feature on the beach is the Rota Wreck which lies almost due south of the pavilion and is a haven for many species of bait on an otherwise barren beach. It is, therefore, an ideal haunt for striped bass. On strong southerly winds these bass are often urged closer to the beach where they become accessible to the anglers on the shore. Starting at the Wreck and running in a general northwesterly direction is a bar which forms a natural funnel leading game fish close to shore approximately 400 yards west of the pavilion.

Continuing our journey eastward, we arrive at the Babylon Town beaches of Gilgo and Cedar, open to town residents for either walk-on access or beach vehicle travel, exclusive of the bathing hours. Gilgo has a parking lot on the north side of the road which is unattended after the swimming season and, therefore, is available to everyone. The use of the parking lots at Cedar Beach is more uncertain. In the past, Cedar Overlook was made available after sunset for night fishermen, but now it seems that the Town has decided to close the Overlook lot and leave Cedar open.

The stretch of shoreline between the Cedar Bar and the site of the old Coast Guard Station, the access point for beach vehicles, is an undeveloped state park. Gilgo State Park is open to all bona fide fishermen who obtain the necessary permits at the Administration Building at Robert Moses State Park. This access is limited to beach vehicles, for the State does not provide parking facilities. Car-bound anglers will have to park their cars in one of the Babylon Town lots, for parking along the side of the road will result in a parking ticket.

This entire section of oceanfront, from West End II east to Cedar Beach offers surf fishermen the opportunity to take fish all season long. From the earliest worm dunkers seeking school bass in mid-April to the hardy souls slinging tin at these same school bass on their return journey in late November, many fruitful hours can be spent seeking trophy sized bass, weakfish or bluefish, from the smallest snappers to those tackle-busters often pushing the 20 pound mark.

In the overall picture, bait fishermen have a definite advantage, with the season being initiated by those fishing worms. Shortly after this run slackens, the sandworms are exchanged for live eels and cut bait in an effort to entice the larger bass which begin to move into these waters around the first of June. Even after the main body of fish passes by, persistent bait fishermen will pick bass throughout the summer and into the fall when monster blues swarm into the area about mid-October. Purists meanwhile continue to work the beaches with a variety of tins and popping plugs, seeking the schools of medium sized bluefish which regularly run the shoreline throughout the summer.

As the chill winds of autumn sweep the land, forcing all creatures to think of warmer climes, the beaches adjacent to the inlets offer excellent oportunities for plug casters to experience some dynamite fishing. The famed mullet run in mid-September, caused by a severe drop in water temperature in the interior bays, has been the highlight of many past seasons. Such great fishing can also be enjoyed in the "Pocket" at West End, especially when an uncommon southerly wind in autumn forces the bait to hug the shore.

Skipping across Fire Island Inlet, we now find ourselves in another State-run complex: Robert Moses State Park. Although the total area of this park is less than Jones Beach, this park has more waterfront to offer the surfcaster. Beach vehicle travel is permitted on the western end of Fire Island, providing ready access to one or two miles of prime shoreline, including the Democrat Point jetty and the eastern edge of Fire Island Inlet. This is an area which can provide continuing action throughout the season starting with school bass in May, which will respond to either sandworms or tin, closely followed by small bluefish,

Blues like this twenty pound, twelve ounce monster have happily been pleasing fall surf fishermen for many years. William Muller Photo.

weakfish, and cow bass through the months of June and July. The remainder of the summer can be spent chasing small bluefish with fast moving schools of bonito putting in an appearance as the summer winds down. Fisherman can expect to catch striped bass, monster blues, and sporadic migrating weakfish during the typical fall run along south shore beaches. Similar to the terrain at West End, the favored areas lie immediately east of the jetty, but wise surfmen react to any changes in the formation of the beach and work the sluiceways, troughs, and pockets wherever they may form.

The parking fields at Robert Moses Nos. 2, 3 and 4 all offer access for surf fishermen, but each is governed by a different set of rules. Field No. 2 is the designated night parking area, while No. 3 provides season long parking, but only from sunrise to sunset. To the east of the Tower lies Field No. 4 open to surfmen from September 15th to December 31st, daylight hours only. The sand bar within the shadow of the water tower is a favorite gathering place for fish and fishermen during the fall season. This is predominantly daytime action featuring tins as the primary lure, but further east in the vicinity of Field No. 4, bottom fishermen join the ranks of tin slingers to seek monster bluefish from the troughs and sluiceways.

The mid-section of Fire Island is restricted to the residents of the shore communities or accessible from the mainland only by boat. When we reach the portion served by the Smith Pont Bridge, oceanfront access is obtainable once again. The William Floyd Parkway leads directly to Smith Point Park, the focal point for approximately 13 miles of shorefront where beach buggy travel is permitted and the fine sandy beach is also available to walkers as far as their stamina and desire can take them. The area to the west of Smith Point is Federally controlled. This National Seashore permits limited buggy access to seven miles of beach to a picturesque location called Long Cove. By driving left, or east after exiting from the bridge, six miles of beach is under the jurisdiction of Suffolk County, who require possession of a Suffolk County Leisure Pass before a permit will be granted.

The inlet, as is normally the case, is the main attraction to both fish and fishermen, producing occasional lunker bass from June through the fall. The adjacent outer beaches do offer repeated sessions with medium sized blues and weakfish until the autumn migration provides the variety associated with this time of the year. The mainstay of this region is bluefish; small blues, medium blues and during the fall, monster blues frequently pushing the 20 pound mark.

Parking lots situated at the foot of the Smith Point Bridge provide surfmen without 4x4s the opportunity to participate in this action. Using either live eels, cut bait, or the now widely favored tin and tube combination, many happy anglers are often seen struggling back to their vehicles loaded down with stringers of bluefish.

The eastern shore of Moriches Inlet is also controlled by Suffolk County. The network of sand bars and sloughs situated just east of the inlet is preferred by many local anglers, particularly when southerly winds combine with an ebbing tide to produce the turbulent seas favored by powerful predators.

As one crosses the Southampton Town line, traveling east along Dune Road, there are many miles of shoreline offering similar opportunities to those which are possible in the Smith Point area. Unfortunately, much of this area is restricted to residents and members of the various beach clubs located here; but once the vacationers abandon the shore with the passing of Labor Day, access for surf fishermen becomes an easy matter. Unlike the shorelines of Fire Island and Jones Beach, this section is studded with numerous small jetties and groins erected by waterfront homeowners in an effort at protecting their houses from the ravages of an angry sea.

Upon reaching the last major inlet on the south shore, we are again privileged to find another Suffolk County park which at least guarantees access to a greater number of fishermen than the local towns and villages. The western shore provides limited parking in the summer season, but once the swimming season has passed, walk-on and vehicular access is available to all. The eastern side offers beach buggy travel along the shore from the inlet to a point less than a mile east all season long for Suffolk County residents. From this point all the way to Montauk, the in-season and out-of-season decree is in effect. A highlight of the after-season activity along this shore takes place when schools of migrating game fish run the beach. Pursuing these fast moving schools with beach buggies is an exciting sport possible only on the wide open beaches of eastern Suffolk County. Chasing these highly mobile schools of mainly bluefish, sometimes weakfish and occasionally, striped bass, requires a four-wheel drive vehicle and is one of the most exciting aspects of our sport. Scurrying anglers hurriedly pluck a fish or two from the school before it moves further westward under its canopy of screeching gulls. A quick race to the front of the school and the process is repeated again until the fish box is filled or the anglers give up in sheer exhaustion. On most occasions, any lure tossed into the maelstrom will ensure a strike, but most anglers prefer to use popping plugs or tin. As the parade of buggies leap-frogs its way west they are periodically joined by crowds of walkers who stream out from every road-end where it terminates at the beach.

But now I am getting ahead of myself, for these many miles of open beach do offer surfcasters other opportunities throughout the season. Under the cover of darkness and occasionally during the daylight hours, patient bait fishermen will be rewarded with striped bass; often of impressive sizes. Because the nature of this open beach is so changeable, specific areas are difficult to determine beforehand, but beaches affected by the ebb and flow of the inlet currents should be given prime consideration.

Directly south of the Town of Water Mill lies a landlocked brackish pond called Mecox Bay, one of several such ponds found along this coast. The shoreline blocking passage to the open sea shows little out of the ordinary except when heavy equipment is brought in to open a breachway. As the mass of trapped bait flows into the nearby ocean, a chum slick of major proportions is set up, attracting predator game fish for days on end. The only difficulty encountered here is to determine the exact time the breach is to be cut.

At the eastern terminus of Long Island's renowned sandy beaches, just east of the Town of Montauk, lies a stretch of beach recognized by veteran surfmen as an attractive haunt for hungry game fish. This is a favorite for surfmen without beach buggies and those who dislike the crowds and treacherous footing associated with fishing "up front." The shoreline from the pocket immediately west of the remains of the lone rock groin at Ditch Plains west through Dead Man's Cove to the rock-strewn point of land known as the Indians, is a natural gathering place for game fish. Here they can await the schools of baitfish as they leave the protection of the rocky shore and begin their journey westward along the open sandy beaches.

Before we leave the sand beaches for an area totally different, it should be noted that little mention has been made of other successful techniques suitable for use along the ocean-kissed beaches of the south shore. One such example can be found when wind and sea are serene, a time for nighttime plug casters to quietly work the water's edge using a variety of swimming plugs. Little is revealed of the rewards these secretive beach rats enjoy, for when the majority of the world is waking to face a new day they are easing their tired bodies into bed for a welcomed rest.

From Ditch Plains east to the Lighthouse at Montauk Point lies one of the most rugged shorelines on the entire East Coast. Rugged yes, but one of extreme attraction to numerous species of fish. Unfortunately, while the fish have little trouble gaining access, the surf fisherman is almost completely shut out. All of the land adjacent to this shore is in private hands, leaving surfmen access only from either end: the State Park at its eastern border and Ditch Plains, the nearest general access point to the west. The intervening section is the domain of the wet suited surfman who, perched on a surf-washed boulder, will work all manner of swimming plugs among the surrounding rocks. Although many plugs will take fish, even poppers during the daylight hours of the fall migration, the seven inch loaded RedFin is the overall favorite.

Places with the legendary names such as: the Fort, Driftwood Cove, Caswell's, or the Coconuts, are all well known testaments of a past era when vast schools of striped bass passed through these heretofore accessible shores. Lateral access is not denied, the only limitation being an individual's stamina and determination. Before concluding my comments of the area known collectively as the Bluffs, let me mention that this region is not exclusively the domain of those clad in wet suits, for long before this apparel was adopted by surf fishermen, anglers wearing the customary waders and top took their share of fish and they continue to do so today.

An open sandy beach might not seem attractive to the majority of surf fishermen who would prefer to spend their time working the inlets, jetties or the more placid, rock-strewn waters of Long Island Sound, but knowledgeable surfmen are aware that given the right set of circumstances, these sandy beaches can produce dynamite fishing. Resourceful beach fishermen, compensating for the various whims of Mother Nature, react quickly to the plentiful opportunities offered by seemingly barren shore. A beach that may seem devoid of life today may, on the morning tide, suddenly provide an experience from which memories are made.

CHAPTER 18

Inlets and Jetties
by Fred Golofaro

Few beaches in the world can compare in beauty to the 100 mile long ribbon of sand which serves as Long Island's buffer to the Atlantic. To the surf fisherman, however, much of this shore provides little chance of scoring with stripers, blues, or weaks, except for those few occasions in the fall when migrating game fish work their way down these beaches within range of surfmen. Instead, the vast majority concentrate most of their surf fishing effort in and around the six major inlets and from atop the boulder-strewn jetties which invariably border these gateways to the sea.

Inlets serve as major thoroughfares through which game fish, and the baitfish they prey upon, move back and forth between the open ocean and the sheltered confines of the south shore bays. Strong currents, created by the funneling effect of bay waters pouring through these inlets on an ebbing tide, provide game fish with an easy meal as baitfish become tossed about, and easily disorientated in the turbulence.

While an outgoing (ebb) tide is preferred by most regulars who haunt the mouths of these inlets, there are occasions when an incoming (flood) tide will produce action. This is particularly true of the beaches immediately bordering the inlets and also of the "backsides" of several of these inlets. Often overlooked by the majority of beach rats, the "backside" refers to those stretches of shore located well within the inlets. These areas frequently harbor large concentrations of bait which, in turn, often results in consistent action with bass, blues or weaks. The quiet nature of these comparatively sheltered waters affords the perfect opportunity to bring smaller lures and light action, seven to seven and one-half foot sticks, into play. During the summer months especially, this lighter tackle can help to put more fish on your stringer.

Each of these inlet areas boasts its own cadre of regulars and if you're exploring an inlet or jetty for the first time, you would do well to pay attention to the specific areas these anglers are working, as well as the techniques they are using.

The easternmost of the inlets and one from which very little is ever heard is Shinnecock. Both the east and west sides of this inlet are bordered by fishable jetties, though over the course of the season, the east side jetty always seems to produce better action, particularly for stripers. Regulars here drift big swimming plugs out off the tip of the east jetty, while others choose to work the rocks further back towards the bay with bucktails or sinking Rebels in either the 5½ or 7½ inch size. The June moon annually seems to produce a good flurry of action with big stripers, some of which are also taken on live eels. Access to the east jetty is via Meadow Lane in Southampton. Both sides of Shinnecock Inlet fall under the jurisdiction of the Suffolk County Parks Department. The west side jetty, which is reached by taking Dune Road east until it terminates at the inlet, often provides lively bluefish action, but its reputation as a bass producer pales when compared to the east side.

Both the east and west side jetties of Moriches Inlet maintain enviable records as fish producers. Here again, both sides of the inlet are within the boundaries of Suffolk County Parks. Cupsogue Beach is reached via Dune Road, westbound. It terminates at the park. The inlet jetty is within walking distance if you lack a four-wheel drive vehicle or the required county permit. Gibbs Bottle plugs and Rebel and RedFin swimmers drifted into the rip off the jetty's tip have produced many fine fish over the years here. On the west side, a deep hole lying off the seaward end of the rock pile has surrendered many trophy weaks, blues and stripers to those drifting live eels into the swirling currents. Junior Atoms, Rebels, RedFins, and two ounce bucktails

While bass are the primary target of "jetty jocks," bluefish often provide good daytime action around inlet rockpiles.

cast along the rocks towards the bay end of the jetty will usually produce some kind of action. While most of the best action takes place after dark, there is often fast daytime action with bluefish on tins. Access to the west side is via a seven mile long beach buggy ride from Smith Point Park.

Fire Island Inlet lacks the traditional breakwater that characterizes the other south shore inlets. The rock pile situated at the tip of Democrat Point on the east side of the inlet is not nearly as productive as the other jetties which are paralleled by deep water and reach significantly further out into the ocean. Yet this relatively small pile of rocks will produce fish on occasion. Most of the fishing here takes place from the adjacent beach on the east side or out on the ever-present bar which inevitably builds up on the west side. Access to Democrat Point is via a nearly two-mile walk from Robert Moses Parking Field Two or by buggy with a State Park Vehicle Permit. Just inside the inlet lies the infamous Sore Thumb. Well known for its production of

Foul weather gear is accepted attire of most oceanfront jetties, affording protection from drenching spray.

blues, stripers and weakfish, this rubble-strewn promontory is off-bounds to anyone not residing in the Town of Babylon. The backside of Robert Moses State Park, opposite Parking Field Two, gets a heavy play from casters at times and frequently provides a better than average shot at tiderunner weaks. RedFins, Eelworms and Whiptails produce well along this stretch of beach. Every now and then a cow striper will intervene, so be prepared.

Jones Inlet is bordered on the east by the very popular and productive West End Jetty. Since there is no beach vehicle access at Jones Beach, the only way to reach this rock pile, which extends well out into the Atlantic, is on foot. It is approximately a one to one and a half mile walk from West End Parking Field Two. If you plan on doing any fishing on the seaward reaches of this jetty, a word of caution is advised. Too many casters have been washed off this jetty in the past and a couple have lost their lives. If there is any kind of sea running at all, limit your fishing out on the rocks to a dropping tide. No fish is worth risking your life over. Needless to say, a good pair of creepers is a vital piece of equipment on this jetty. The waters adjacent to this jetty further back in the inlet have yielded many memorable catches, as have the rubble-strewn shores bordering the Short Beach Coast Guard Station on the inlet's "backside." On the inlet's opposite shore at Point Lookout are two small, but productive rock piles from which many big stripers and slammer blues are taken. Live or rigged eels or chunks of mackerel or bunker seem to take their share of fish here.

Another inlet jetty from which very little is heard, but one that is known to produce many fine stripers even in the leaner years, is the Silver Point Jetty in Atlantic Beach. Bordering the east side of East Rockaway or Debs Inlet, this area is well canvassed by a small group of hard fishing regulars who speak little about their nights' labors. Big swimming plugs and rigged eels are favorites for big stripers here, while 5½ inch Rebels and RedFins take their toll on school bass and weaks.

Some of the best surf fishermen on the East Coast toil atop the rocks bordering the westernmost inlet of the south shore. Rockaway Inlet and its accompanying Breezy Point Jetty get a heavy play from the Metropolitan Area surf crowd, and for good reason. Many fine stripers are taken from these boulders on two to three ounce bucktails, surface swimmers and rigged eels. Also productive here are sinking Rebels and "loaded" RedFins, both in 5½ inch sizes. Breezy Point falls within the realm of Gateway National Park and is accessible to four-wheel drive permit holders and, depending on current regulations, parking may or may not be available for cars. Here, too, a good pair of creepers is essential if you plan on fishing the tip of the jetty, and pay heed to sea and tide conditions.

A useful tool for any of these jetty fishing situations is a long handled gaff with a handle of eight or so feet in length. Foul weather gear makes better sense than a pair of waders for maneuverability and such garb is in the best interest of safety should you be caught by surprise and washed off a rock pile.

Like an oasis in the middle of a desert, the south shore inlets beckon game fish and those who seek them.

CHAPTER 19

Long Island Sound West
by Andy Regina

Ah, surf fishing! The very mention of it conjures up visions of stalwart fishermen, clad in rubber from head to toe and brandishing fishing rods the length of telephone poles, being buffeted by mountainous, crashing waves. If these same visions come to mind when you think of surf fishing in western Long Island Sound, dispel them immediately. Such is not the case in this instance. Here, our surf fishing is a much subtler art, performed with normal tackle on friendly shores. Here the roar of the surf is replaced by the happy gurgle of lacey wavelets, giggling up a gravel shelf or tinkling merrily as they scurry back into the Sound. There is no loud boom of exploding water, merely the gentle hiss of foam tugging at your boot heels. And, because we normally do our fishing from the water's edge rather than actually being in it, I guess that our surf fishing could more truly be called fishing from shore.

Accessible north shore beachfront property is almost a memory now. What acreage is not consumed by industrial conglomerates is ceded to smaller industry, and the remainder is jealously hoarded by private real estate, except for some slight concessions made for state and local parks. The scraps leftover to the general public are few and far between, and needless to say, are not the best fishing areas in the world. But, we make do with what we've got, clinging tenaciously to every inch that affords us a toehold onto the Sound. We utilize the shoulder of any service road that skirts saltwater, every inch of riprap along some causeway or beneath a bridge, and our public beaches and parks. Surf fishermen sometimes trespass on private property. There are worse crimes committed everyday and though most fishermen are not criminals by any means, they do bend the law from time to time in pursuit of their sport. Almost always, they end up on a private beach simply by walking through the wash from a nearby public access point. Never do they call undue attention to themselves by making unnecessary noise, showing any lights, or, as an afterthought, leaving behind any debris or litter. And many times, even if they do get spotted by property owners, they are seldom chased anyway. There may be times when you may have no choice other than to actually trespass over private property to reach a favorite beach though, so some hard-earned tips may be in order at this point.

Be extra careful of barbed wire. This stuff can surely raise hell with waders and, in fact, seems to be especially attracted to them. Whenever and wherever possible, avoid it if you can. If you must climb over it, you make it more safely if you carry your waders at this stage of the game and climb into them later on, down on the beach, and reverse the process when you leave. Beware of barking dogs! Most of the time the beast will be chained in the yard somewhere, but a lot of dogs run around loose, too. Freeze at the first bark and try to analyze your situation. Some mutts keep yapping and some shut up, and some come running while others stay put, chain or no. Keep your gaff handy for use as a billy if needed and proceed slowly. Never run unless it is vital to your health! I've had dogs follow at my heels all the way across the front lawn and through the back yard, growling all the way to the beach, but a slow pace and some soothing talk saw me safely through. Another good reason for not running are those damned guy wires some frustrated gardeners install on skinny trees to keep them upright. Up high that stuff always hits you around the head, either knocking your glasses off or nearly decapitating you; and down low, it always grabs an ankle to trip you.

But, you can avoid all these problems simply by fishing from public land, and though it's not the best in the west, it ain't too bad. The causeway in Cold Spring Harbor can be productive at night. We get bass on worms there in the

Big tide runner weaks like this one are a prime attraction along western Sound beaches during late May and June. William Muller Photo.

spring; bass, blues and some weakfish on cut bait and plugs in the summer, and some nice bass on plugs at times in the fall. Close by, in Roosevelt park in Oyster Bay, some big blues fall to bunker chunks from the jetty near the town beach, all summer long. The park is restricted to town residents and windshield stickers are required as proof, but visitors can have access for a minimum fee that includes the parking lot, launching ramps, beach, and park. West of Oyster Bay, the shoulder of the service road runs along the water all the way to the Bayville Bridge, and you have access to this any time you want it. In the spring there is a herring run under the bridge, and herring runs are

Stripers start early and leave the western Sound late. That means good catches can still be made even when its so cold that you need heavy clothing. William Muller Photo.

synonymous with big stripers. I was alerted to this little-known fact by Dick Mermon some years ago and have taken some nice bass by live-lining a lively herring right under the bridge since then. The town beach at Bayville is your typical, sloping sand beach and gives up a fair share of bass, bluefish, and weakfish, too; but you must be a town resident and have a windshield sticker, and there is a curfew imposed at any rate. We get in some good early spring and early fall fishing by visiting that beach before Memorial Day and after Labor Day, when restrictions are off. Some good plugging can be had in the fall, off the jetty on the western end of the beach, once again for bass, blues and weakfish.

Closer to home, the shoreline from Peacock Point west of Matinecock Point, in Glen Cove, is about the best on this end of the Sound. It boasts rocky patches, boulders, sand and gravel beaches and jetties—just about everything a beach rat could dream of including, believe it or not, fish! And it produces consistently, from the spring through the summer and far into the fall season, depending upon existing water temperatures. There is a parking lot near the town beach at Prybil, but naturally, both lot and beach are restricted to town residents and there is a curfew enforced at 9PM. You do not need windshield stickers to park there though, and although your license plates get checked at the guard shack, we have never been refused entry yet. Of course, being the gentlemen true sportsmen should naturally be, my pal and I never do anything to call attention to the fact that we are legally trespassers there too; but if they don't complain, we certainly won't.

Mott's Point, Prospect Point, Sand's Point, Barker's Point—all productive areas as you work your way west along the Sound, but also almost all private property. Here you either know the landowner, seek his permission politely, or trespass! I do not know any landowners and a polite request could be answered by a polite rebuff, so I sneak on these beaches. I'm not telling you what to do. You do as you want, or as you must, but there is some good to excellent fishing to be had at those points at times. Late spring and early summer always seem to give up cow bass

Bass are available from May through November in the western Sound. Shallow water and heavy boat traffic means that night tides will be more productive. William Muller Photo.

for a week or two, and cut bait seems to catch just about as many fish as live baits do, the live baits being bunker almost exclusively. The fun comes in when the bunker are cavorting inside Barker's, for instance, and the bass are off Sand's. You'd think that the two would be found together, but such is not always the case. We snag two or three baits, then carry them in a pail of sea water back to where we want to fish, usually the jetty under the light at Sand's, and replenish baits as needed.

For many years we have touted the shoreline of Little Neck Bay as some of the best accessible surf fishing real estate available to the public, that strip of land that runs parallel to the westbound Cross Island Parkway, from the shadow of Northern Blvd., up to and under the Throgg's Neck Bridge. And so it is, still remaining highly popular today because of its ready availability, its ease of access, the legal parking available close by, and the fact that some fish are usually always taken from there on a fairly steady basis, especially school striped bass, which seems to have set up a nursery or playground in that area. It's truly amazing that such good fishing is available so consistently there, because there is no water at all there at low tide, which means that your productive periods are severely limited to only half of the incoming tide and maybe about the first half of the outgoing tide, if that much at times. When the tide is dead low, the entire bay is one giant mud flat, at least on the Northern Blvd. end anyhow, and that is the end that seems to get the most attention. We almost always take the first striped bass of the year from there each spring; spunky schoolies caught on worms fished directly on bottom from holstered rods. Later in the season, larger bass and some big bluefish fall prey to cut baits and plugs, especially at night in late summer. The shoreline directly west of Fort Totten and the two jetties thereon attract a lot of fishermen on balmy summer days, but this might be due to the easy parking condoned in that immediate area and the casual, family picnic-like atmosphere that prevails. Serious surf nuts hit this same area and those jetties in the dark of night and drill out bass, blues, and some weakfish all summer long. You never see these guys in daylight, 'cause they're long gone when the sun pops up!

The Whitestone Bridge has a public park at each end, Whitestone Park on the Long Island side and Ferry Point Park on the Bronx end. We mention these two parks merely to alert you to the fact that there is still some public fishing land available to the beleagured John Q.! It might not be the most productive place to be, but one can while away a few pleasant hours with the wife and kids at such a place, fulfilling marital obligations while wetting a line. Here, because you never expect to catch anything anyway, every fish taken is treasured that much more and dear old dad is a hero to his family again, at least until he tries to start the charcoal fire anyhow! However, once again, if you know what you're doing and when to go about it, these same parks give up bass and bluefish almost all summer long.

Bass of mixed sizes will swim together. One cast could produce a shore while the next could produce a cow. Medium tackle will do the job for both. William Muller Photo.

Here a lot of patience is demanded of the angler, especially if he seeks his fish with bait, which is always a sit and wait affair anyway. Float-buoyed worms seem to get a lot of bass for us in late spring and early summer at these parks, and when we convert to cut bait in early summer, we could pick up a jumbo blue on one cast and a school striper on the next. Weakfish are few and far between, but we do get some here from time to time; a bonus, so to speak. In late summer and throughout the fall, nights see a lot of plugs being put to use, and the results are fairly good too, especially when bluefish are herding bunker.

In the Bronx, this same action gets duplicated under the Throgg's Neck Bridge and from the riprap alongside the toll booths on the north side of that span, but only more-so. The same methods and techniques take the same assorted species during various parts of the season, with perhaps one

Serenity is a key word when describing the attraction of fishing western Long Island Sound beaches. William Muller Photo.

extra little-known bonus thrown in to boot. Some big striped bass are taken on fly rods from the backwater between the toll booths on the north side of the bridge and the old Bronx Beach and Pool. It doesn't happen all the time, but on gentle summer nights when there is little or no breeze and not too many anglers disturbing the area, a guy with a long wand can have a ball, casting streamers to rising bass.

The entire shoreline along the Tremont-Country Club part of the Bronx, from the Throgg's Neck Bridge to Pelham Bay Park, is striped bass territory. The numbers of bass consistently taken out of these waters is truly amazing, and many anglers do not believe it to be fact. This is what leaves that area underfished, that lack of belief. The believers, like me, are few, but we revel in being able to fish without being crowded out, and continue to catch fish year after year. The usual methods apply here also, and the seasons are the same, too.

Eastchester Bay yields a lot of school bass into teen weights and some really big jumbo bluefish, from the bridges spanning Eastchester Creek all along the shore running up to Turtle Cove, and beyond, past the police pistol range at Rodman's Neck. The Cove is noted for its striped bass, but like Little Neck Bay, it holds no water at all at low tide, so here you are also severely limited to only a part-time shot at some fish. Here, too, is ideal fly rod territory, and practitioners of the long wand can be found along the grassy sod banks more often than not, although the most productive times for stripers are the same here as virtually everywhere else: after dark, when most sane men are asleep, or at least at home, keeping the wife happy one way or another. Up a bit, past the pistol range at the point of Rodman's Neck, some of the biggest bluefish in the Sound are caught with a steady consistency that defies imagination. Most always, the fish are never small or of mixed sizes; only those biggies we so fondly call jumbos. My personal belief for this is the proximity to Rodman's Neck of a huge underwater reef called Cuban Ledge, although the Ledge itself is too far off to reach from shore. This reef is a known holding area for big blues, who must be attracted to that structure because of the vast amounts of bait it can itself attract, both for feeding purposes as well as protection. Knowing this, predators patrol the reef on a regular basis, so it is not entirely out of line to imagine some of those hunters venture off those grounds a bit in search of a meal. While cut bait on bottom does a good job throughout the summer and fall, some of our better plug casting is had here also, and

Quiet waters and good stringers equate to a satisfying night's fishing. William Muller Photo.

swimming plugs account for their fair share at night.

Walk along the shore towards the City Island Bridge and beyond, up to the first jetty at Orchard Beach, and you can catch fish almost every foot along the way, concentrating on the area directly under the bridge and alongside that jetty. It's a good area to work with plugs because not only is the rugged structure hell on bottom rigs, it is ideal holding structure for bass, and many of our legal schoolies are taken while walking this beach in the early morning, pre-dawn hours. That jetty at Orchard Beach and the jetty at the other end, as well as part of the ensuing shoreline of Pelham Bay Park, also produce at times, once more for school bass and bluefish on both bait and plugs. Directly beyond the last jetty and the remaining scrap of the park, lies Hunter Island, a decent spot from which to get big blues on bait and plugs, and some fairly nice striped bass on plugs at times, at night. Here we come into our own because we set up a bait rod in a sand spike and plug happily away with our second rod as we wait for that insidious chunk of bunker to do its lethal work for us.

Stretched out beyond the Bronx, and running along the Sound all the way to Connecticut, is the rugged shore of Westchester County, long famous for its striped bass. Pelham, Rye, Larchmont, Mamaroneck—pick a spot. The beaches running from one small town to another are strewn with jetties and littered with boulders, ideal striped bass habitat if there is such a place. And the fact that it is lightly fished makes it all the more desirable. But, like anything good, it does not come easy! Mostly, private property predominates once again, and these owners do not like strangers walking on their beaches. The public parks and beaches are limited to town residents, a fact strictly enforced throughout Westchester County, and permits are required and demanded by local police. While your car will be stopped at the entrance to the parking lot, it seems that a guy walking by never is! I park up the road apiece, take my rod out and lock the car, and walk right by the guard shack, most of the time waving and calling out a cherry "Hi!" as I go by. And, best of all, I've never been stopped yet!

If nothing else, you owe it to yourself to try the breakwater at Larchmont or one of the jetties at Mamaroneck, some sweet summer night, or any other place we have mentioned, in fact. And, when you have bass busting all over your half-ounce floating plug or some big and sassy bluefish headed for the ocean with your bait in its mouth, I'd love to be nearby, just to hear your comments on the caliber of the fishing that can still be found today, in western Long Island Sound!

CHAPTER 20

Long Island Sound East
by William A. Muller

A discussion of where to fish anywhere in Long Island Sound is a problematical situation for any writer confronting the reality of ever-decreasing access and township rules and regulations regarding the use of beach facilities by non-residents. Heap on top of these difficulties the fact that in the last decade or two more aggressive youth, acting out adult activities without a sense of adult responsibilities, and you have a picture of rising vandalism and increasing reluctance by town officials to allow nighttime use of the beaches by fishermen. Unfortunately, politicians equate crime and mischief to those who use the beaches rather than analyzing that only one segment of the user groups is responsible for 95 percent of the problem. Therefore, youth crime, mischief, and vandalism results in more and more beach closures every year. Be certain that I do not refer to all youth. As with all things that prick the skin of our social order, it is the arrogance and blatant disregard for the law by a few that cause untold difficulties for the majority who pay their taxes, obey the law, and only want to proceed privately with their lives. About a decade ago, as an example, Oyster Bay closed their beaches to general night fishing, and for town residents required a special permit that must be shown to a guard at the gates of beaches. Smithtown does much the same, as do many others. Problem is, it's a small town and the guard isn't paid a great salary. Therefore, sometimes the guard is there and sometimes not. You can make a trip only to discover that the gate is locked and there is no guard in sight. Last year Brookhaven closed its beaches to night fishing in a unique way. They stopped parking adjacent to the beach, which effectively stopped the fishing. Isn't it a shame that police and town officials don't solve the problem with greater surveillance and more arrests rather than restricting the rights and access to facilities for the vast majority who cause no problems. Over the last half-dozen years we have convinced the Long Island State Parks and Recreation Commission that surf fishermen on the beach can be an asset and a deterrent to crime. We hope to do the same with municipalities in the next decade.

Okay, with that rhetoric out of the way so that all understand that access to the spots I'm about to mention can be a problem, where can we fish? Eaton's Neck is generally considered the eastern edge of the western Sound, so I'll begin my discussion at that point.

Eaton's Neck itself is virtually closed to surf fishermen because the Coast Guard Station is at the end of the point. There are persistent rumors that some local surf fishermen have privileged access and we have called the Vice Admiral for the Coast Guard in this region. He looked into the feasibility of access and called back to say that official regulations prohibit civilians on military bases, except during special activities. I asked if we could set up a special permit system and he responded "NO." If you live within walking distance, the east side of Eaton's Neck, called Ashroken, and the point itself are excellent spots from May through November. If you live within walking distance, you can utilize the whole area. In May, stripers begin to work the beaches. Generally, the fish first show near the point at the top of the tide and move along the east side into Smithtown Bay with the falling tide. In July, excellent runs of weakfish have been known to occur, but boat fishermen get to enjoy most of the action. In September, big blues make an appearance. In October, very good runs of teen blues can be experienced. The fish often show up in the early morning and late afternoon, as well as at night and will take baits or plugs. In November, bass return and although most of the fish from the beach will be school fish, a few teen-sized and even up towards 30 pounds are taken to spice the action and anticipation.

Smithtown Bay offers many possibilities. Once again, most of the beach front is restricted, but there is one jewel amongst the costume jewelry called Sunken Meadow State Park. A permit is available to anyone free. Simply go to any state park or to park headquarters in Babylon, show your car registration, and ask for a *night fishing permit.* Show this permit on your dashboard and you can fish the area at night.

There are two parts of the park that seem to produce best. The first is the area in front of and to the west of the extreme western edge of the parking lot in front of the Administration Building. This location produces school

Bass and weaks are often swimming companions during the spring run along the Sound's east end beaches. William Muller Photo.

bass, small blues, and weaks in June and July, although every year is not productive. In October, large and small blues arrive and respond to popping plugs as well as chunks of bait. To the east is the Nissequogue River and the eastern boundary of the park is the western side of the river. In spring, white perch and school bass are taken and throughout the summer there are occasional raids by school bass, blues, and weaks, although these are not very predictable. In the fall, often late October into November, migrating shoals of small bait attract schools of blues mixed with bass and weaks. This fishing is not consistent, but when it does happen, the action can be impressive.

There are town beaches and private property along the stretch of beach from the Nissequogue River to Port Jefferson Harbor. Most of these beaches represent very difficult or downright impossible access. There are exceptions. Some surf fishermen report little difficulty gaining access to West Meadow Beach, for example. Whether or not some villages allow access is really not the issue. What is important to note is that local residents do have access to their town and village beaches. All of these beaches have potential to produce outstanding catches at times from May through November. All of these beaches tend to be rather inconsistent, however, and thus, we suggest that local residents seek year to year, month to month, and week to week information from local tackle shops.

Just to the east of Port Jefferson, White Beach, and Mount Sinai is Miller Place. The beaches from Miller Place to Rocky Point and Wading River used to be mainstays for the surf fishermen. In recent years access has been restricted. However, access is still possible to some beaches. For example, an interested fisherman can obtain a Town of Brookhaven Beach Vehicle permit. This permit, at least at the time of this writing, is available to non-residents as well as residents. The beach vehicle permit allows one to get around the problem of no parking rules. Also, we've been informed that fishermen are permitted to park in the lots between 6PM and 9PM; and this includes non-residents.

Those rules do not represent open access, but certainly are an improvement over some towns where no non-resident access is permitted.

Riverhead beaches boast solid potential for big bass in June and then large blues in the fall. However, although access to these beaches is less restricted, anglers should use caution because there have been reports of angler-youth confrontations on these beaches.

The beaches near Mattituck Inlet produce weaks and small blues in June. This action sometimes lasts into early July. Some big bass are taken from the tip of the West Inlet jetty in late May and in June as well. Rigged eels and large plugs seem to be the recommended approach to fool these fish, as well as plying the waters in the deep quiet of late night. Small blues are commonly seen at dusk and sunrise for most of the late spring and summer close to the beach at places like Bailey's Beach, the Firing Range, Duck Point, and Peconic Village beaches. Access to these beaches is not very restricted in spite of regulations requiring permits. The reason for relaxed enforcement is because vandalism and other problems have not reached the epidemic proportions they have elsewhere. Thus, police patrols are less common, citizen discomfort with people on the beach at night is less, and most police will let you fish if they see by your equipment and demeanor that you are a serious fisherman. Please remember, whether you are a town resident or non-resident, to be quiet and do not leave any garbage behind.

Some of the spots mentioned above have already brought us into Southold Town beaches. Perhaps the best known of these beaches are found more to the east. Kenney's Beach, Horton's Point, Truman's Beach, and Orient Point are names familiar to many surf fishermen. Some have long standing reputations of producing big fish in quantity, and access, up until a few years ago, was virtually unrestricted and today remains only semi-restricted. The ease of access referred to pertains to that part of the fishing season before Memorial Day and after Labor Day. Since swimming is the primary activity at town and village beaches, fishing is always more restricted during the swimming season.

In the mid-1970s, there was a fantastic run of blues weighing up to 20 pounds and a bit more along these beaches. The beaches were often crowded with fishermen lined up shoulder to shoulder. The residents out there tend to be less sophisticated surf fishermen, while non-residents who fish there tend to be the more experienced and hardest working fishermen in the sport. The action was frantic and some impatience developed among the "pros" with the residents whose casts often went astray and who fought fish for interminable periods of time. Hostile and unkind words were exchanged. Some of the unwise words were leveled at a town big shot who called the police and prodded the town board to institute stricter parking regulations. I offer these details to point out how important good manners are for non-resident fishermen on town beaches. You can usually

Light tackle works fine at most spots during the spring and summer. Gentle waves and gradually sloping beaches facilitate the landing of even good size fish. William Muller Photo.

spot the locals. Give them room, offer to help them with landing the fish, give them a lure to use that works if the ones they are using are not producing, be quiet, and leave no garbage behind. Sticking with these rules will help develop, as well as maintain access to otherwise private beaches.

The Southold Town beaches produce weaks and small blues in numbers beginning in June or even late May. This fishing is often sporadic, but can be top-notch at times. As elsewhere in the Sound, sand eels are the main baitfish since the early 1970s. The summer is usually dead along these beaches save for an occasional flurry. It's almost as if the fish and the beach was resting in anticipation of the fall blitzes. Sometime in October, the sand eels along with some mullet and bunker return to these beaches, and with them come big blues. Sometimes small bluefish are caught, too, but more often than not, the blues start at about eight pounds and go all the way to 20 with many fish in the low to mid teens. These fish respond to popping plugs and tins, as well as bunker and mackerel chunks. We prefer the start of the falling tide occurring with daybreak for best results, but midday blitzes in calm, bright sun at dead low tide are not so uncommon as to avoid mention. Many times I've arrived at sunset with ideal conditions only to find out that three guys fishing bait murdered the fish between 11AM and 1PM. Of course, I caught nothing under ideal conditions.

The fishing along Southold Beaches holds up surprisingly late into the season. In most places, the blues are gone by late October, but it has been true along these beaches that the best fishing for the largest blues doesn't occur until the first week in November. In addition, some blues are taken until Thanksgiving Day; enough big blues to make the effort worthwhile. When the blues finally depart, the bass move in. Often the schools of school bass are enormous even in these days of declining stocks of bass. From time to time, larger fish mix in, but 99 percent of these bass are shorts to five or so pounds.

It is interesting to observe how the fishing scene changes through the decades. In the 50s and 60s, the mainstay bait

In recent years the Sound's eastern beaches have produced many weakfish in the teen size range. William Muller Photo.

in the surf was "silver dollar" sized bunker. Vast shoals of these fish would be worked over by game fish. We almost never saw a sand eel in those days. Small bunker are a better bait for catching fish than sand eels. Sand eels are often small but very numerous. Game fish may swim through a school and not select individual sand eels, rather swim with their mouths open. They can't do that with bunker. They must select targets and thus the game fish are more aware of your plug. Also, the bunker race around more trying to escape and thus a more frenzied feeding pattern is created. Anyway, back a few decades we fished Horton's Point and the accepted game plan was to go to the Lighthouse parking lot, stand on the top of the cliff and watch the water below. When large bass, sometimes as big as 40 or more pounds, would chase the bunker into the surf, we would see huge black shapes slicing through the clear water over the sand. That was our signal to rush down the steep steps and charge the beach. In those days, huge bass were common catches along the Southold beaches. The run of fish would only last a few days or tides, but fishing was outstanding. After that short burst of hot action, there would still be some good innings, but blitz fishing was a matter of a limited period.

The entire Sound offers some phenomenal fishing opportunities for surf fishermen. The problem is access. However, local fishermen are encouraged to try the surf zone along their town beaches. It may take time to learn the area, but the investment in time will be well worth it. For non-residents, we can still work some town beaches and there is Sunken Meadow State Park as well as Wildwood State Park. I haven't said much about Wildwood Park because there aren't too many surf fishermen who fish there consistently, although I suspect that a great potential has been overlooked. I've been there several times and the water looks good. Small to medium blues seem to be the most common visitors to this beach and popping plugs are preferred.

CHAPTER 21

Cape Cod
by Frank Daignault

Mere mention of Cape Cod to the average surfcaster evokes thoughts of dark, swirling tide rips, wind-swept foam-topped seas, and backing surfcasters with bowed sticks. When that picture takes form in your mind, there is no way that the imagination can do it justice. The Outer Cape has some 40 miles of white sand beaches flanked by bars on the outside that are too trecherous for boats, and dunes on the inside that are too high and too hostile for the permanent encroachment of man and his inevitable civilization. And, on occasion, the Atlantic reminds us that this real estate—half land, half sea—belongs to it. Consequently, it is by default the domain of the surfcaster. Whatever the Cape is to the casual, non-fishing observer—"quaint," "natural," or "unspoiled"—it is at times a marine garland to the beach man. It might be whales surfacing off Race Point, their spouts bending like wind-blown steam; or a landfall of squid stretching for five miles that provide a sight worthy of a place in our memory. The tide could change or the wind could pick up as though some Divine signal had been struck and enough bluefish for each caster to set on several, before a firm hook-up, could be all over the wash. That could be every person with a rod east of Race Point Station. Miles.

But the preeminent quarry of the surfcaster is the striped bass which can be found just often enough to dwarf the imaginations of any who have fished for them elsewhere. While there have been some lean years—a time when many were saying that there were no stripers—the Cape continued to yield more and bigger fish than anywhere else;

you could still drag a fish up to the buggy with two hands while grappling with a back-of-the-mind feeling that there can't be *that* many bass.

A couple of years ago my wife and I came upon a school of linesides at a spot where we had taken them before. I don't tell this because of the number of fish involved, but rather to illustrate how the mind, what we are told, can be influenced, almost subverted, into believing that the last shovel of earth has been spread upon this fine game fish. Anyway, I could see Joyce's feminine form backing toward the buggy in the moonlight when the first contact was made, her spinning rod flat with the horizon. I was rushing my retrieve to go help her when my eel was hammered by a cow. By the time my fish was in she was pushing hers in the surf. With this kind of furious action, I simply changed plugs on her outfit and she had another on before I could get my fish to the buggy. This went on until the first dull glow in the east, the both of us so exhausted by then that we could barely function. The stripers weighed from 36 to 51 pounds and because we had not made contact for ten minutes, I told her that we had either hurt or caught every bass in the spot as we lay perspiring. In the next few minutes, the light had improved enough so that the shore was bathed in the dull copper of dawn. And for a mile in each direction there were bass porpoising in the sun. Decidedly, we had not taken them all.

Small wonder that most of us perceive Cape Cod as Mecca.

THE BEACH BUGGY

The Outer Cape's surfcasting's impressive reputation is largely attributable to the beach buggy. By definition, a "buggy" is usually a four-wheel drive vehicle, outfitted for fishing, that can be divided into two categories: the self-contained vehicle which is a pick-up truck with a slide-on camper equipped with plumbing; and the chase vehicle, which is a smaller 4x4 in the Bronco, Blazer, Jeep style of auto. Because it is illegal to camp in the open on the Cape, you must have a self-contained vehicle if you want to stay

This Cape Cod trophy fell for a rigged eel which can be seen dangling between the reel and the body of the bass. Frank Daignault Photo.

on the beach during the hours that you are not fishing. Those equipped with a chase vehicle must leave the beach when through fishing at night. The debate rages about which type of equipment serves the surfman best. The larger campers are better for family fishing because they provide both creature comforts and shelter from the elements. On the other hand, they are restricted in some instances and more heavily regulated; they are also less mobile for those who plan to hunt for bass. Only two beaches—but they are the major ones—allow self-contained vehicles: Nauset Beach in the Town of Orleans and Chatham, and the Provincelands of the Cape Cod National Seashore. At the latter, self-contained buggies are required

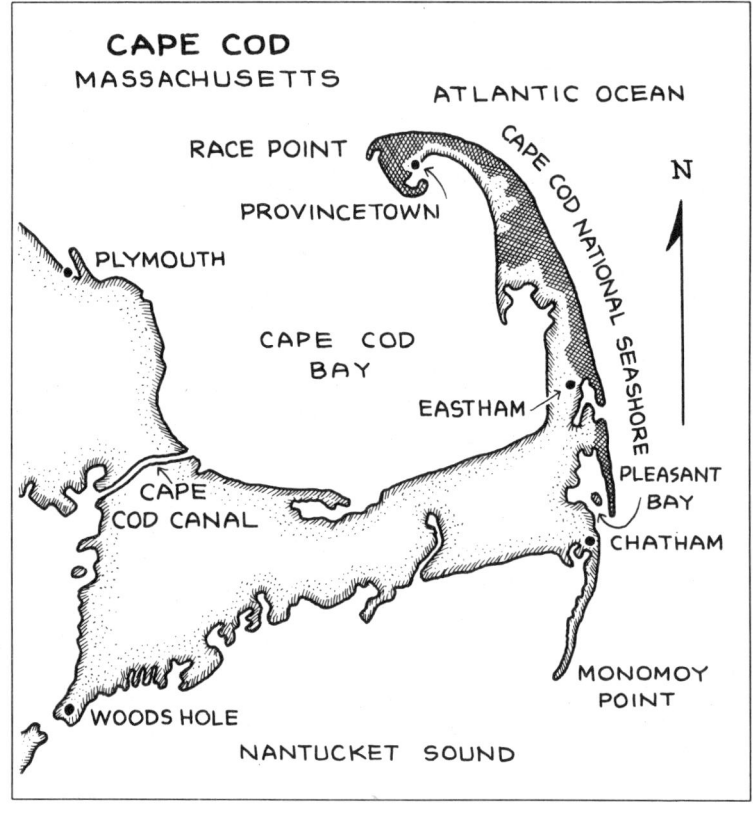

by regulation to park in "Self-Contained Areas," which are usually crowded and confined to very close quarters. Whatever your choice of buggy, keep in mind that the sands of Cape Cod are softer than what you'll find anywhere else and four-wheel drive is not to ensure mobility. *All*, and I must emphasize this with no exception, have to lower tire pressures to assure both flotation and traction on the sand. These pressures can be quite variable with the heavier camper equipped family machines, depending upon the weight of the rig and the tires that it is fitted out with. With the chase vehicle, a good starting point for tubeless, preferably radial, tires is 13 psi.

NAUSET BEACH

Nauset Beach is a natural peninsula flanked by the Atlantic on the east and south and Pleasant Bay on its west. Consequently, there is only one access point which is guarded by a police check-point at the north end in the Town of Orleans. After the required permit (which costs, at this writing, $25 for the season and $2 additional daily) there is a one mile back trail ride south through the dunes to a high dune that has vegetation. There the trail splits and the left fork leads to a large, bowl-shaped impression called Pochet Hole. There has always been good structure there, though changeable in its natural design, but invariably attractive to stripers that seem to delight in the avenues of sand carved by the wind and tide. Bars and sloughs, many dark enough to invite use, flank Pochet Hole and it is indeed an unwise caster who would pass the spot up on any tortuous drive south to Chatham Inlet. That is not to say that there are not other spots for those who care to read a beach. But anything else between Pochet and the beach's end is too variable from year to year and I cannot guarantee its location. Some years, weather depending, the 12 miles from check point to the end of the beach is a veritable garden for surfmen. Other seasons, Pochet is the last thing worth seeing before you get to the end. But any surfcaster with a measure of salt in his grog is accustomed to a roll of the dice.

Cape Cod surf fishermen can also catch cod in season using a variety of baits from sea worms to squid. Frank Daignault Photo.

We first looked upon Chatham Inlet in 1964. I say *we* because the kids were small then and we were together in a $200 converted bread delivery van that suffered from a smell of yeast and the interminable leakage of every fluid system in its design; the odometer long dead after its second pass at 30,000 miles. Here we discovered a surfcaster's nirvana where the tide rises in one direction and the wind-blown surface the other, causing the water to clap straight up over a myriad of bars. Between two fields of bucking seas, the one in our fore, and the more distant one that stretched south to Monomoy, lay a green, winding channel—a trail for vessels and a passing place for Pleasant Bay's tides. The children caught stripers on every cast just often enough for my wife, Joyce, and I to agree that we had found our spot.

The theory hereabouts is that the fish lay offshore until they can come in on a rising tide, when water has covered the bars and enough darkness is at hand to make them feel safe from predation above. If feeding opportunities present themselves—usually sand eels in astronomical numbers—the bass will chance the shallows. Bowed rods aside, their presence is often betrayed by the noisy sloshing and wallowing of big fish rolling for bait. And Chatham Inlet is no dead-water. On the contrary, Pleasant Bay is either filling or dumping with powerful currents and the slackwater that occurs between the flows is often the best of what can be a most memorable night. For the inlet fisherman, swimming plugs are best, what with bluefish. However, a friendly dispute endures the test of time about whether live eels are better. Evening tides are best—those that are high at 8PM. The favored wind is west or sou'west. A half-mile east, away from the currents and lines of casters, there is excellent sea worm *(Nereis)* fishing on the bottom. The inlet can be thronged with casters from all over the Northeast when fish have been showing; indeed, it is a spot well known for what it is. While it saddens me to divulge any of Chatham's intimacies, I do so with no greater sadness than that which Joyce and I both experienced when we found that detailed maps were sold and that a city fellow bragged in a weak moment in P-Town to hungry casters there. The secret is dead and there is now little use in keeping the oath I once made to myself about writing of it.

PROVINCETOWN

Any old-timer can tell you that an abiding ingredient to good striper water is movement. These fish didn't get of a two-handed size by swimming madly about in search of forage. Rather, they have an expert talent for utilizing the tide to bring them nourishment. Any surfcaster who accepts the fact that humping tide-rips translate to feeding stripers would do well to keep his eye on P-Town, more specifically Race Point. "The Race," as it has been fondly called by both sport and commercial fishermen for centuries, guards the very edge of the opening to Cape Cod Bay. At full tide, the qualities of good bass water become apparent. Whatever the Race is, it is more of it when the onshore sou'west howls. Nutrients are against the beach and bait and its tormentors follow. The ideal tide is one which is low after dark and optimum fishing is two hours either side of low. Thus, wind and tide are common sets of conditions here that can produce uncommon results. While this is prime plug water, recent years have witnessed throngs of bait fishermen using sand eels anchored to the bottom. With either method—plug or bait—the Race is a worthy first stop.

Just east of Race Point Light the shore deepens at a spot named when commercials maintained fish traps there. "The Traps" can be good on the incoming just after the Race goes dead; apparently stripers and blues (both species act the same) move east against the incoming tide. All hotspots are subtle to those fishing the Provincelands for the first time and names are in the minds of regulars as there are no signs. Moving east from the Traps another half mile is the "Second Rip" where currents form against the beach the first three hours of the drop. Most drift big swimming plugs: Gibbs, Dannys, Pikies and big Atoms. When these come in straight, it is time to move.

All of the above is to the west of the Ranger Station where over-sand vehicle permits are issued. There is a seasonal fee for buggies similar to that at Nauset, but without a daily charge. The mobile sportsman will find the Seashore Park more reasonable in its over-sand mileages than those at Nauset Beach because no point on the shore is more than a few minutes drive from the hard road. However, trails to the shore are hilly and P-Town sand is of a larger grain which makes driving more difficult. Beach erosion invokes certain hazards at places where the sea threatens a dune base and

Large crashing waves and strong backwashes can make landing a bass by hand a difficult proposition, especially if the bass is a big one. Frank Daignault Photo.

tight crossings or low tide risks to a buggy are not unusual; this more likely on the "Back Beach."

East of the Ranger Station, after a short back trail run, the rounding of the shore faces a more easterly sea and a greater surf is in evidence. Known as the Back Beach, the area affords the surfcaster the opportunity to read water from a number of points formed by the tides for about two miles. After that, a pesty weed, locally called gunk (this is natural marine growth and not pollution) is of great enough abundance to make fishing impossible. Many years the weed will stretch five miles, clear to Highland Light. (Also known as Cape Cod Light.)

A brief, reiterating lesson in geography: West of the Ranger Station—the Second Rip, the Traps, Race Point, then a small estuary called Hatches Harbor. To the east, the Back Beach. For most surfcasters, a generalized itinerary would be to fish the Second Rip three hours down from high tide. Rest an hour. Fish the Race the last two hours of the drop and the first two coming in; check the Traps for an hour, then cast the Back Beach the last three hours of the incoming.

ON FOOT

While the Cape's reputation as a Valhalla for surfcasters was built by mechanized anglers, that is not to say that its sands are the exclusive domain of the beach buggy. On the contrary, some of the best spots—no longer in-bounds to vehicles—are accessible to the caster on foot. For instance, from the Nauset Beach (Orleans) parking lot you can go left or north, and fish a surf that is influenced by Nauset Inlet, the only estuary facing east on the Outer Cape. It is neither necessary nor in your best interest to walk the full mile plus to the Inlet as beach structure immediately north of the swimming area, which is barren at night, is usually the best this side of Pochet. North Beach, the part of the beach above the Inlet, is also a worthy hunting ground for the on-foot surfman.

All access points to the Outer Cape shore are best found if the angler were to pretend he wanted a bathing beach.

Cape Cod may be best known for its huge bass, but out-sized choppers are common along Cape Cod beaches and provide tackle busting fun. Frank Daignault Photo.

Frolicsome day swimmers have no effect upon stripers foraging in the deep night. Besides, the Cape shore is bounded by impassable dunes that are sheer cliffs to the water, in some cases as much as 200 feet. Bathing beaches offer a safe access point as well as place to park. Spots like Lecount and Newcomb Hollows, Balston Beach, Head of the Meadow—all well marked along the highways—have given up more than a measure of 40-pound-plus linesides. Bars, sloughs and deep holes, if you can keep your notes straight, should be read during the day at the approximate tide you plan to be there at night. Unlike the many hotspots that

If you want to release a big bass on any beach the gaff must remain holstered. However, it is no easy matter to work a big fish up the beach for unhooking by sliding it up feet at a time with each crashing wave. Frank Daignault Photo.

beach buggy jockeys collect at in numbers that approach absurdity, the outer beach affords a solitude that could stand upon its own merit without the moby stripers that can be found there. Late summer has an edge on these Outer Cape bars when, it is said, bluefish have "taken over" the better rips at Chatham and P-Town.

By the way, one of the best bluefish hotspots for the walking surfman is at Race Point Beach which is adjacent to the Ranger Station at the end of Race Road. A falling tide and hard blowing sou'west are mandatory conditions for the place to pay off, particularly if the tide is moving strong during sunrise. Use a popping plug with a rapid retrieve.

Fluke or summer flounder fishing is subject to the whims of marine cycles and a high point has been the early 80s with fantastic numbers in P-Town. Herring Cove or New Beach, which is neatly placed between Wood End and Race Point, is both accessible and productive. Refreshingly, this is daytime fishing and early morning is a good time to beat the bathing crowd. Use frozen sand eels, which can be bought in most Cape tackle shops and slide them along the bottom slowly.

TIMING

The surfcasting season, by virtue of natural timing, not regulation, is school stripers at Nauset around May 15 and big fish, say 20 pounds up, arriving May 30 throughout the Cape. Bluefish dribble in from mid-June on, but the fishing for them does not peak until mid-August. There is always a run of these killers in P-Town at that time. I've seen casters on foot below the Ranger Station that stretched in both directions as far as the eye could see; and the place was not short of beach buggies, either. Still, every man, woman, and child holding a rod either had a fish on or was taking one off and the sea there looked like a berserk mine field what with fish blowing up the plugs... We are supposed to be talking of the seasons here. Summer ends more quickly in P-Town, around October 20, usually with one hell of a blitz. In Chatham, weather depending, November 1.

No guarantees, surfcasting is a craft of strong back and

noble spirit that calls for an all-abiding optimism in what sometimes seems like a hopeless cause. It can only be done right by those with a boundless enthusiasm. Otherwise, the nights are too long, the elements too harsh. Here the primitive tenets of a man on the beach are still in place; no graph recorders to tell him when it is time to fish. Ours is a mid-watch hunt that pits itself against the inseparable variables of wondering whether we fish empty water right or a striper laden sea all wrong. High adventure here has somehow evaded the plastic, high tech world that seems to have conquered all else. And while the magic of a shimmering silver sea captures the imaginations of us all wherever we fish, a big bass lunging at your plug etches it in your memory. It happens more often on Cape Cod. No one can tell you *when* it will happen, but I can tell you that it will: the wind will unaccountably rise sometime after the sun touches down; whitecaps will form and from somewhere they will come—big bluefish and way bigger stripers. There will be two groups of casters—those who were there, and those who wish they had been. It happens every season.